# INNOVATIVE THERAPEUTIC LIFE STORY WORK

*by the same editor*

**Life Story Therapy with Traumatized Children**
**A Model for Practice**
*Richard Rose*
ISBN 978 1 84905 272 6
eISBN 978 0 85700 574 8

**The Child's Own Story**
**Life Story Work with Traumatized Children**
*Richard Rose and Terry Philpot*
ISBN 978 1 84310 287 8
ISBN 978 1 84985 428 3 (Large Print)
eISBN 978 1 84642 056 6
*Part of the Delivery Recovery series*

*of related interest*

**Life Story Work with Children Who are Fostered or Adopted**
**Creative Ideas and Activities**
*Katie Wrench and Lesley Naylor*
ISBN 978 1 84905 343 3
eISBN 978 0 85700 674 5

**Life Story Books for Adopted and Fostered Children, Second Edition**
**A Family Friendly Approach**
*Joy Rees*
*Foreword by Alan Burnell*
ISBN 978 1 78592 167 4
eISBN 978 1 78450 436 6

**A Guide to Therapeutic Child Care**
**What You Need to Know to Create a Healing Home**
*Ruth Emond, Laura Steckley and Autumn Roesch-Marsh*
ISBN 978 1 84905 401 0
eISBN 978 0 85700 769 8

**The Simple Guide to Child Trauma**
**What It Is and How to Help**
*Betsy de Thierry*
*Foreword by David Shemmings*
*Illustrated by Emma Reeves*
ISBN 978 1 78592 136 0
eISBN 978 1 78450 401 4
*Part of the Simple Guides series*

# INNOVATIVE THERAPEUTIC LIFE STORY WORK

## DEVELOPING TRAUMA-INFORMED PRACTICE FOR WORKING WITH CHILDREN, ADOLESCENTS AND YOUNG ADULTS

### EDITED BY RICHARD ROSE

FOREWORD BY DEBORAH D. GRAY

Jessica Kingsley *Publishers*
London and Philadelphia

First published in 2017
by Jessica Kingsley Publishers
73 Collier Street
London N1 9BE, UK
and
400 Market Street, Suite 400
Philadelphia, PA 19106, USA

*www.jkp.com*

**Library of Congress Cataloging in Publication Data**
Names: Rose, Richard, 1965- editor.
Title: Innovative therapeutic life story work : developing trauma-informed
    practice for working with children, adolescents, and young adults / edited
    by Richard Rose.
Description: London ; Philadelphia : Jessica Kingsley Publishers, 2017. |
    Includes bibliographical references.
Identifiers: LCCN 2017007463 | ISBN 9781785921858
Subjects: | MESH: Stress Disorders, Post-Traumatic--therapy | Narration |
    Psychotherapy | Self Concept | Child | Adolescent | Young Adult
Classification: LCC RJ506.P55 | NLM WM 172.5 | DDC
616.85/2100835--dc23 LC record available at
https://lccn.loc.gov/2017007463

**British Library Cataloguing in Publication Data**
A CIP catalogue record for this book is available from the British Library

ISBN 978 1 78592 185 8
eISBN 978 1 78450 468 7

Printed and bound in Great Britain.

MIX
Paper from
responsible sources
FSC
www.fsc.org    FSC® C013056

# DEDICATION

In writing and editing this book, I have had the honour of sharing, learning and developing alongside social care practitioners across the world. For each and every one of them, I thank you. Over the last 20 years I have used therapeutic life story work as an intervention that supports children, young people and their care providers, each and every one has left their mark and shaped my practice, my profession and my view of the world. For that I am eternally grateful.

Finally, my love and thanks are for my family, Paula, Ben and Callum. My vocation often takes me away from them; although I am absent with leave, I have always felt them near me.

# CONTENTS

# FOREWORD

Richard Rose has created a child-centric life story, or narrative, model, for children/teens after placements through child welfare. His approaches are sensitive, playful, and imaginative – yet coherent over time as he works with children, co-creating their life stories. Rather than supplying a narrative that adults want children to have, or working from a check-off list of essentials, his narrative starts with the unanswered questions of children. He includes foster and adoptive parents (carers) within the meetings in order to enhance children's experiences of felt safety. His work increases the empathy and insight that carers have for their children, as well as for themselves. He reaches out to birth family members, obtaining information and exchanging questions and answers. He builds bridges between experiences and behaviors; between birth, foster, adoptive families; and over disconnects due to trauma and placements.

This is in contrast to the experience that many children describe to me. Imagine being a child with a concrete understanding of your world, and auditory memory problems due to high stress. Now imagine that a nice caseworker is giving you critical information in simple language, but that she is still using abstract concepts and generalizations. You know that the caseworker's words are vital to your understanding of how you have ended up in a different family. But, you simply do not understand the concepts or generalizations that you are to apply. And, she talks a lot, exceeding your processing load. You must somehow hold her abstract information within your auditory working memory even as your heart is pounding. Then, you must retrieve information from auditory memory in order to deduce how you came to be in this home, this family. You can't, so you fill with shame, thinking, 'I have something wrong with me. I can't remember and I can't understand. But, I am angry.' The caseworker asks you if you have any questions. You shake your head, 'no'. In fact, can't even phrase a question. This typifies the experience of many children in child welfare. They wonder, 'how does "my parents had many problems" mean that I go in a car with a stranger to a home with other strangers?'

Richard gives a kinder and child-centric alternative. By itself, that would be compelling. But, to my delight, his work is fun and imaginative. My colleagues and I have been in Richard Rose's training. I have also heard feedback from Portland State University's Post-Graduate Foster Care and Adoption Therapy Certificate students. They range from skilled to beginning therapists. We have shared our exuberance with his model. The 'scroll' that he co-creates with children is both enjoyable to do, and profound. It contains visual imaginary, facts, and evokes sensory memories. Richard models a right-brain led approach, which is successful for children who need empathy and help with stress regulation. His approach is playful but respectful.

The work within this book can be adapted as a whole within child welfare organizations. Alternately, parts of the model can be applied within individual practices. He has a variety of playful activities that will enliven the work between children/teens and caseworkers or psychotherapists. This is a great 'idea' and activity book.

I particularly enjoyed the sense of integrity with which Richard Rose approaches children/teens and families. He models treating families with dignity throughout the book. Rather than boiler-plate approaches, he describes the process of individualizing children/teens as they create their unique narratives.

As a field, we recognize the power of secure attachments in enhancing resilience and helping with recovery after toxic stress. Approaches like Richard Rose's enhance sensitivity and nurturance of parents (carers), which, in turn, supports children's movement into patterns of secure attachment. His model is helpful in reducing the impacts of grief and trauma as children/teens integrate their life events. The activities assist children in moving from a disorganized pattern of attachment into a more secure pattern. I heartily recommend this book to caseworkers and therapists alike as they have the privilege of working with children and families.

*Deborah Gray, MSW, MPA, LICSW*
*Nurturing Attachments, Kirkland, WA*
*Author of:* Attaching in Adoption:
Practical Tools for Today's Parents,
Nurturing Adoptions: Creating Resiliency
after Trauma and Neglect,
Attaching with Love, Joy, and Hugs

# PROLOGUE

*You can't connect the dots looking forward, you can only connect them looking backwards. So, you have to trust that the dots will somehow connect in your future. You have to trust in something: your gut, destiny, life, karma, whatever. Because believing that the dots will connect down the road will give you the confidence to follow your heart, even when it leads you off the well-worn path.*

*Steve Jobs, Apple (Stanford Commencement Address 2005)*

Welcome to this book – the third I have published about therapeutic life story work. For the last 20 years of my professional life, I have been delivering training and promoting therapeutic life story work. This book details the work that has evolved from my travels across the world; as individuals and groups I have encountered have become enthused by therapeutic life story work, they have gone on to develop their practice in new and interesting ways, including making adaptations for their own cultural environments.

This book recognises innovators in the process of therapeutic life story work across the world and is designed to be a space for their expertise and voices to be heard.

## My story

As this is a book about life stories, it makes sense for me to start it with my own.

Having been brought up in the care of my mother and then, from three years of age, my father (I am 'step-parent adopted'), I shared my early life with six sisters and brothers in an interesting environment outside the home, but a loving one within.

By the time I was in my teens I began, with others, to raise money for a local children's home. This was quite successful, and by the time I was 17 I was working as a staff member in a children's home in Wiltshire, England.

The children's home was a small 12-bed unit called Red Gables in Purton, near Swindon. This home was not set up as a specialised centre, but as a generic residential home for children and young people. At that time, the home was very much run as an independent unit managed by a wonderful head of home called 'Aunty Ann'.

At 17 years of age I found it a daunting task to suddenly have the care and protection of 12 children; but as a keen, sometimes ever-present care worker (for the first three years I lived as a residential care officer at the home) and, although I was supposed to work 12 hour shifts I just worked continually throughout the time I was resident.

I was a senior member of the team by my 19th birthday but, following an abuse inquiry in a London borough children's home, it was decided that those in a senior role had to be 21 or over. I was therefore offered a secondment to study to be a social worker as an alternative to being reassigned. I found it very hard to leave the children in my care as we had grown up together, sharing our lives and our stories. In the four years I was at Red Gables only five children had moved on. It gives me great joy that I am still in touch with some of the children 35 years later.

One thing I remember doing at the children's home was a project around storytelling: each child was asked to help write a story with me. This was long before I understood about the value and attachment potential of therapeutic stories and story stems. It was done so that I could help the children share a thought, hope or desire, or perhaps speak of their fears, hurt or pain through symbolic application. I still remember the story by one of the children, Michael, which introduced Herbert the Hedgehog and his trip to Mars – we called this 'Hedgehog L'Orange'. When I eventually retire, I hope to write these stories to honour the children back in the 1980s who provided me with the foundation of childcare knowledge and therapeutic healing.

Several years later, while I was on my 'second practice placement' of my Certificate of Qualification in Social Work, I was able to work at a leading drug rehabilitation centre called Phoenix House in London. Phoenix House was a groundbreaking organisation in 'residential community living' catering for adults whose lives had been affected by drug dependency and who had engaged in crime and consequently been incarcerated for this.

Among other interventions, I was able to do family history work with the residents. This took the form of timelines, exploring wishes and feelings, grief and loss, and trauma. At the time, I did not know of the concept of adult attachment interviews, but intuitively I was doing just that. What I noticed was that the use of the adult's personal narrative in helping to unpick complex life events was an essential tool.

While working at Phoenix House, I was able to interview people in prisons throughout the country – those who had been found guilty, were on remand and were awaiting sentence. Using a narrative approach, hearing their stories of their identity and not just the story of their offences, gave me the opportunity to consider their sense of self and in turn identify their potential for change. What was of interest during these early thoughts about stories and healing was the number of people I interviewed who had suffered disruption, abuse and hurt in early childhood. As we thought through this together, I was minded of the long-term effects that such early life trauma can have on people that, if untreated, visit on those around them (friends, family and dependants).

In 1989, after qualifying in social work, I started working in a children and families team in a social work department. The notion of life story work was rarely considered and, if done, was not influenced by the work of early contributors to the process (Fahlberg 1984; Ryan and Walker 1984; Usher 1984). As a therapeutic intervention or a therapy, the powerful nature of your own narrative as a potential healer was not considered. At this time, the work by Professor Gordon Turnball and the use of narrative therapy with those who are affected by war (post-traumatic stress disorder) was only just surfacing.

Since then, there have been a number of research papers attesting to the effectiveness of narrative therapy, including the celebrated work of Michael White (1990, 2007) and David Demborough (2014); commentaries from Baynes (2007); and books detailing the process of life story work through Edith Nichols (2005), Rose and Philpot (2005) and Ryan and Walker (2007).

Although I worked with children in long-term care placements, as well as being asked to work alongside adolescents in crisis, not one child had the opportunity to undertake identity work, life story work or reflection. This is not to say that I noticed this, but more an admission that I didn't consider it. In essence, I was in that unconscious–unconscious paradigm – I didn't know that I didn't know. Looking back at my time in local authority work between 1984 and 1997, I wish that I had been in the position of being 'consciously unconscious' – that I had known that I didn't know and therefore more keen to learn and to develop my practice.

There were many children I could have helped to understand and move through their present by using their past and looking to a positive future. Many of the children I worked with became the parents of some of the children I later worked with. It was this more than anything else that persuaded me to take a role in a private therapeutic care agency.

I started work as a life story worker at an organisation called SACCS (Sexual Abuse Child Consultancy Service) in 1997. There were 32 children aged between 4 and 12 years of age on admission, and on average each child was placed in the organisation for three years. I was aware of the techniques of using scrapbooking and third-party books about children, but felt that we needed to engage the child in an explorative journey through their life in the company of their primary carers. This engagement and subsequent model of intervention has been the subject of my two previous books (Rose 2012; Rose and Philpot 2005).

In 2005, I was in a position to offer training in life story work and began to establish a specific model of intervention called 'therapeutic life story work'. This training began to influence the delivery of life story work for traumatised children in the UK; and then, gradually from 2008, it was introduced internationally. From 2011, having left SACCS, I began to establish therapeutic life story work in the community for placement support, traumatised children and attachment disorders. I now own and direct a small organisation called Child Trauma Intervention Services. In 2011 I was honoured to be appointed as an Adjunct Associate Professor in Social Work and Social Policy at La Trobe University, Melbourne, and have jointly authored papers on foster care with colleagues at the university.

In 2014, the Professional Diploma in Therapeutic Life Story Work was launched in London at the Institute for Arts and Therapy in Education and validated by the University of East London. The Diploma is now delivered in London, Melbourne and Sydney and will be delivered in Portugal from 2017, and in the USA and New Zealand from 2018. Therapeutic life story work is now established in Australia, Portugal, Japan, New Zealand and the UK. I am fortunate that I supervise teams in the majority of these countries. Given the establishment of the intervention in these regions of the world, this book hosts chapter contributions detailing the work in a myriad of cultural and professional settings.

This book is my opportunity to provide you with an insight into this work. It is my hope that this will enthuse you to consider, engage and develop therapeutic life story work as a process to allow children and young adults (and adults) to reframe their sense of self. I hope it gives you the opportunity to assist children and young people (and adults) to understand who they were, what they are and that they can fashion their own future without being led by their past. This is essential for their own recovery and for them to achieve brilliance of self.

## The therapeutic life story journey

This book presents a selection of therapeutic life story interventions across the world, but also represents differing clinical settings and approaches. I have asked that the contributors share their approach and hope that the reader will gain an understanding of the work and ideas for future practice and trust that we all can make a difference.

*Richard Rose*

# PART 1

# INTRODUCING THERAPEUTIC LIFE STORY WORK THEORY AND PRACTICE

Chapter 1

# INTRODUCING THE THERAPEUTIC LIFE STORY MODEL

## ALL OF US SHARE SOMETHING IN COMMON – WE ARE ALL A COLLECTION OF STORIES

*Richard Rose, Child Trauma Intervention Services*

*If you want to know your past – look into your present conditions. If you want to know your future – look into your present actions.*

*Rinposche (2002)*

For every case I am currently involved in throughout the world there are recommendations which state that life story work would be helpful, is a necessity or is under way. As we read more and more about how life story work is therapeutic, supportive and, in some cases, liberating, we also see that it is rare that such work has been carried out. It is for this reason, with the support of Margot Sunderland and her team at the Institute for Arts in Therapy and Education, that we have a Professional Diploma in Therapeutic Life Story Work. I have been delivering this year-long course every year since 2014, and I have provided the same course in Melbourne and Sydney since 2016. The aim is to develop hundreds of trained practitioners across the world who can then support traumatised children and young people to be who they can be and not be led by who they were.

For some time now specialised services have called themselves therapeutic, but we are all in the childcare field working to provide 'healing' for hurt children. These courses are designed to promote therapeutic thinking and practice in care as a standard of intervention for all.

In November 2014, the National Institute for Health and Care Excellence (NICE is an independent, non-department public body), which reports on English medical, social and health issues, but also makes recommendations for UK-wide awareness, stated that all children in care of English local authorities have a right to have life story work. This stance was supported by the UK government introduction of the Adoption Support Fund (ASF), which is centrally located and supports direct work for children who are adopted and need therapeutic services. In May 2015, when this fund was launched, it recognised that therapeutic life story work (enhanced life story work) was a provision that could positively affect the care of children and young people as well as providing stability for adoption placements.

In May 2016, this fund was widened to include children and young people who were subject to special guardianship and those who were internationally adopted. It is my hope that the countries that are starting their therapeutic life story journeys can lobby governments and social fund streams to finance this incredible and essential approach for children in the looked-after system.

The phrase 'life story work' is commonly used in the social care field, to indicate that an intervention around the history of the child is undertaken. The child's story is collated and then, in some cases, discussed with the child before a book is produced which details a chronological illustration of their life journey. What is most commonly seen, however, is a collation of 'known facts' contained in a short book that represents so little of the child's real story and so much of the social work recorded file history. Across the world, I have seen that one thing is commonplace: children and young people in care will often experience three or more placements in their care journey and three or more (often many more) social workers. Each of these placements and case managers will deliver different values, morals and perceptions of the child. This will be seen in the files that are read and interpreted before becoming core parts of the 'life story' written for children.

Life history work is often referred to as life story work. However, in most cases the approach does not involve the child in the process. A clear example of this is adoption life story work, where a book is created to enable the child to understand in future years why they are subject to an adoption order. Life history work is a process where the child has the opportunity to understand their history. It is often provided by a social worker, foster carer or student and has the aim of providing a written account of the child's life journey from their separation from their parents to the current date. Life history work has been widely considered as a default service for children who are subject to adoption and latterly for children that are placed in permanency. As early as 1984, life story work was encouraged as an opportunity to provide children with a narrative to explain the life events and the sequence of their journey from birth to their current placement. However, the child does not have the opportunity to explore their own understanding of events or to talk to those who have had a significant impact on their lives. Nor are they able to identify the role that guilt, shame and responsibility play within this. Much of the life history work that takes place across the UK involves a collation of the 'easy to find' information which is often untested and taken as truthful accounts. This collated information is then placed within a story, loosely based on a chronology, and presented often as a completed piece of work to the child.

Most of us who have been employed in social services will acknowledge in our more relaxed moments that our recording in files, often carried out days after events, was not as accurate as we would have liked it to been. These events are often based on opinion and are therefore subjective, and again most children within the social care system would have experienced multiple placements and multiple social worker changes. For example, I have recently finished working with two children who, over nine months, had seven different social workers, each with slightly different approaches, beliefs and ethical stances. It is highly probable that there are different interpretations of the problems facing the children and therefore different thinking and solutions for their best interests, and thus different recording systems.

It is clear that much of the life history work collation is taken from the social work files and reinterpreted for the child in an (occasionally) age-appropriate life story book. I have had the opportunity to view hundreds of life story books, which are in most cases held with great value by the child and their carer(s). These books vary from a few pages to photograph albums to beautifully created stories: whichever sort the child received often depended entirely on the professional involved, the time they had and their skill and commitment.

These life story books commonly fail to include the difficult situations that are often the very reason for the child being placed in the care of others and not with their families. Examples of these include books that are lovingly produced for the child, but contain the positive events and not the abuse, the deaths or the more 'ugly' sides of the child's experience. I once worked with a 13-year-old child who was keen to show me her life story book. It was a series of photographs with a paragraph, or at least a few lines of information, about each picture. The child was able to tell me who was who, and who they were in relation to her. She was not able to connect the pictures of the people or the places to the story of her life; she was not able to identify who did what to who and when, or where or why it had happened to affect her reason for her abusive experiences, her care episodes, her adoption or its subsequent breakdown.

I have worked with parents of children who have been placed within the care system who explain how life story books, far from helping their children, have caused more sadness, difficulty and distress. One parent explained that a social worker delivered her child's life story book to the child on a contact visit. Once she had given the book to the child, she announced that she (the social worker) was leaving the authority. The child, on receiving the book, immediately flicked through to find out who her father was and found that this had not been included. She turned to the social worker, asked her why this was not included and was told, 'You're old enough to know; ask your mother.' At this the child turned to ask and the parent stood up, left the room and contact between the two was disrupted and eventually further contacts between the two were cancelled.

Life story books are often completed on behalf of the child, especially for children who are under three years of age. These approaches may not be as helpful as currently viewed, as they commonly have sparse information contained within them, and it is rarely applicable in later life when the child begins to ask the questions about her identity. On numerous occasions I have called for 'moving from and moving to' books to replace life story books for adoption and permanency placements for the under-threes, so that when the appropriate need for life story becomes clear, there is no confusion between the two. In most adoption cases, children are provided with a later life letter, which is an account of why they were adopted. These letters can be very detailed and contain reasons such as their birth parent(s)' alcohol dependency, domestic violence and/or sexual abuse, physical neglect and emotional harm. I have long argued that this practice is poor, and full of challenges for the receiver – imagine a child brought up with a story of why they could not remain in their birth family. Often the reason is minimised to protect the child and so 'mummy was poorly' rather than mummy was addicted to drugs, or 'daddy had troubles with his anger' rather than daddy killed someone. When they get to 18 and leave the security of their adoptive family, they are given a letter that pulls few punches:

> When you were born, your mother was addicted to heroin; this affected her judgement and so she could not care for you safely. On one occasion, your mother left you in a park and, a few days later, she came to see the social worker to have you placed back with her. Your mother was a prostitute so that she could get enough money to pay for her drugs; you would be looked after by neighbours when she was doing this.

Surely while the child is in the care of loving, therapeutic parents would be the time to talk about, to make sense of and to be at ease with the history we come with? To wait and to then provide challenging accounts just when the young person is making their own way in the world is nothing short of cruel. I have argued that children subject to adoption and special guardianships should be offered the opportunity to explore their stories at seven to eight years of age. This supportive service will explore the past, secure the present and allow for growth in the future – an intervention which would be provided alongside their permanent carers so as to build on the attachment relationships at a time when most children are asking 'Who am I?'

I worked with a 13-year-old girl who told me that she had been sexually behaving with her father when she was three; she felt that it wasn't so bad, and she must have been okay with it as she could have stopped him if she didn't want him to do it to her. For many years, this young person had been told that it wasn't her fault and that her father had been responsible for hurting her. The reality was that this fact had not been internalised; she had nodded as it was said, but not believed it. The opportunity to work through these issues with young people can provide internalisation; to sit with the awfulness of these experiences and to reflect on those involved. This young person, with her carer, was able to think about what a three-year-old can do, think and feel – we used the beautifully written books of Judith Trowell, *Understanding Your 3-Year-Old* (1992). We then spoke of the role of 'dads' and how fathers learn to be dads. Over a period of time we were able to consider what had happened and, although she was not able to think that her dad had done wrong, she was able to understand that she was not able to 'stop him, even if I had wanted to'. It is a wonderful thing to see children and young people conclude that they were not to blame, that the things that happened to them were not their fault.

Another pressing issue supporting therapeutic life story work in the earlier years of a child's life is the threat and opportunity offered by the internet and the ease of social media in providing information instantly for those that look for it. These are extremely useful tools, but in the wrong hands can be incredibly damaging to our hurt children. Gone are the times when we can protect children from hurtful information by not discussing difficult things with them. I once worked with a young child whose step-father was in prison for murdering another child in the family, in the presence of the other child. This child didn't know that her birth father had also been in prison for a similar crime against another child. There had been much confusion as to who and what could be shared with her by the professionals around her. One day, when a computer had been left on at the local library, he decided to put her birth father's name into the search engine. She was immediately directed to articles and news sites detailing the deaths, the nature of the killing, the court case and the sentencing. We should have been there to assist her, to tell her the detail and work through the story – if we don't then someone else will, and that someone may not have the child's best interest at heart. It is clear that Facebook and other social media provide resourceful platforms for those looking for their (lost) children, siblings searching for their (lost) family members and, if we are not mindful about this, more and more placements will become fragile and sadly, for some placements they will fail.

I am aware that many are concerned that young children cannot hear distressing details of their family of origin, but as Fahlberg (1981) states, the very fact that adults hesitate to speak of difficult things with a child could mean that the child believes it is so terrible that even the caring adult is unable to cope with it. A few years ago, when I was supporting children in the court system, I was asked to work with a child who had a parent in prison. The parent had been convicted of rape and the assault of a child. All those around the child were worried that telling the child about the real reason would be harmful to him. His foster parents were very worried that the information would be too much for the child to bear, and became very challenging as we came closer to the telling. On the actual day, the foster mother chose not to be involved, leaving the foster father with me and the child. When it came to talking about the issues, I asked the child why he thought people might go to prison. He replied with little hesitation that people go to prison because they rape and hurt people. I stated that that was an interesting thing to be told, and he commented that he knew this was why his dad was in prison as he had heard his carers talking about it when he was supposed to be asleep. The carer was amazed by this, but children are vigilant and they know to listen in order to be aware and prepared. I have an '80/20 rule' regarding children in care – they know 80 per cent of what is happening around them compared with their carer(s)' 20 per cent. They know when things are not okay, when their carers are not well, angry at each other, worried or unsafe, because their survival depends on this attuned awareness.

It is my experience that children and young people can hear difficult things if those speaking with them are confident, caring and informed. More to the point, once they have been able to speak of these hurtful times, then the weight of this information is removed somewhat and the children are able to move forward with a slightly lighter step.

In 2006, the Commission for Social Care Inspection (CSCI) conducted a survey of young people who had been adopted, exploring the areas of confusion, if any, around their past. The CSCI published the fact that children wanted to know why they could not stay with their birth families, who the people were who gave birth to them and what had happened to them in the past; they also wanted to know about their birth and other relatives, particularly siblings. These details are basic, yet hold countless other stories which, when handled safely, can provide assurance, stability and hope to all involved.

Over the last 20 years I, along with other practitioners, have developed approaches which assist children to engage in direct work that affords an explorative narrative of their life and that of their parents and grandparents. The life story book published in 2005 (Rose and Philpot) described a life story approach within the structure of a residential therapeutic children's facility. Since 2008 I have developed a therapeutic and creative programme that has proved to be effective in working with children and adults within a community setting.

There has been for some years now the concern that life story work can be retraumatising for children, but in my view it is hard to retraumatise a traumatised child. Of course, it is certainly possible to harm a child if the approach of the therapeutic worker is carried out with undue care and undue haste. I am reminded by the observations of Vera Fahlberg (1984), who said, 'A major aspect of direct work is listening for the child's perceptions. Until we do this, we won't know if we are to expand their information or correct their misperceptions.'

Therapeutic life work is different to story work or life history work because it works with children and their primary carer from the beginning of the process to the end. It is designed to work on the attachment between the carer and the child by inviting both to consider the events of the child's individual journey and that of their family of origin.

> It is generally accepted that life story books should answer the what, when and why questions about a child's life experiences. They should also be used as a means to allow the child, without undue pressure, to express feelings about these events. Life [story] work is a means of unravelling confusion and discarding some of the negative emotional baggage which the child has carried for so long. (Connor *et al.* 1985)

As a social work intervention, life story work is often referred to as a therapeutic task rather than a therapy in its own right. It can be an effective tool to support children and families in moving forward from one state to the next as well as a tool to assist children and families to understand significant issues from the past.

Rushton (2002) identified that the value of such intervention was hard to measure and that for some children it may be helpful, but for others it may create more difficulties for them.

> Although preparation of children, especially 'Life Story Work', has been described and promoted by practitioners, studies are lacking on how this subsequently affects the child's development and placement. It also raises many unresolved therapeutic concerns such as whether reawakening abusive experiences from the past serves to resolve or to enliven the ill effects... Researching this area is extremely difficult and no large-scale trial of the effectiveness of pre-placement work has been attempted. (Rushton 2002)

In my last book, (Rose 2012) I acknowledged that research into the effectiveness of therapeutic life story work had not taken place: it was the variable approaches to life story work which led to the difficulty in evaluating it. I am pleased to state that research has now started to happen in Australia on the therapeutic life story model I have championed, and

I am sure that the findings over the next few years will be invaluable to the further development of the approach.

Up until this stage I, along with practitioners in therapeutic life story work, will continue to promote the approach and to establish standardisation of the intervention.

Chapter 2

# THE VITAL PROCESS OF RECOVERY

*Richard Rose, Child Trauma Intervention Services*

*The Moving Finger writes; and, having writ, moves on: nor all your Piety nor Wit Shall lure it back to cancel half a Line, nor all your Tears wash out a Word of it.*

*Fitzgerald (1859) translation of The Rubáiyát of Omar Khayyám*

## Introduction

This chapter considers the essential concept of recovery. I decided to call life story work 'therapeutic life story work' to emphasise the healing opportunities of the intervention. Our stories should not be simply a review of life, or a tale of events, but more about the importance of our current and future journey not being led and orchestrated by our past. We cannot change the past, however hard we might want to try, but we can make sense of it and, in doing so, move to a healthier future. Many years ago, I heard a residential care worker telling her child that her trauma wasn't who she was: that her trauma, although part of her, was not a life sentence. We all have experiences that shape us (Perry 2012; Ziegler 2002), but shaping is not permanent. To allow the opportunity to continually shape provides the journey to recovery: 'You are today where your thoughts have brought you; you will be tomorrow where your thoughts take you' (James Allen 1910).

Developments in neuroscience have supported our thinking on the impact of trauma on our brains and on our bodies (Centre for the Developing Child 2015; Ziegler 2002; van der Kolk 2016; Perry 2012). Similarly, there are recovery concepts that suggest that neural pathways can be reworked and, with effective therapeutic intervention (Sunderland 2009; van der Kolk 2003; Rose 2012), recovery can be achieved. It is an essential 'known' that all those working with traumatised children understand that trauma is treatable and that children are able to move forward and be healthy, loved and loving. Not one of us has a pre-ordained script that maps out our life. We all have authorship of our future, and with courage and hopefulness we can all be what we want to be.

The process of recovery is not simple or straightforward, but it is always possible. Recovery is a right for children who are affected by trauma, and it is a duty to those who support them to promote all we can for this to be successful. Childhood is our learning place: we learn how things are, we learn how things work and we learn the rules of life. In short, we learn how to be. Providing love, boundaries, clues, commentary, engagement, stimulation, education and opportunities for success and support influences a state of healthy childhood. The question therefore for all of us involved in the care of children is – can we show love to the children and young people that we care for, in the hope that these children will be able to give love and support for those to come in their future lives?

## Therapeutic environments

I believe that our best work with traumatised children should not be judged on whether the child falls down but how we can help them to pick themselves up, how we support them as they heal and how we guide them by modelling positive outcomes. Traumatised children are not monsters; they have simply had monstrous things happen to them. They have experienced events that have shaped their internal and external worlds, and their brain architecture has developed to react and to cope with these catastrophic life events – to be safe and to survive. Researchers at the Center on the Developing Child at Harvard University found that children who learn to cope with adversity engage in a healthy process of development. Children who endure 'unrelieved activation of the body's stress management' and are without protective supporting carers can be challenged in their learning and mental health. Most children who enter care do not come with visual injuries: nevertheless they are as hurt, in as much pain and often as immobilised by their injuries as a child who has suffered a physical injury such as a broken bone. If we consider a child who has broken an arm, how would this injury be treated? One would hope that the child receives comfort and reassurance, that the child's arm is assessed in a 'triage approach' and then gently wrapped in a structure that is strong, supportive and resilient when under pressure. After a while, the arm is re-assessed and, if ready, the structure removed. But the arm is continually cared for therapeutically until strong enough to function.

Our interventions with traumatised children need to provide the same structure, support and love as they do for our physically injured children. The child needs to experience an environment that will protect and heal wounds they have experienced and that will foster positive outcomes. It is our role to provide comfort with structure and to ensure that this structure is strong, resilient and encompassing. In essence, we need to provide comfort, reassurance and safety. The 'hurt' will need assessment, and if necessary, the child should be surrounded by strong boundaries and clear structures so as to protect the child and promote a safe environment. Over a period of time, the hurt can be addressed therapeutically and then, as it is understood, accepted and safely achieved, the child can function healthily.

When considering the most effective therapeutic environments for recovery, we need to have predictable, consistent and repetitive elements that provide safety, security and boundaries. An environment that is designed to promote and develop recovery will provide healing, strength and focus for the child and thereby afford the child opportunities to be lovable, to be loved and to belong.

Education, care and the provision of a loving environment will create the ideal nutrients for children to develop. Lanyado (2003) suggests that recovery can be achieved through providing a nurtured and healthy space, 'taking the tender seedling (the child) and replanting it in a place where it has a better chance of growing. This is an enormously difficult task – attention to detail in their everyday life is vital in bringing about this rehabilitation.'

Therapeutic environments encourage children and young people to engage with those who wish to promote an open and honest approach. They require us as therapeutic life story workers to do the same. When an adult or child uses his or her power to control unhealthy spaces, confrontation and battles flourish. Displaced children often learn to defend themselves against the adults around them who are not able or interested enough to meet their needs. These children have a need for a high level of fairness, sometimes exercising it at the cost of their own wellbeing. As Charles Dickens said, 'In the little world in which children have their existence, whosoever brings them up, there is nothing so finely perceived and so finely felt, as injustice.'

## All behaviour is communication

Children and young people placed in care, especially those who have experienced poor parenting and abuse, may have particular behavioural issues that create challenges for those caring for them.

'All behaviour is communication' is a much-used phrase that considers how children communicate trauma to those around them. Those who had authority over them or responsibility for them in previous environments, such as their birth families or former substitute care placements, as well as their current carers, need to heed their behaviour as much as to listen to their voices. It is also equally important that we understand and ensure that the children in our care are listening to us.

In my experience, traumatised children learn to assess threats: these are identified by reading body language and non-verbal clues rather than by relying on verbal expressions. Once they identify a threat, children do not always follow a self-protection route. For many the trauma is an anticipated inevitable outcome. Often these children have been let down and thus have become entrenched in negative outlooks and are angry confused about the situations they find themselves in. Sadly, they are familiar with these and actively channel any alternative options away so that they can cope with the hurt as they have always done. As Barton *et al.* (2012, p.53) explain:

> Experiences of trauma create states of hyperarousal and fear in children that cause the brain to produce adrenalin, which stimulates the mind and body to be prepared to fight or take flight. This can be seen as a normal healthy response to danger that improves the likelihood for survival. We take flight from the danger rather than stay in its proximity. However, when a child is continually in a state of danger, the brain is in a constant state of arousal and the excess of adrenalin that is produced actually damages the brain's development. Additionally, the part of the brain that reads danger signals becomes hyper vigilant and begins to exaggerate warning signals. Danger is increasingly read into situations that are not actually dangerous. Hence the child becomes highly anxious and hyper aroused by ordinary everyday experiences.

Ziegler (2002) comments that the brain continues to signal to the body that trauma is still occurring long after the actual trauma has ceased to apply (hence the analogy of a trauma as a wound that has yet to heal).

The best therapeutic interventionists are those that champion the children they work with. Therapeutic life story workers need to be accepting, consistent, active listeners who can respond to and nurture children. It is crucial that they show respect and that they value and promote their children. However, the best of us are those who can show love, for this is a crucial part of our childhood and threads its way throughout our lives. To love is to be loved.

Children look to their carers as nurturers, and the 'relational aspect' of care is as important as any practical process. Therapeutic life story work is designed to nurture the relationship between the primary carer and the child through modelling, direction and emotional congruence. If children believe that you care for them, they will care for you. This in turn will provide opportunities for the children to model care and to learn its benefits for when they are adults and require skills to do the same for their own children. To be loved, to love and to belong is the right of every child; therefore, it seems logical to state that to be cared for, to care and to attach is a need that we all share. For a therapeutic life story worker, a good start is to model Bronfenbrenner's (1994) observation that children need someone who is crazy about them:

> Somebody's got to be crazy about that kid, and vice versa! But what does 'crazy' mean? It means that the adult in question regards this particular child as somehow special – even though objectively the adult may well know that this is not the case… For the child, the adult is also special – someone to whom the child turns most readily in trouble and in joy, and whose comings and goings are central to the child's experience and well-being.

Our children in care need to feel loved to know how to love others. For me and those who know me well, I often consider fictional writers and their ability to say the things that I most want carers to be aware of. My favourite film of all time is the *Wizard of Oz*, and the line that the great Oz speaks to the tin man is: 'A heart is not judged by how much you love; but by how much you are loved by others' (Baum, screenplay 1939).

## What is recovery?

> The core task for professionals where a child or young person has experienced significant harm is to assist them and their families or their carers in their journey to recovery. (Bentovim 2009)

There is much written about the effects of trauma on children and their development, and many organisations responsible for their care refer to 'trauma-informed practice'. The work of Dr Bruce Perry (2008) and Dr Daniel Hughes (2004) has done much to share thinking on the impact of trauma on children with carers and social care workers. The therapeutic life story work process provides the opportunity to review life events of the self and of those who have conceived the self.

Through this exploration, there is a chance to 'make sense' of the world, of our parental and authoritative figures and our own sense of self. Terry Philpot and I put forward the following view:

> The life story worker picks up the shattered shards of a child's life, putting them together with great sensitivity. A long process begins to help children internalize understandings and to explore the meaning of their life and identity. Without the opportunity to integrate this work into the rest of the therapeutic task, the chances of children being able to make sense of what has happened to them and put the past into place are very slim. (Rose and Philpot 2005)

The approach is not always an easy option, but it is an essential one – in England and Wales the National Institute for Health and Care Excellence has stated that all children in care require life story work. Indeed, the England and Wales Adoption Act states that all adopted children have a right to understand their family of origin and their history. The therapeutic life story work intervention serves as a vehicle to take a child from the past and to the future and, in doing so, allows the internalisation of a safer, more accurate narrative of self.

For recovery to be effective, we need to involve primary carers in the work. I have long held the view that when trying to resolve challenges in the care placements, working with a child alone might help the child with child issues; working with the carer alone might also help the carer deal with carer issues; but working with both the child and the carer will deal with the challenges of living together. Caring for any child can be difficult, but caring for a child who has learnt that adults can be dangerous, threatening, sneaky and dishonest can be almost impossible. Therapeutic life story work is designed to be an opportunity to coach those involved to care with knowledge, understanding of the self and acceptance of each other for who we are.

Therapeutic parenting is a skilled approach; there are many publications that consider the essentials for caring for traumatised children, including the Sexual Abuse Child Consultancy Service (SACCS) series of books around recovery work for traumatised children.

Others have also contributed to this essential approach within the family home as well as within schools and communities. Essentially, therapeutic carers need to provide safe environments with predictability, consistency and repetition at the heart of their care. With a clear emphasis on protection, attachment and belonging, caring adults have essential roles in providing opportunities and guidance that lead to the healthy development of their children. We trust that parental figures commit to keeping their children safe, and in doing so they model essential clue sets for when their children begin their own adult relationships and, in most cases, their parental journey.

We all need to be loved, and children who have been loved unconditionally have the ability to return this love to others. Many children who might find love a complex, potentially frightening and empty emotion need those around them to make sense of these feelings and to support change. Making time for these children and ensuring that they know that their carer(s) are available to them, that they can enjoy consistency, predictability and trust and have their needs met, will provide surety that promotes their recovery.

As children develop, they will look for clues from those whom they are dependent on. This role-modelling is an essential task for the child to understand how to react, control, behave and show appropriate emotion. It is important that the carer is able to demonstrate internal control, to remain calm and to express their own internal thoughts and feelings with commentary for children to learn. Children who have been traumatised are sensitive to emotion and both verbal and non-verbal communication. In many cases their survival has depended on this skill. Traumatised children learn and adapt to the environment and culture they are in: they adopt emotions, and adapt behaviour that shields their true feelings behind such emotion. Some children will laugh at times when sad things have occurred, which can often be as a result of learned coping behaviour. Underneath the facade the child may be confused and hurt, but not be able to communicate this or risk showing a vulnerability that they feel they cannot afford.

To be a caring adult, you must be able to use the skills that you have to ensure that you can communicate with the child and that the child is able to communicate with you. As Margaret Hodge, the former Minister for Children, Young People and Families, states (DfES 2004), 'Children need to be at the heart of everything we do. Listening to children across all ages will ensure they get the support they need at the right time to achieve their full potential.'

Recovery work with children and their carers also requires competency in listening skills. We are in no position to engage therapeutically with children unless we actively listen to what is being said and what is being communicated.

I have listed three types of listeners below based on the work by Egan (2002).

## Pretend listener

Pretend listeners use gestures and paralinguistic responses to put forward the impression that they are engaged, but, as the name suggests, they are pretending. Often when pretend listeners are active, they are thoughtful of their own issues and concerns. Children who have been traumatised can be very effective at recognising the thoughts and feelings of those around them and often identify (through this attunement ability) who is worth communicating with and, more importantly, who isn't. Paralinguistic responses include the use of tone, pitch and non-verbal cues and expressions.

Think about the times you have had conversations and found your mind wandering to the agendas outside the interaction – my own children used to catch me out and so test me by saying something impossible, such as they had just got back from the Moon, but I would keep nodding and agreeing with everything they said.

## Limiting listener

Limiting listeners limit their listening to their own agenda. The problem with this is that often the listeners are allowing themselves to only hear the things that they consider affirm their views or, at the least, those views that are not challenging. Often children within therapeutic life story work will speak of many things, each one having the possibility of helping them to make sense of the world. If, as a therapeutic life story worker, I am only listening to a part of the communication that covers a particular life event we are discussing, then I will miss the rich material that will be available, as the whole message from the child has not been heard.

## Self-centred listener

Self-centred listeners have their own problems, and the interview is a vehicle for them to sort out these problems. For example, they may have low self-esteem and involve themselves in conversation simply because they like to see others being dependent on them and valuing them.

All of us who work with people, especially children and young people, have engaged in the above types of listening in our professional as well as our personal lives.

Egan introduced the following process, which he termed *active listening*. Active listening is an active process. As you listen to the person speak and watch their facial expressions and body language, you're actively asking yourself the following four questions:

- What is or was this person feeling?

- What exactly did this person experience?

- How did they react?

- What is the essence, the core message, of what is happening to this person?

While you're not necessarily looking for a pattern or the big picture, you want to integrate the particular feelings, behaviours and experiences into a meaningful whole message.

I mentioned paralinguistic language earlier, as it is Egan's preferred way of encouraging the story of the listener. An active listener will use language such as 'Umm', 'I see', 'Go on', 'Yes' and 'Interesting'. As the conversation unfolds, you will find that the child will convey their story, and by modelling good paralinguistic skills you can help children develop such skills in the future. Active listening involves picking up accurately what the other person is communicating, such as repeated words or phrases, emphasis on particular words, instances of volume and tone, as well as words used.

As well as hearing *what* the person has said, it is important to observe *how* things are said. Just as the therapeutic life story worker expresses body language with clues to the young person, so the body language of the child or young person can give clues to the therapeutic life story worker. It is important to be aware of actions such as facial expressions, body positioning, physiological responses such as sweat, and eye contact or eye focusing. There have been many times when I have engaged with children and witnessed them de-focusing as they leave our conversation and think of other things. With the active listening process, I respond by asking where they are and acknowledging that I have lost them. This acts as an opportunity to refocus for both of us.

Positive active listening can help improve poor self-concept. If we take an interest – if we listen to, care for and protect children – then we will improve their internal esteem that informs them that they are worthwhile, valued and loved. Some children who do not feel loved and lovable in their immediate family can develop feelings of self-worth if a relative takes an interest, a teacher appears concerned and caring, or a therapeutic carer responds with kindness and consistency and actively listens to them.

## How long does recovery take?

Recovery is an individual journey: it takes as long as it takes. Trauma is loss – a loss of self, of a part of you that you either once had, or that you should have had. The earlier that recovery can begin, the more likely that the time it takes is shortened and the more effective it is likely to be. Trauma is heavy, and as time goes on, it becomes heavier, to the point that the weight of such trauma becomes unbearable. Early work with children is essential to stem the development of potential mental ill-health. The roots of trauma develop coping mechanisms, often for defence purposes, and for some children such defensive actions become the default behaviour, and as they mature so does the complexity of the coping mechanism.

One important implication of the fact that recovery is likely to be a longer-term process is the importance of assessment. We need to know that what we do with children supports their recovery, and therefore therapeutic life story work has developed its own assessment process. This has been based on the work that was carried out in the SACCS in 2006 and by the Argyll and Bute Fostering and Adoption Team, led by Jill Hughes, a pioneer in supporting hurt children in adoption placements in 2011 (Rose 2012) where we designed the model alongside the SHANARRI outcomes (2009).

## Therapeutic life story assessment model

This model helps therapeutic life story workers to consider and contribute to the recovery of the children they work with. The model has been replicated by numerous organisations such as SACCS and Lighthouse Project Melbourne. It is based on the work of Patrick Tomlinson and myself to track the developing recovery of children through child development domains. The therapeutic life story worker, following interviews with the child's carer and educator as well as a therapist if involved, completes the first assessment. This assessment compares seven domains of the subject child in relation to a healthy child of a similar age. In doing so, they would score the child between 1 and 4 (1 being serious concerns and 4 representing no concerns). As well as scoring, the therapeutic worker is required to provide evidence and examples as to why they have scored the child as they have. Once completed, the shape of the child is plotted and the 'zone of proximity' (Vygotsky 1978) is identified.

The process described below is now the accepted assessment for all those engaged with the therapeutic life story professional qualification. The assessor considers the presentation of the child by comparing them with a healthy child of a similar age in the community. If the assessor feels that the presentation is similar and therefore not concerning, the assessor would score a 4 and explain why (the examples of what to consider are included in the scoring tables). If the assessor scores a 3 they have some worries; if 2, then clear concerns; and if 1, there are major concerns for the child being assessed.

## *Achieving and learning*

1. School is currently not working well for the child. They are unable to complete most/all of the work, which they say is too hard or too boring. Homework is consistently not completed or handed in late. Their behaviour in school is often disruptive to themselves and others, and they are regularly asked to leave lessons; they seem very preoccupied with things other than learning in school and may be on a behaviour plan. There is a general consensus that the child is not achieving academically and not reaching their potential.

2. The child often appears anxious about going to school, expressing that they would rather not go while accepting that they have to. They have a small number of friends but complain that they can feel a bit lonely and left out of things, especially at break times and lunchtime. They find lessons hard and can find it hard to concentrate while sometimes disrupting others in lessons. They are reluctant to ask for help. They are below target in some subject areas.

3. The child likes school, has a number of friends and mostly enjoys lessons. They do not find lessons too difficult, and if something is more challenging, then they are not worried about asking a teacher for additional help. They are happy to go in the mornings and seem to cope well with the more unstructured break times and lunchtimes. They are able to manage their homework without too much prompting and hand it in when it is due. They are achieving their potential.

4. The child really enjoys school and has lots of friends there. They appear happy and included at break times and lunchtimes, rather than finding more unstructured times difficult. They ask for help at appropriate times and in appropriate ways. They have good relationships with the school staff and know who to go to if they feel worried or unsure about something. There is a general feeling that they are doing at least their best in subjects taught

and they generally find the work not too difficult. Homework is completed and handed in on time.

## *Attachment to primary carer*

1. The child has a negative internal working model; for example, they feel that they are bad, unlovable and worthless, their carers are hurtful, unresponsive and untrustworthy, and the world is an unsafe place and not worth living in. They show no empathy and do not seem to have a conscience. They retract and push away any love and care that the primary carer attempts to give them, and the child may be very controlling, angry or helpless. Their attachment style is largely disorganised.

2. The child is either very 'clingy' to their primary carer, needing almost constant reassurance that they are there for them, or they appear ambivalent to needing care and are very self-reliant. There is still an overriding sense that the world can be a very unsafe place and they do not wholly trust their primary carers.

3. The child has a fairly positive internal working model and feels that they can trust their primary carer who responds well to them. They like the family that they live with and they feel accepted. They have a consistent routine and know that they are going to be kept safe and cared for. They know that their carers want them and that they want them to be happy and to achieve. They seem to understand that they are staying within their current family for a long time and they are happy about that.

4. The child feels very safe and happy with the family that they are living with. They have secure attachments where they feel loved by their primary carers and they are able to love them back. They feel understood and listened to and they know how important and cared for they are. They have developed a conscience. They are able to seek comfort and affection when needed and feel that they are worthwhile and lovable; they have a sense of belonging and know that the world is not always a scary place. They are

settled where they are and know that they are wanted. They are able to have time away from each other (to freely explore) with the reassurance that the carer will still be there for them and is keeping them emotionally in mind. The child has a positive internal working model.

## *Physical health and development*

1. Overall the child is not in good health and finds it difficult to self-care or to accept help from others. They have little motivation and energy to do any physical exercise. The child finds going to sleep at night very hard, and when they do eventually sleep, they usually have broken nights, waking up regularly throughout the night. They appear anxious and afraid at night times. They do not care about their body and have little self-respect for what they look like; they are considered by some others as being unclean and scruffy, and they have a poor self-image. Eating can be a difficult area and they may be significantly under- or overweight. Some of the things that the child does are considered not in their best interest and are a risk to their health.

2. There are some health concerns, which are either being managed or investigated. The child is not motivated or interested in doing physical exercise but will with encouragement. Their personal hygiene could be described as 'hit and miss'; sometimes they forget to wash and keep themselves clean, so they need reminders and a lot of support to do so. They need help to relax and know that they are safe and protected at night time. Their diet is not that healthy, and they probably eat too many foods that are not that nutritious in place of healthier options.

3. There are no significant health concerns; the child has a good diet and exercises regularly. They usually sleep well at night time and know the importance of personal hygiene, having enough respect to look after their body in a normal way appropriate to their age and development.

4. The child has good health and there are no major concerns. They have a healthy appetite and a balanced diet. There are no difficulties with going to bed and sleeping through the night. Regular appointments with the dentist and other health professionals take place when needed. They have respect for themselves and know that it is important to look after their body; they ask for and accept help with this when needed. They are very active and participate enthusiastically in sports both at and outside of school.

## Emotional intelligence

1. The child avoids talking about their feelings and consistently feels angry and cross about most things. They keep this inside themselves and find it difficult to manage, resulting in hitting out or being destructive, hurting themselves or others in the process. The child does not consider how others are feeling and shows little or no empathy. They are not able to take responsibility for their own actions.

2. The child feels sad, cross and worried more often than happy and consistently finds it hard to express how they are feeling to others. They sometimes have thoughts about hurting themselves or others, but don't usually carry this through. They can find it difficult to concentrate on what people ask them to do. It is rare that they take responsibility for their own actions.

3. The child expresses that they are happy most of the time, and when they do feel sad, cross or worried then they are able to tell others so that they can receive support. The child is able to reflect on their own actions and take responsibility for the choices that they make.

4. The child is able to appropriately identify and express a range of feelings, including happiness, sadness, disappointment and crossness, to people whom they trust. They can also identify other people's emotions and show empathy, having the ability

to cheer up or calm down another person. Mostly the child feels happy and settled and enjoys life. They have a positive outlook and are looking forward to their future. They act responsibly and are fully aware of the consequences of their choices and actions.

## How included the child is

1. The child does not seem to have any friends and says that they feel left out and out of things most of the time. They feel disliked and rejected by their peers and feel that they are different to them. They find it difficult being with people their own age and knowing how to interact appropriately. Clubs they have joined have not gone well, and they may have been excluded from them due to their behaviour. They usually spend time with others who are either a lot younger or older than them, and this causes a concern for the adults in their life who care about them. They have been described as a 'loner'.

2. The child has few friendships but is known within their peer group. They do not receive invitations to different activities like birthdays or going to people's houses. It does not appear that they are truly included and they find it hard talking to people their own age. They spend more time on their own than with other people their age.

3. The child has quite a few friends but no one really close or a 'best friend'. They do go to clubs and participate well, and also receive invitations to different events.

4. The child has lots of friends both in and outside school and has some closer friends too. They are accepted and included in their peer group and are a member of some clubs; they are popular. Friendships are appropriate to their age and are reciprocated. They are truly included in both their current family and the wider community. They receive invitations to different things. The child is not trying to act older or younger than their age. They have a sense of belonging to where they are now.

## *Identity*

1. The child has lots of questions about their past and many gaps in their knowledge. They consistently think magically, making up possible scenarios. They seem to be very confused and preoccupied with their past, and their behaviour is often a challenge to others. They do not understand why they are living where they are now and why they cannot live with other people from their birth family. They do not know who they are and appear very lost.

2. The child has minimal information about what has happened in their past and how they came to live where they are now. They have a collection of stories from other people, and they do not know which are true events and which are made up. They are confused about their past and spend significant amounts of time thinking about it. They often feel sad, hurt and rejected and do not always express these appropriately.

3. The child seems to know why they are living where they are now, although they do have some questions. There are some gaps in their knowledge, but they are aware of mostly all of the significant things that have happened in their life so far. They have quite a positive self-identity but need help and support with understanding their story.

4. The child has had help to understand why they are living where they are now and how and why life has changed for them. The questions they had previously have been answered, and they have internalised why things happened and why people behaved in the way that they did. They have a sense of identity and culture, and they have worked through all of the things that they were confused, cross and sad about. There are no longer big gaps in their knowledge and they are not demonstrating magical thinking. They have accepted their past and are able to live mostly in the here and now, without feeling that their past controls them — overall they have a healthy sense of self.

## *Ability to concentrate and be physically settled*

1. The child finds it incredibly difficult to concentrate on any activities, especially within school. They may complain of always having a head full of thoughts, mostly about bad or negative things or questions that they don't know the answer to. They find it almost impossible to sit still and be physically settled and usually need to move around and/or talk loudly. They present as being hypervigilant and anxious and wary of the environment around them. Others can see them as hyperactive, obstructive or very demanding.

2. The child often finds it difficult to concentrate and 'flits' from one space or activity/subject of focus to another fairly frequently. They find sitting or being physically still a challenge, finding it easier to move in some way. Other people may describe them as a fidget. They complain that bad or difficult thoughts come in to their head quite often and they can't get rid of them easily.

3. The child is able to concentrate most of the time and can stay still and settled for fairly long periods. They are able to focus on a task and see it through to the end without too much difficulty.

4. The child is able to concentrate well both in school and also more generally on everyday tasks. They are not constantly thinking about bad thoughts and do not appear to be preoccupied with their past or other things that they are worried about. They participate well in home life and school and in clubs and activities. They are able to be physically still and settled when it's needed, as opposed to constantly moving and jumping around, talking and fidgeting.

Once you have decided where your child/young person/adult is in relation to a similarly aged 'healthy' child, plot the scoring on the charts shown in Figures 2.1 and 2.2.

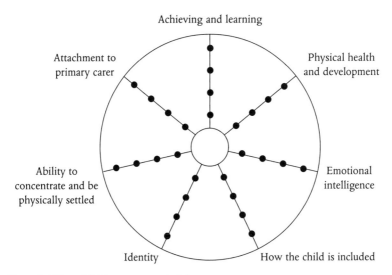

*Figure 2.1 Your child/young person/adult*

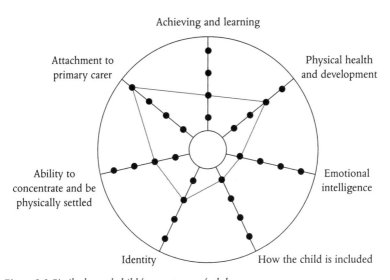

*Figure 2.2 Similarly aged child/young person/adult*

Child's name: . . . . . . . . . . . . . . . . . . . . . . . . . . . . . . . . . . . . . .

Child's age: . . . . . . . . . . . . . . . . . . . . . . . . . . . . . . . . . . . . . . .

People supporting this therapeutic life story work are:

. . . . . . . . . . . . . . . . . . . . . . . . . . . . . . . . . . . . . . . . . . . . . .

Why is now a good time to do therapeutic life story work?

. . . . . . . . . . . . . . . . . . . . . . . . . . . . . . . . . . . . . . . . . . . . . .

. . . . . . . . . . . . . . . . . . . . . . . . . . . . . . . . . . . . . . . . . . . . . .

Child-specific outcomes for this piece of therapeutic life story work:

. . . . . . . . . . . . . . . . . . . . . . . . . . . . . . . . . . . . . . . . . . . . . .

. . . . . . . . . . . . . . . . . . . . . . . . . . . . . . . . . . . . . . . . . . . . . .

. . . . . . . . . . . . . . . . . . . . . . . . . . . . . . . . . . . . . . . . . . . . . .

Therapeutic life story workers complete this assessment at the start of the intervention on their own; then after three months they complete another assessment and ask the carers, teachers (if attending education), therapist (if one is engaged) and the child themselves (if age appropriate) to complete one also. Nadine Jay, a therapeutic life story worker in Peterborough, has designed a 'child-friendly' assessment. With her permission, I have added the chart shown in Figure 2.3.

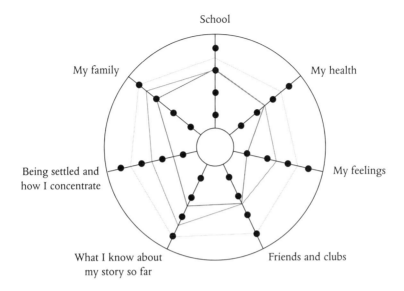

*Figure 2.3 Completed chart*

The domain headings are more child specific for discussion, and in this example Nadine has plotted a child's assessment over the life story programme – as you can see, the child believes that she has recovery in all areas of her development. As children and young people see that they are feeling more positive about their world, the more committed they become to achieve parity with their peers and secure greater esteem.

# Chapter 3

# COMMUNICATING WITH CHILDREN – THERAPEUTIC LIFE STORY WORK TECHNIQUES

*Richard Rose, Child Trauma Intervention Services*

*We cannot become what we need to be by remaining what we are.*

*Max DePree (1997)*

All the contributors to this book have undertaken therapeutic life story work training and, in most cases, are clinically supervised by me. I have noted that many discussion techniques that were first introduced in my second book on life story therapy (Rose 2012) have since been updated and improved. To this end, I have decided to rewrite two of the chapters by way of an update and also to support new readers with an insight into the skills and tools used, and to assist them in their practice. I would still recommend that new readers consider the 2012 book for guidance and other techniques. I would also recommend that readers access the life story (activity-based) books written by Katie Wrench and her colleague Lesley Naylor (2014), as well as the excellent books from Joy Rees (2009) and from Tony Ryan and Rodger Walker (2015).

## Initial visit

I am frequently asked how I start the intervention after receiving the instruction. My first port of call is often with the primary carer(s) as I hope that they will assist me in the delivery. This first meeting helps me to consider and walk alongside the carer(s)' world and to assess their potential capacity to engage in the work. I then use the assessment tool that I have introduced in Chapter 2 to aid in understanding the strengths and challenges for the child referred. Finally, I ask the carer(s) to assist me in completing a behaviour tree (this is discussed later in this chapter) so that I can help to identify the history of the child that is known by the carer, the behaviour and emotions communicated by the child on a day-to-day basis, and how the carer relates the child's history to their current situation.

When I first meet children to undertake life story work, I normally arrive with some good quality colour crayons/pens such as Stabilo or decent Crayola and a roll of 'lining paper' (wallpaper will be as useful) that is thick enough to take felt, ink and paint (and glue!). I am often asked in countries that do not have wallpaper where therapeutic life story workers might be able to get some – luckily in this global age, wallpaper can be exported from the UK across the world, and more and more is finding its way to Australia as you read this. I also bring a pack of Jenga on my initial visit: for some children there is concern about how they might welcome me, so I take the Jenga blocks in a decorated old wine box. As I walk into the house I gently swing the box, and the wood rattling around inside makes an intriguing noise – children cannot resist and so will ask: 'What's in the box?' As the child has asked me to engage, we have a level playing field where I am not asking – they are. I often bring an A3 art pad to encourage drawing and to write on if the wallpaper feels a little overwhelming at first.

## Jenga (tower blocks)

Jenga is a brilliant game for the introduction process and relationship building. Its very nature is to construct and then to deconstruct, only to construct again. Jenga is a high-end tower building game, which costs around £13 per set in the UK and seems to be slightly more expensive when purchased in other countries. Most countries do sell similar tower block games for a much cheaper cost; this includes Kmart, Woolworths and Toys R Us. As I have previously said, each child I work with has a set at the beginning of the introduction process, and every time I have used this, the results have been very positive.

A typical set has 54 rectangular bricks, and each tile is placed in groups of three to form a tower which is 18 bricks high. The idea of the game is to carefully, on a turn-by-turn basis, remove one brick at a time using just one hand. On each successful removal the removed brick is placed on the top of the tower, thus increasing the height and leaving the structure a little less stable. As we begin the game, the child, the carer and the therapeutic life story worker each take a turn, with the oldest going first!

As the process begins I am interested in how each play the game – whether the child plays to win, and whether the adult does the same. I am interested in alliances, support, encouragement and engagement; as well as the verbal communication, I am particularly keen to identify the non-verbal. As the game becomes increasingly difficult, I observe body language, feelings, emotional expression and tolerance. Built into this, I am also looking for cause-and-effect thinking, planning and strategy. One can often identify the true course of the placement by watching a child and their carer play this game, as the interaction and the relationships are fascinating. As an example, I was playing this game with a foster mother and her looked-after child. Each time the child managed to remove a block the mother congratulated her daughter, but this was very awkward as the child was irritated by this and eventually sabotaged the game to stop her. We were able to think about this over the following sessions and assisted the foster mother to be more strategic in her praise and the child to see that such praise was a reward and not an overbearing threat.

The game can explore feelings of success, anxiety, nervousness and anticipation; each affords the opportunity to make sense of the communication of those involved. My checklist for consideration is as below:

- How do the child and carer risk assess?

- How do the child and carer approach the task?

- Is either the child or carer overtly strategic in their thinking?

- How do the child and carer cope with anticipation?

- How do the child and carer manage with pressure and tension?

- How do the child and carer encourage, engage and strategically play?

- Do the child and carer play by the rules?

- How do the child and carer offer support, advice and guidance?

- How do the child and carer demonstrate relationship and allegiance?

- How do the child and carer react when successful?

- How do the child and carer react when others are successful?

- How do the child and carer show empathy?

- How do the child and carer react to the possibility of failure?

- How do the child and carer react to failure?

- Are the child and carer kind, thoughtful and caring?

- Are the child and carer unkind, thoughtless and dismissive?

- Are the child and carer able to communicate the feelings that they feel?

- Does the child enjoy play?

- Can the carer play?

Once I am happy that the game has given as much information as possible, I ask the child if I might be able to take the game away and add things to it. I then take 20 bricks and write a question on each; ten questions are benign/fun and the ten others are particular to the child and the known history. Benign/fun might include asking the child the following questions as well as completing statements:

- If you had £1 million, what would you buy?

- What animal is most like you?

- What makes you laugh?

- If you had three wishes, what would one of them be?

- If you could go anywhere on holiday, where would you go?

- My friends are...

- The best song is...

- My favourite food is...

- My favourite book is...

- If I could have an animal it would be a...

Child-specific questions could be asking them to complete these statements:

- I am scared when...

- I dream about...

- I cry if...

- You know I am angry when I...

- My safe place is...

- I miss...

- I hate it when...

- I am sad when...

- If am worried I tell...

- I wish I could...

The game is then played with the carer, child and life story therapist, and as the bricks are removed and placed on top of the tower, if there is a question on the brick, then it is read out. The person who pulled the brick from the tower asks the question and everyone has a chance to answer it (including the person who asked the question itself). I have found that the simple act of sharing information and hearing and being heard is a valuable introduction to the life story process. Many children I work with are upset when they do not choose a question brick and at the end of the game will go through the questions and ask each one. The information gained from such an exercise is incredibly valuable and, as it is wrapped into a game, the stark questions can be dealt with in a non-threatening way.

I use this part of the game when we are getting to know each other; but it can be used well with those undertaking wishes and feelings work and child assessments. I once played this game with an 11-year-old boy: he loved the game and insisted that he should have a question on each of his bricks. I explained that, as the Jenga was his game, he could write a question on all of his bricks and we could go through them in our next session. Two weeks later, he had the Jenga ready and it had 34 more questions added to the 20 already set. As we worked through them, he told me to write each of the questions down on his wallpaper, and his carer was asked to record the answers from him in red, mine in blue and her answers in green.

This game is played for a few times over two or three sessions and then I ask if we can choose a colour each. Together we then colour 18 bricks each, so this should lead to 18 bricks with red ends, 18 with yellow ends and the last 18 with blue ends; these colours are changeable to whatever suits the child. This part of the game is played by the child and not by the adults. The carer and I are there to encourage the child to play. They are informed that the colours have rules and then the child is able to play. Red means the child can ask a question about the story being discussed at that session. Blue means the adults can ask the child a question as long as it is about the story shared at that session. Finally, yellow means that they are encouraged to consider how the people we are talking about in that particular session may have been feeling. The one rule for this version of the game is that it lasts ten minutes and is not governed by the fall and rise of the tower. The game is played, and it is important to ensure that any questions from the child or the adults have to be related to the subject of the session only and not about things outside the session. As an example, if we were discussing the child being removed from their home, the questions must relate to this event. The beauty of this session is simply that the child becomes the facilitator and can manage the interaction. Each of the questions and the answers are written on the wallpaper as they occur so as to honour the importance of the child's narrative.

Again, I play this game over a period of three or four sessions so that the child can get used to the process. There have been many times when a child has asked to play Jenga during later sessions when they feel that it might prove useful.

## The importance of play

Games, such as Jenga, are an essential medium to reach children, and I use many to engage and to practise relationships, be they of the storming, forming or norming variety. Janet West (1980) has explained how play helps a child to:

- develop physical skills

- find out what is 'me' and 'not me'

- understand relationships

- experience and identify emotions

- practise roles

- explore situations

- learn, relax and have *fun*

- act out troublesome issues

- achieve mastery.

Play is symbolic communication and acts as a bridge between conscious awareness and emotional experiences. In play, children embrace the numinous and the luminous, as well as the practicalities of daily life.

Play does not occur on its own. It is symbolic of who we are – our values, our understanding, our thinking and our experiences. Important events and relationships, as well as our understanding of the world we live in, become part of the play dynamic. Children will represent what they perceive in life – be that the roles of parents, carers, doctors, policemen, soldiers and teachers. Often these roles are gender specific or reflect the cultural world we live in, but rarely does play enact just the actual events witnessed or experienced: indeed the role of imagination, fantasy, hope, desire and despair will be present.

The act of play is to engage, share, learn and achieve. When you play with children, helping with construction, creative art, physical activity and communication through enactment, you are entering a form of communication that is full of opportunity and discovery. The action of the play becomes a portal for those involved to share a common activity that ultimately brings down the barriers which often exist between the child and the adult.

> …my work with both children and adults, and my contributions to psycho-analytic theory as a whole, derive ultimately from the play technique evolved with young children…but the insight that I gained into early development, into unconscious processes, and into the nature of the interpretations by which the unconscious can be approached, has been of far-reaching influence on the work. (Klein 1955)

Social workers will often state that the best time to talk with a child is in their car. Much the same occurs for family support workers and other direct service providers, and they are, of course, correct. The fact that other activities are ongoing allows the child to take more risks to engage in discussion; as the attention of the adult is drawn away from the direct one to one, the child is able to talk, think and act out how they feel inside.

Think of a game that you most like to play, then consider why.

- Do you think you are likely to win?

- Do you enjoy the challenge?

- Do you enjoy the social context?

- Do you want to become better through practice?

- Do you enjoy beating people?

- Do you cheat?

Then consider what games you think children enjoy, and why.

- Have you thought about why they like it?

- What are you like with the game?

- Do they always win?

- Do they enjoy the time with you?

- Do they want to practise more?

- Do they cheat?

I love to encourage children and their carer(s) to play strategic games such as chess or draughts, or dominoes. In the process of therapeutic life story work we are helping children and their carer(s) to consider sequential patterns, behavioural responses and instinctive defence mechanism responses. This would be pointless, though, if we were only identifying challenges: the core activity is to understand, then to accept, the past and look to the future. This can be done as the child begins to understand that not only is there cause and effect (an action followed by a consequence) but there are also ways in which they can identify and change outcomes by thinking through the likely consequences and choosing to do or not to do the action. In chess, to be successful, you have to consider several moves ahead – if your opponent moves his knight next to your queen, do you take it because you can or do you consider what your opponent can do if you took it? This requires time and space; it slows down the automatic reaction, and you might decide to ignore the knight and move your queen to safety. I consider this to be the ultimate way to model cause-and-effect thinking. When mastered, we are in control of our environment rather than our environment being in control of us.

Games that are successful in working with children who have been traumatised through early life experiences and have low self-esteem include, but are not limited to:

- Snap

- Happy Families

- Uno

- Guess Who?

- Frustration

- Ludo.

All these games are quick and action based, and the child, the adult and the therapeutic life story worker are able to succeed or fail. If the child says that they were rubbish at the game, the adult can discuss it, ask how the child feels, and relate that to other feelings. In much the same way, quick games like Snap allow children to consider lots of emotions as they win and lose; again the adults can explore the feelings with the child, and model how they (as adults) feel when they win or lose.

## Vocabulary of feelings

It is important for the direct work process that we have the opportunity to think about, experiment with and identify the myriad of feelings that we all have the capacity to experience. I have devised several ways in which to explore feelings through activity-based tasks and, like all these tried and tested interventions, they can be used as tools for communication with children.

One thing that I have noticed is the limited literacy of feelings children and adults seem to share when speaking of emotions. Over the years I have tried many differing techniques to get feelings 'on the table' – but recently I introduced a process that has never failed to reap rewards. Rather than asking children or adults to think of feelings, I ask them to identify a space on the wallpaper and to each choose a colour. I then get my watch, or phone, out and explain that we are going to have a competition. We have 60 seconds to write down as many feelings as we can think of – we are not worried about spelling and, if need be, the child can ask me not to do my list, but to write down each feeling they can think of. So far, every child has chosen to do their own list. On average, the child identifies 12 feelings, and adults 10 to 14, so within moments we have more than 20 feelings written on the wallpaper. The child is then asked to identify the same feelings that we all thought of in our individual lists. These are written down on a separate space on the wallpaper. Therefore, if I had feelings such as 'happy', 'sad', 'angry', 'silly', 'frustrated' and 'scared', the child had 'happy', 'scared' and 'angry' in their list and the carer had 'scared' and 'angry' in their list, then we would have 'scared' and 'angry' in our separate list.

We typically end with six similar feelings, and then we are able to add one feeling each to the separate list from our individual lists. For example, we might end up with the following feelings in our separate list: scared, worried, silly, angry, confused, mad, excited, tired, lonely. We are then in a position to explore these feelings – when they come about, how they are used, and what we do when we have them.

## Charades

I find this activity fun, and fun is a very important part of therapeutic life story work. Having played charades with 500 people on the same occasion as part of an international conference presentation, I know that it is fun for all kinds of people.

Even with the most resistant of children and their carers, the game creates a complex list of feelings which in turn are acted out and identified, or helpfully misidentified. With the feelings identified by the timed game above, we would write all nine feelings on nine bits of paper. Each piece of paper would then be scrunched up so that we cannot see the feeling; all nine pieces are then put in the middle of the table and one by one we take it in turns to choose a piece and act out the word. The task for the two watching the 'acting' is for them to guess what the feeling is that is being acted out. Be aware of the guesses, as each provides a clue to the child and the carers' awareness and understanding of how each feeling is felt and how each is communicated.

Emotional regulation and emotional expression are both vital to the therapeutic life story process. Being able to see how children and their carers act out feelings has always been helpful as both a reference point and as a visual non-verbal assessment of how children and carers are coping. For some children, acting out feelings can portray hidden feelings and memories, and often there is an opportunity to consider how these feelings affect us both outside and in. I have experienced children acting out 'lonely' and it comes across as contentment or sadness, anxiousness or fear. I have also seen carers acting out the same word and children interpreting this as 'upset', 'cross' or 'dismissive'. There is, with all similar exercises, a risk: we have to be thoughtful with the child. It is important that we play with the child and that in the play we share what feelings mean to us. The more open we are in this respect, the more engaged the child becomes. The child can make sense of the feeling interpretation that they have relied on within their placement, and it is often the case that children will tell their carer when these interpretations have been mistaken. The child can reflect on a feeling that might overwhelm them in the process, which is helpful if the therapist can support the child through this. I have found it useful to use the A3 art pad as a recording medium in these early stages and record the feeling and the associated memory so as to demonstrate its importance to me and the ability to safely hold the memory shared. It does not help if the memory is heard and left to the side: the message may then be received by the child and interpreted as a lack of interest.

The fun generated by the competitive nature of the game needs to be accompanied by a reward, and for this I often arrange a small prize, in most cases chocolate. Once the game has concluded and each has had a chance to act out the feelings, the next step is to consider some of the times that the feelings have been experienced. In the past I have used a simple grid system and plotted Sunday to Saturday of the week. Then the child, the carer and I think about the week we have just had and plot feelings that we have experienced. To do this we all have a separate colour and produce a grid similar to the one shown in Figure 3.1.

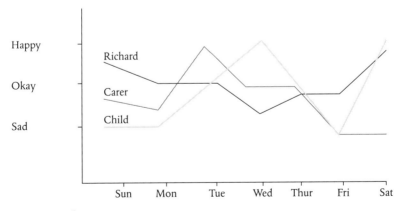

*Figure 3.1 Feelings*

You can of course add different feelings to the column on the left and a different timescale on the horizontal. What is helpful to the child, the carer and the therapist is that the child can see that we all have feelings and that sometimes we feel good and sometimes not. Going through the week with the child and the carer(s) allows them to think of why feelings are changeable, and the reasons behind these feelings, so that we can begin to choose which activities make us feel better and which make us feel worse. In effect, I am beginning to explore ways to help the carer understand the child and the child understand the carer.

## Feelings theme charts

With the same nine feelings from above, it is then helpful to produce a feelings chart. Together the child, the carer and the therapeutic life story worker consider the feelings list under a theme which allows a symbolic representation of each feeling to be created and understood. The most beneficial way of producing this is to collectively think of a theme which would be a fun topic to base the feeling themes on. Over the years the themes used have included food, shoes, hairstyles, plants and animals, as well as the circus, funfair rides and cars.

The theme establishes the focal point, and together, in discussion, the three decide which feeling could be symbolised as part of the overall theme. As an example, the nine feelings identified earlier could be grouped under the theme of weather:

- Scared – lightning

- Worried – dark clouds – no rain

- Angry – clouds with lightning coming out

- Confused – the sun and rays hiding behind a cloud that has rain coming down

- Mad – tornado, cyclone

- Excited – sun with a big smile

- Tired – yawning clouds

- Lonely – a single cloud with one raindrop.

As the feelings are drawn, there is ideally a discussion about each of the feelings which relates them to the child's past. It is important not to relate it to the past of the carer or the therapeutic life story worker, as this exercise is to create the child's feelings chart and not the adults'. Once completed, the symbols are photocopied (or digitally photographed). It is ideal for the therapeutic life story worker to make several copies of each feeling and bring them to the life story sessions once the wallpaper work is introduced. With my work, I will often have 20 copies of the feelings listed above and then invite the child to pick one feeling at a time when they want me and the carer to understand how things felt or feel as we are working through their story.

Children hate being constantly asked how they feel, so the chart allows them to communicate this when they wish to, and the results are very positive. In some cases, the child will seek to use a symbol and decide that it does not reflect what they mean by a feeling such as 'angry'. Perhaps the 'angry' that they have is not the right kind of 'angry', so they create a new symbol for 'very angry' or 'a little angry'. This creates the opportunity to think about different levels of feelings, which add colour to the child's range instead of the 'black and white' concept that they often have. Thus they begin to understand the different shades of feelings.

## All About Me books

I am quite wedded to the concept that the more unique something is, the more value it has. It is for this reason that I do not use the All About Me books that one can purchase from bookshops and various other places.

It is important that children are able to understand their present and feel anchored within a safe port before the visitation of the past. Children need to understand that they are safe, that they are cared for by the primary carer. One way that I have achieved this is through the process of an All About Me book produced exclusively for the child. This is a PowerPoint production that is designed around the child and exclusive to their current placement. The book can sometimes be accompanied by a disposable camera for the child to take pictures of those things around them that are important to them. Ideally the book is left with the child and carer to complete in a two-week period between visits, but often I have sat with the family and they have done this with me, writing directly onto the wallpaper.

I have completed hundreds of these books and can recommend them as a way to capture the current thinking and feelings of the child who completes it. I was asked to do some work with a child who had been described as emotionally 'empty' and, in one sad note from a previous foster carer, as 'the girl with dead eyes'. Having completed the feelings game, the welcome book and the feelings chart, it was clear that the child had many valid feelings and was equally guarded as to whom she would expose them to. The All About Me book invited her to share her current situation and interests, and what I received was a brilliant representation of who she was.

Once the child has seen their book, they are able to consider the opportunity to have a much larger book about their past, which details how they have come to live where they currently do.

I am always concerned about how we involve children in their reviews and how we assist them to have their voices heard, recorded and responded to. The All About Me book could be used as a six-monthly recording process, detailing the current experience of the child. It identifies their likes, their dislikes, their previous placements, their contact, their feelings of being in care, what they love, what they hate, their home life, their school life, their wishes and their feelings. Over a typical five-year care period, children would have prepared ten All About Me books (200 pages of their snapshots of care), which show changes in their interests, hobbies, favourite things, loved ones and so on. For those of us who care for the child, we also get to witness change, growth, identity formation and, if we do the job properly, recovery. Gradually, I am seeing more and more organisations develop these booklets and, as such, carers and children are becoming more aware of each other. I now recommend that carers who have children placed with them also complete All About Me books so that their children can share their interests. This will encourage potential attachment and attunement opportunities.

Two children I am currently working with gave me a Christmas present. They asked me to open the present while I was at their home, and so I agreed to. These children had written an All About Me book for me – it included how they thought about me when they first met me and how they now felt. Then, as they did not know about me, but that I knew about them, the children and their mum asked me to fill the book in, explaining about me and my journey. I thought that this was a great way to illustrate how relationships can be formed when working with children in this way. Many people believe that carers, social care workers and others engaged with supporting children professionally should not share their information with the child they are working with, but it is important to share your story. Of course, there are sensible precautions to bear in mind, including not sharing your unresolved trauma, not sharing problems that you might currently have in your relationships and family, and so on. It is important that you share how you think, how you cope and how you celebrate and embrace opportunity as a role model in a way that is tangible and achievable. I often talk about my interests, my trips and my family, and in discussion provide clue sets for how the children may choose to engage with these.

## Fact, fiction, fantasy and heroism

When working with children, I often find that they are concerned that they will not be believed, that their carers will always be believed and that it really doesn't matter what they say because their truth will never be heard. I considered this over a few years and in 2004 came up with an idea of how to help children become free to tell their story without fear or favour. This started with the premise that 'there is no such thing as absolute truth'. I base this on years of experience where my perception of the truth is my truth, not necessarily the truth. I know from my 'poor' social work in the early 1990s that I rarely recorded the absolute truth. I often recorded what I thought was the truth and, when I did record (or had the time available), it was based on memory some five or more days after the event. Those of you in social care will know the reality of recording and understand that we record what we can but not necessarily when we should. It was with this in mind that I came up with the idea of the fact, fiction, fantasy and heroism exercise (the chart of which is shown in Figure 3.2). This has been very useful when working with children on the confusion of life, the 'he said – she said' moments and differing versions of the same event. The role of therapeutic life story work is not to interpret but to facilitate interpretation and exploration, and as such truths and non-truths are treated as equal in weight and effect.

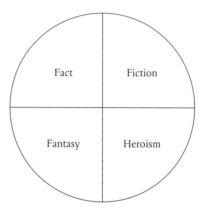

*Figure 3.2 Fact, fiction, fantasy and heroism exercise*

Taking each domain separately, we can explore the concept of each with the child and the carer.

## *What do we know about ourselves that is fact?*

We may say that we know when we were born – but how? Well, we have a birth certificate with a date on. We may say we know who our father is – but how? 'Well, I was told he is', 'He looks like me' and 'He is in all my photographs when I was little'. Birth certificates are only as reliable as the person who completes the paperwork and those who provide the information. I have had plenty of occasions when the birth record has proved to be inaccurate, both in name and date, which has a massive impact on the fact of our lives. We all watch soap operas where babies are conceived out of a relationship and nothing is said; we know of DNA tests that confirm that the fathers people thought they had were in reality not their biological fathers.

Take a moment to recollect your earliest memory. Often the first memory that comes to mind is a painful event, such as hurting yourself or being separated from your parents who seemed to have left you alone – my son reminds me of this often even though he is 24! Now, consider how old you were when this memory was located. For example, my earliest memory is when I fell off a garden gate and 'cracked' my head open. I was about five at the time! Most of us have a verbal memory at around three to five years old; some have memory recollection younger and some older than these years. If, however, we take an average of four years of age for the first memory, then how do we know the facts of our lives before this time? The simple answer of course is through the stories of our parents, relatives and other reference points. Children in the care system may not be able to access this source of information and consequently have little understanding of their early lives.

## *What about fiction then?*

I was born at home in Bristol; my mother having had two children before me was very comfortable in labour (so she tells me!). When my time was due to enter into the external world she informed the midwife that she was not going to give birth to me until the credits rolled at the end of her favourite TV soap opera, *Peyton Place*. Sure enough, the credits came at the end of the episode and I was projected out and onto brown paper. Now this is probably not true, but it has no doubt been shaped along the years by my retelling and is a story. I mentioned this in my last book and my mother reminded me that it was a newspaper I shot onto and not brown paper. However, it is my story, something that makes me unique, and so it becomes a truth about me.

We all have stories that make us who we are, and these stories can be dramatic, exciting and worthy of telling in the same way as other stories are forgotten, not retold and become lost to the teller and the receiver.

How many of us lie? I know I have and will at times continue to do so. What is a lie? Is it for good, to protect, to encourage? (Perhaps, in truth, the picture of a horse that your six-year-old child has done does not look like a horse, but you respond that it is a brilliant picture of a horse.) Maybe the lie is a lie to cause harm, to avoid, to pass the blame.

The thing about lies is that, if you say them long enough and hard enough, they become your truth, a truth that is much more solid than all other truths. The children whom I work with have these kinds of 'truths'; they are the 'truths' that prove hard for their carers to understand, hard for us to deconstruct, and in most cases they become an unshakeable defence for children and young people.

We are, as I said earlier in this book, a collection of stories. It is in the telling of these stories that we understand who we truly are, how we perceive ourselves, how we see others and eventually how we are able to understand how other people see us.

## What about fantasy?

We all fantasise, whether it is about winning the lotto, having a better home or a better job or manager, or similar. Fantasy is a very important part of our truth and who we are, providing us with the opportunity to think beyond our current situation. I have trained many people from all over the world on therapeutic life story work, and fantasy is an extremely vital section to understand. Without the ability to fantasise, many of our children in care would not survive. Their reality can overwhelm them, and so through fantasy they create a coping mechanism that allows them to project away from the awfulness of their current situation. I am sometimes concerned when people state that their child lives in a fantasy world, when in truth the child is demonstrating an ability to manage the chaos and sadness of their reality. I urge carers not to break down this fantasy but to engage with it, to understand it and then to gently support the child to address it with the provision of safe care and messages of belonging.

I worked with a child who told me that when she lived with her mother she had six white horses in the garden of her home. I knew that she had lived in the middle of a city centre in a block of flats and that there was no garden to have horses to live on. I could have said to her, 'Look, this is important work and we do not have time to pretend', and told her that her mother and she lived in a block of flats. Or I could have asked her to tell me what the horses' names were, whether she liked them, rode them and what she fed them on, and then asked if we could draw them on the wallpaper. I hope that you considered that I would do the second, and this is what happened. Listening to her fantasy of the horses – their names, which were her favourites and how we could tell them apart – led to being engaged in the fantasy and exploring the story behind it.

At the end of the wallpaper work, we went on a life story journey and visited the places that she had lived before. We arrived outside the flats where she had lived with her mother; she saw that it was quite neglected and that there was no green area where her horses could have lived. I am sure that she thought about the horses (we had, two weeks earlier, walked through her wallpaper to acknowledge her life journey). On our return, she asked to see her wallpaper and placed the words *I wish* in front of her statement about the horses; the sentence on her wallpaper now reads '*I wish* I had six white horses'. It is this that we all try to get to, where a child can equate her fantasy to her reality and protect them both.

## Where are the heroes?

I often ask carers if they believe that they are heroes to their children and the majority respond by stating that they are not. Children need their carers to be heroes, to champion them, to claim them, to protect them and to love them. Most of us in social care understand that we are role models for our children, offering clue sets that they can follow and, it is hoped, succeed with. We all allow our children to infect our lives, we allow our care to impact on our own family and relationships, and all of us do much more than what we are 'paid' to do. We do this because we want our children and young people to be valued, to feel worthy and to know that they hold an important part in our thinking and feeling…and dare I say it, in our hearts. We cannot expect children to develop a sense of worth if they cannot experience that they are worthy, a sense of loving if they are not loved and a sense of belonging if they are not claimed.

# Using the fact, fiction, fantasy and heroism chart with children

I have used this to help children and young people to problem solve – it has been especially useful for those who are struggling in placements and schools, or who have experienced issues such as self-harm and challenging events in the past. For those children who have challenges in the school environment, the best way is to have the circle available on the wallpaper. Ask the child what is true about school – Do they like it? Do they have friends? What are they studying? What do they find hard? Once done, move to the next quadrant and ask what people say about school, or about the child – Do they like you? Do they say unkind things? Do they think you are good enough? Again, record these and move to the next quadrant – How would you make school more positive? Different lessons? More time? Less homework? More help? And then move to the final quadrant – Who can/is helping you? Who might be the best to help you? Who can advocate for you?

It is a problem-solving technique, but you demonstrate that you are not only listening to the child but also that the child can work with you to explore change and understand reality. I have had great success with this – one child I worked with wanted to go on holiday with her carers, but she was not allowed to go and so went to respite care. In reality, the carers were at a religious retreat where they could have a week of silence to contemplate their faith, something this particular child would find the most 'boring' of experiences. Once it was explained and thought through, she was able to enjoy her week away from the family knowing that it wasn't that she was not wanted, but that it would have been terrible for her. In most cases, children will identify a challenge and take on the blame for this in order to cope; by exploring their understanding of the truth, the stories, the fantasy and those who might help, we can, together, make all the difference in the world.

# Preoccupation – bar charts

Every so often children within the therapeutic life story work do something that either completely alters the thinking or supports it.

A 12-year-old child I worked with was struggling with the concept of life story work and why she should tell people what she thought about her life and the people who had played a part in it. I tried all the things that have been covered so far in the book but none of this actually worked for her. One day she came into the life story session shouting to me, 'I got it, I got it'; I asked her what she had got and she explained, excitedly, that she now understood what life story work was for, and (more importantly) why it made sense for her to do it. She got hold of the paper we were working on, having not started the wallpaper at that point, and told me to draw bar graphs.

She explained that she was learning about bar graphs at school, and during a maths lesson she found herself thinking about her mother and her brother and whether they were safe. She thought about her abuse and her sadness and that she was having problems with other children in the placement. She was worried about her father and whether he would find her, and concerned that people in the school would find out all about her.

I listened and then asked her how she had worked out the need for life story work: she replied that the bar graph had helped her to understand that all the thinking she can't stop herself doing meant that she was too full in her head. She identified that this meant she had too little space left to make sense of new, and sometimes complicated, things. She stated that this was why she was struggling at school and not doing as well as her friend. Again, I said that she was really clever to have worked that out, and she replied, 'If I tell you about all the things in my head, then you can write it down on the wallpaper and we can make sure that it is kept safe.' I agreed that we could do that, and that the wallpaper would make sure that the information was not lost, not forgotten and accessible when it was needed. 'So,' she continued, 'if I get to empty what I am thinking all the time, then I will have space to learn new things and feel better about myself.'

I was amazed at this reasoning, as she had given a great explanation for preoccupation: if you ever lose something valuable and you cannot remember where you have put it, it begins to invade your normal thoughts. Another confession – a few years ago I thought I had left a court report in a hotel room in Sydney, Australia, having remembered putting it in a safe in the hotel room. Picture me on a plane travelling to Perth, suddenly thinking, 'Where did I put that report?' All worries of flying, which are constant as I have an unreasonable fear of it, were immediately put to one side. For the next few hours I was unable to think of anything else but the court paper: Where is it? What if someone finds it? What if the court is informed? What about my job? I was exhausted by the end of the trip, and when I got to the baggage lounge at Perth Airport I tore open my bag and found the court report neatly stored in my luggage. The relief was amazing, but it taught me a little about the preoccupation that some of our children have when they are constantly bombarded with the most traumatising thoughts, yet have to try and survive in the world of education and in society in general.

As an aside, there is a lot of talk around providing 'level playing fields' for children in care. This has led to the provision of laptops, tuition and other services. None of these would work for children who are traumatised and, as a consequence, they are always at a disadvantage in relation to others. The only way I believe that children can be provided with a 'level playing field' is if we can help them to gain an understanding of their preoccupation, which inhibits their learning opportunities. Therapeutic life story work can provide this, and when I work with children's preoccupation they begin to engage with education. Many of these children have gone on to achieve outstanding results in their GCSEs and further qualifications.

All the children, their carers and I now complete bar charts of our thinking in the process so that we can understand each other and what is stuck and how we manage this.

## Behaviour tree (psychodynamic thinking)

I have also developed a version of the behaviour tree, which is loosely based on the Tree of Life (Denborough 2008), established by the Dulwich Centre Foundation based in Adelaide, South Australia, and an organisation called the Regional Psychosocial Support Initiative (REPSSI), active in South and Central Africa. I also considered the 'damaged goods tree' introduced by Suzanne Sgroi as a useful representation of the effect of the past and how it governs current behaviour. In doing so, I have designed tools which continue to prove highly successful when working with family and foster breakdown, behaviour management and, in this instance, understanding ourselves and the roots of who we are. The behaviour tree is particularly useful when working with children struggling in a school environment where there is a breakdown of communication between them and their teachers.

The Tree of Life was introduced as a process of assisting children to make sense of their trauma and the narration around their life journey. It has been used extensively with children who have been affected by HIV/AIDS in South Africa, and is now used extensively as a trauma-related identifier in countries such as Russia, Canada and Australia. Children are encouraged to draw their tree by visiting the roots of their background and then moving up the tree and considering their skills and knowledge. The tree encourages children to identify those people who are important to them, who protect them and who help to realise their hopes and dreams. The process also promotes group thinking and group healing, whereby groups of children can share their trees and together create a forest of 'trees of life'. Through the process of sharing and exploring their differences and similarities, they are also able to identify their similarities and draw strength from each other.

Sgroi (1988) introduced the notion of the damaged goods syndrome and based her thinking on the effects on children who had suffered sexual abuse. She identified ten impacts of abuse, which included 'guilt', 'fear', 'inability to trust' and 'pseudo maturity'.

Most of the children I work with believe that life story work is done because they have been naughty and, as a child told me, they are 'messed up'. It is important to 'out' these issues as soon as possible and before the child's own story is explored. By using the behaviour tree based on Sgroi and Denborough, I have found a way in which children, with the support of their carer(s) and the therapeutic worker, can consider and develop understanding of their behaviours.

## *The process*

Ask the child to draw leaves at the top of the page (it is best to use A1 flipchart/butcher paper for this exercise or wallpaper if you have started or intend to use this). It will help if you assist the child in drawing the tree. Aim for about 15 leaves. Once done, consider the different feelings and behaviours and write each one on a separate leaf. It would be helpful to consider positive and neutral behaviours as well as those that are more problematic and destructive. Once done, spend a little time talking about the identified issues and consider the way in which they are shown and the reasons, if any, that the child has for exhibiting them. Reflection works well in this process, and also some mirroring of the carer and the therapeutic life story worker's own feelings and reasons that they are present. I also would encourage using speech bubbles to record the responses that seem important so that there is validation of the exchange.

Some children may find this hard, but if you are patient, engaged and attentive, the rewards of the child identifying their own behaviours are more than worthwhile.

Once you have completed the leaves, move to the bottom of the paper. Draw some roots which should be tangled and plentiful; I would normally have ten roots, but there is no definitive number to use.

For each root, identify and label one of the issues from the child's past. The carer and the therapeutic worker will need to think together about the events and to ensure that the child understands that they are aware of them. It is for these reasons that they want to help the child to understand the effects of the past. It is most effective if the roots are firmly based in the child's history and that of their family before they came into their current care placement. Sadly, multi-placed children experience repeated trauma within the care system and these placements are not to be dismissed. For example, a child who has been told that they are going to move to a 'forever family' and then experiences that the placement was far from that is likely to have internalised repeated rejection, repeated loss, repeated separation, repeated neglect and ongoing emotional harm.

By identifying the past issues, the carer and the child have an opportunity to consider the reality for the child and to make some sense as to the difficulties within the current placement.

As with all trees, a trunk is required, and so the roots and the leaves are joined together; the carer and the child draw this so as to symbolically link the roots to the present.

When the tree is complete, the child is encouraged to draw the grass line, which in turn allows all to see that the roots are hidden, often forgotten, and that the leaves are the only visible part of the child. The child and the carer can then see that some of the behaviours, feelings and actions are communications of the roots hidden below the ground. Some of the behaviour can be seen as appropriate, if not helpful, for the child. In most cases, the behaviour that is shown could be seen as being legitimate, and it is that legitimacy that assists carers to see that it is not simply a behaviour chosen to attack, disappoint or reject the carer, but merely a learnt, tried-and-trusted process that keeps the child in control (or in some cases purposefully out of control).

The therapeutic life story worker can then start to think with the child and the carer about how the behaviour they have identified is helpful or unhelpful. This then leads to a collective thinking about how to protect the behaviours, feelings and actions that are healthy and to change those that are not. The therapeutic worker needs to discuss how the child uses their behaviours as a form of communication as well as a process of defence and a coping mechanism. I worked with a child of 14 who had some very aggressive behaviours and had found himself in a secure environment due to this. We worked on his tree, and as we discussed his roots and then retraced upwards he stated, 'So my leaves might grow more healthily, and those that are unhelpful and get me into trouble might fall away.'

When I have worked with potential family placement breakdown, this tree exercise has proven to be a placement-saving process. Carers who struggle with the demanding and often confrontational behaviours of their children frequently feel exhausted and consider themselves to be drained from the attempt of caring. In some cases, they 'give up', as they have no obvious effect or positive response to their interaction. When working through the tree (on these occasions without the child being present), carers can see that much of the anger, hurt, rejection and verbal aggression presented to them by the child is not about them and probably never was, but is a result of what the carers represent. The child's internal model and 'shaped by experience' brain installs alerts to the threat of harm, the threat of betrayal, of the unpredictable and the unknown. As an environment becomes more unstable, more unpredictable and more stressful, so the behaviour becomes more protective, more defensive and more attacking of the self and of the external representation of the threat, the carers.

> Carers may benefit from understanding that traumatised children are likely to find it difficult to utilise reasoning and logic to modify their behaviour or reactions… Carers can be supported to understand the purpose and meaning of trauma based behaviour in children, helping to shift their interpretations away from blame to greater acknowledgement of the ongoing impact of children's abuse experiences. (Mitchell 2008)

A recent illustration of this occurred when I was asked to assess kinship carers who had stepped up to care for their grandson. They were struggling with his behaviour as he was hurting them, the pets and himself. The child had some testing tantrums which led to him being placed 'on the thinking step' for long periods of time. He had begun to take the behaviour outside the home and this was causing difficulties with the neighbours. The tree process helped to identify the past experiences that the child had lived through and the legitimacy of some of the behaviour he had adopted. I referred to the importance of providing a secure base (Schofield and Beek 2014), which was as predictable, as consistent and as repetitive as possible. It became apparent that the maternal grandmother in this situation had assumed responsibility and guilt for not protecting her grandson from the abuse visited on him by her daughter and her daughter's partner. In exploring this and how her behaviour impacted on the care of her grandson and the relationship she had with her husband, she was able to give herself permission to see that the behaviour she was struggling with was in part a reflection of her own trauma.

I once worked with a young girl who had been sexually hurt by her parents, but for her it was not sexual hurt but love. She had been brought up to believe that the sexual hurt visited on her was how she needed to love her parents and how they showed her that she was loved. From the age of six months, she was regularly 'loved' and made to 'love' in this way. By the time she came into care, at three years of age she was clear that she knew how to love someone. She was placed in care to caring adults, who provided care, food, warmth and kindness to her. As time passed they began to love her and told her so. This child knew exactly what to do to show love – she placed her hands on the foster father's privates and placed her hand up her foster mother's bra. They became distressed and told the child off, telling her that her behaviour was wrong and that they do not do the things she did in their house. To the child, this was a demand that she did not show love towards them and that she could not be loving as this was wrong. The concept of sexual hurt to this child was an understanding of love – her roots taught her to behave in the way that she had. By understanding this, we were able to help her and her carers redefine safe and unsafe loving and caring.

We can make such a huge difference for children and young people in care if we take the time to understand their roots, how these have developed and how these are communicated in the behaviour (leaves) of the child. By doing so, we can then help to identify whether the roots are still powerful, present or influential. As we find that the past is not the present, then the leaves, although understandable, are no longer needed. Therefore, new and healthier leaves can grow.

## Family tree

The next session should then introduce a family tree process and here the concept of the typical tree can be used; for much better results, my version of the tree may prove more constructive. A typical tree approach involves the drawing of a tree with heavy green foliage, and then for the child to name the family members and for each an apple is labelled and placed in the tree. The visual process is interesting, and the child's understanding of who is in their family should not be questioned at this time. Often if the child misses a family member, there is a reason for this, and the inclusion of family members or foster family members is neither wrong nor right. Currently an eight-year-old boy I am working with decided that he did not want apples but wanted to attribute a fruit to each member of his family. He also decided that his family included birth and foster parents and siblings that were and are part of his life. His father was an orange, his mother a pear, his foster mother an apple and his foster father a tomato! This was fun and descriptive, and led to lots of conversations about the fruit he chose and the fruit he did not. It was also of interest that he would not refer to himself as a fruit. He insisted that he was a monkey – not a chimpanzee as they were too violent, but a monkey. He explained that they were cute, but a little naughty.

For some children, I introduce family tree work in a different process. When asking who our parents are, it can be a simple response that has not demanded obvious thought – in my case Barbara and Robin. I have not had to think too hard about them, and when asked about my siblings, it is the same – Mandy, Becky, Matthew, David, Lizzie and Kate. It is a rhyme, and as such I have not had to consider who they are, just their names. This is a technique that all three people in the therapy can engage in. On the wallpaper, ask the carer and the child to draw their family tree – demonstrate what you want by producing yours first. The tree needs to be three generations and will look a little like mine in Figure 3.3.

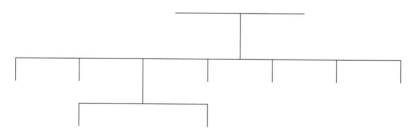

*Figure 3.3 Family tree*

When the tree is completed, the task is to ask the carer and the child to draw something that reminds them of the people who are in their family and place these pictures where the names would normally go. It is important that the therapeutic life story worker helps the child to draw the family members and not the carer's: this is because the carer and the child will need to exchange the stories of their own drawings. As I am asking the carer and the child to think about the people on their tree, they have to think about each person separately; this will require all three to think about and remember the person by recalling memories, and for some this will then produce a mental picture of them. The next thing that occurs is that there is an unconscious and conscious filtering of the memories and thoughts on how to represent them. In effect, the person thought about becomes present, and this enables discussion of and reflection on them. With the completed trees, the therapeutic worker can then ask about the pictures and the reason for them being selected. For a family tree as above with 11 people included, this represents 11 stories about me and how I see those I am related to which are ready to share. The information shared can be very useful and encourage awareness and attunement between the carer and the child.

If I thought about my mother, I might choose to draw a plate with some food on – I would then hope that the child might, and certainly the therapeutic worker would, ask why I selected a plate of food. The story would then be told, which would have, as in most stories, a beginning, a middle and an end. In this case, as one of seven children living in a small home and having parents who did their very best to provide for us from little income, I found that there was always an issue around food (the beginning). I remember having a plate of food which contained a very small piece of meat and a very small potato, and that was it. I was aware of a charity push for the hungry in Sudan and that a television programme was raising money for this. I ran upstairs, grabbed the family camera and took a picture of my plate of food. My mum asked me what I was doing and I replied that I had taken a picture to send to the TV programme, so that they might send some of the money raised to us (the middle). My mum was far from impressed and reminded me that the children in Sudan were really starving, and sent me off to my bedroom to think about what I had said. Looking back as a 51-year-old at the ten-year-old I was, I know that it was very wrong to have done that.

However, it was a fair representation of my thinking then and how I have matured since (the end).

For the task, I have now told those who read this book an awful lot about me, and if I went on to tell you ten more stories, imagine how much more you will understand me. I use this family tree work for all the children who I currently work with and for children where I am engaged in assessments. At the risk of repeating myself, we are a collection of stories – it is what defines us. To take time to tell the stories, to hear them and to discuss them is therapeutic; for the carer and the child, the act of sharing their stories encourages them to become closer and to understand much more about each other.

Over the next few sessions the wallpaper becomes the focus of the intervention, and the introduction of the details contained within the information bank is slowly worked through. The carer and the child are supported to consider, debate and explore the events of their family life, and as the child begins to understand the lives of their mother, father and siblings we find that they are also able to consider their present. There have been numerous occasions where children I have worked with suddenly make 'aha' statements, which are often insightful. These become 'healing moments'. One such statement was: 'So it wasn't that she didn't love me, it was because she didn't know what love was.'

The chronology of the child's story will get to their birth, and this invites the carer and therapeutic life story worker to mark this with as much information as possible. Birth certificates are essential and, alongside this, weight, height and birth stories are very useful to consider the importance of early life care. There are times that the birth of the child is very much central to the success of the life story. I have worked with a child who told me when I informed her of her birth weight that she was too heavy. She announced that she was too fat and should have been much lighter, perhaps 1lb instead of the 6lbs 6oz that she was. Her carer stated that she would have been a very poorly baby if she was that small, and the child replied that she might have died but it was better than 'being the size I am now'. The carer was shocked by this, but on reflection the child had given us a real insight into her sense of self and into her body image. There will be plenty of occasions where children will make statements that will cause concern and responses from the carer which will be an attempt to make the child feel better or worse. It is better, however, to allow the child to express themselves and to follow their thinking. In that way, the real issue for the child may surface, and the urge for us to problem solve for them needs to be held back.

As the wallpaper work continues to tell the story of the child, as they become older on the paper, their own memories will kick in and the connections that they make will be evidenced on the paper. Over the years, people have told me about their abuse, their sadness, their secrets and their lives. These have been recorded, thought about and 'made sense of'. The use of thinking cycles is a helpful technique and allows the therapeutic worker to think with the child and to consider their action in choice making, reflection and action.

The use of thinking cycles can be very helpful when engaging children on expanding their information and communication. The cycle works by thinking through each stage of the communication, therefore resisting the inclination to respond on automatic. Often when talking with children, adults allow interference to dictate their involvement, yet children often state that the adults who care for them never listened to them. Most respond by stating that the adults would solve their problems, react for reaction rather than through thought, and forget the individual and unique nature that each child presents. By following this thinking cycle, the adult can:

- *listen* – do not interrupt, shut off the communication or continue to do the other hundred things that need to be done. Listening intently to children involves complete attention. Allow the child to express themselves and encourage them through the use of non-verbal encouragement – nodding, eye contact and open body posture

- *interpret* – as the child talks, reflect on what has been shared, explain to the child that the information they have shared is important and that they deserve the time to think through the communication. Consider what lies behind the statement, the way the child verbalised the information, the body language, what was said and what was meant

- *evaluate* – whether the information changes the known issues that the child has, and whether the thinking behind the communication is safe or unsafe. The adult can evaluate whether the child needs affirmation, challenge, empathy, direction and/or clarification

- *respond* – responding to the child in the best way that assists the child to begin their own listening cycle. The response can be detailed, direct or requesting more information. It is important to consider an opportunity to encourage, discourage, comment or conclude.

The thinking cycle looks complex, but it is something that we do all the time. It is the carer and the therapeutic worker's opportunity to think with the child, to reflect on what they are communicating and respond to it. Many children will spend time testing the carer and the therapeutic worker. Their tests will include the carer and therapist's ability to cope, respond and give protection, direction, barriers and permission. As the carer and the therapeutic worker develop relationships with the child, they have to be mindful that they do not ignore these opportunities to build effective relationships. Avoiding the age-old habit of 'problem solving' for children is crucial, as is remembering that high quality care of children is not based on over-protection, thinking and acting for the child. Rather it is the engagement in providing opportunity and a role model and communicating through commentary and support that will help children to problem solve, to think and act responsibly and to realise effective, healthier self-protection.

There are many approaches that are useful within the wallpaper process, and I have detailed a few of these communication exercises below.

## Memory jar/boxes

In some cases, I have introduced the memory jar process, which is promoted within a 'solution-based therapy' approach. The memory jar is a visual way for children to add their memories to a jar by using coloured sand or coloured beads. Each colour represents a feeling around the memory, i.e. red sand for a happy memory and yellow sand for a sad memory. The child can write the memory down on corresponding coloured Post-it notes which are then placed on the underside of the lid. The more memories the child brings to the session, the more sand is placed in the jar. The therapeutic life story worker should encourage plenty of different colours, which will allow the child to consider the different feelings that memories evoke. Once the jar is three-quarters full, the therapeutic worker seals the top of the open jar and then the lid (with all the Post-it notes taped to the underside) is placed on top and sealed to the jar with more tape.

There are other ways to do the above: often I will ask children to draw a box on their wallpaper; once done I then encourage them to fill the box by writing down their worries, scares and confusions. Often children fill the boxes up and ask for a chance to draw another box for what they have forgotten: I merely point out that they do not have another brain, so they should write over what they have already written. Once done, many of the children will say, 'No wonder I am so confused!' With the memory jars or the boxes, we can then think about our preoccupations and work slowly through these so as to 'declutter' the fragmented memories.

# Air balloon

For some children, the opportunity to be apart from the activity that they have experienced is an important process. I have found that the use of an air balloon as a symbolic view of life is helpful for children.

On the wallpaper, draw a hot air balloon and ask the child to draw themselves in the balloon; once they have done that, ask them to draw an adult that they feel close to. Then ask the child what they can see when they look over the edge of the basket. As they describe what they can see, the carer or the therapeutic life story worker will draw underneath the balloon what the child details. On completion of this, the child is then told that the balloon has been blown across to a scarier place, where the wind is strong and the clouds are bursting with rain. The balloon is struggling to float, and then suddenly the wind drops.

The child is then asked what they can see over the edge of the basket and this is drawn; often this is a more troubling sight and the child will describe the scene (sometimes in great detail). The balloon is then gently blown towards the next place, where the weather is calm and sunny, and lots of birds are drawn around the balloon. Once done, the child is asked to look over the edge again and is asked to describe what they see, and again this is drawn by the carer or the therapeutic life story worker. The balloon then needs to land and the child is given the choice as to where they would be prepared to settle with the balloon and asked why. I have used this for children who are struggling in placement and the carer is exposed to their worries. In most cases, the carer realises that the child is drifting and unable to settle due to their need to be held safely and loved. This, alongside the behaviour tree, helps to shore up placements long enough for me to engage in the more challenging areas and to offer appropriate support to reach a stable placement.

The wallpaper concludes as the chronology meets the present day. Then the child and the carer are encouraged to walk the length of the wallpapers (normally between three and six rolls) and the child is encouraged to tell their story. The process is then followed by a little celebration between the carer, the child and the therapist before the work is taken by the therapeutic life story worker in order to create the life story book.

## Squiggles

In 'getting to know you' times, the above games are useful alongside hangman and Tic Tac Toe. It is possible through the use of these approaches to encourage the most defensive of children, as games and competition can often override suspicion or resistance. More importantly, they are fun, and when you have fun you make relationships. Winnicott (1971) and Thurow (1989) consider the therapeutic nature of squiggles – their use in the interactive therapeutic space and also as a diagnostic tool. In Donald Winnicott's book *Therapeutic Consultations in Child Psychiatry* (1971), he spoke of the use of squiggles in his work with children and young people as an interactive form of therapeutic communication. He suggested that drawing with children could aid those around them to understand them more fully. It is fair to state that many of the squiggles that I have done with carers and children have been accompanied by the narrative of the drawing itself. Winnicott considers that the action of playing the squiggle game provides a process whereby the child records on paper their current problems, emotional conflicts or stress at that moment of the client's life (Winnicott 1971). I am not convinced that squiggles can so easily be assessed as a deep, meaningful activity full of clue sets in establishing the child's current emotional and psychosocial view – I just know that when we play the game, children and adults learn something that is vitally important. On our own we make little sense; together we can make sense of anything. The game itself is as simple as it is brilliant. The three people in the intervention letter themselves A, B and C. On the wallpaper, A will draw a single line in any way, shape or squiggle. Once done, then B and C openly discuss what picture they can make from the line already drawn on the wallpaper. It is often the case that A will join in with this discussion and finally either B or C will complete the agreed picture by using the already drawn line as the starter. On our own, our individual lines might make little sense – together we can think about our lines and agree to make sense together from it.

This game is played regularly and all have a chance to draw a line and a chance to make a picture from it. Very much like the therapeutic life story work, on our own our stories might lack definition and they might be sparse and needing more detail. Together, the carer, the child and the therapeutic worker can add to the story, explore what it might look like and create a healthier, clearer and more helpful picture of the child's life.

## The box game

Many children find it hard to talk about themselves and, believe it or not, the same can often be said of carers. The box game is a great game to play if this is the case. Draw on the wallpaper 16 dots (four rows of four dots); then take it in turns to join two of the dots together with a single line – horizontally or vertically, but not diagonally. Once everyone has had a go, repeat the turns, all the time trying to make a box. When a box is made, the person who has completed the box places their initial in the box and tells the other people an interesting thing about themselves. In the end, the game provides the chance of learning nine things about each other; in the later sessions, it is good to theme the box game on subjects such as family, feelings, school, friends and memories. There have been many children who have requested this game in order to talk about certain things – they set the subject, and together we listen and make sense of things.

## The stuck child

The past is something that must be faced. It does not go away; it cannot be avoided. We all have monsters in us, but for some the monsters escape. The past may not always control, but at times of stress it becomes a very powerful and heavy burden. Life story therapy, similarly to other therapeutic interventions, can only succeed if the child wants to be involved. Much of my time is spent creating relationships for children who have little trust and providing them with the opportunity to ask for the service. Other children take part in the process as a means of encouraging exploration and because it affords an opportunity for them to ask questions. It is for these children that I offer myself as their 'private detective' who can go away and find out the answers to questions that might be raised. When those questions evoke painful answers, they may conclude that it is safer to go no further, to seek comfort in the unknown. It is the way in which the response is given that will support the child and prevent them from being upset to the point that they cannot continue the process.

There may be very simple and easily remedied reasons why a child seems to be stuck. For example, they might not gel with (or even like) the worker, or the environment in which the work takes place does not suit (for example, it is too noisy or too quiet). Then there may be other things happening in the child's life which make life story work more difficult than it would otherwise be (for example, the child is going through a bad time in therapy or has had contact with someone from the past who evokes disturbing memories). Again, it may be that someone important to the child, like a foster carer or social worker, is leaving the child's life. Alternatively, it may just be that the life story worker has not planned the sessions properly so that they sit well with other parts of the child's life.

There are times when something as simple and everyday as a game played between the child, the carer and the therapeutic life story worker may reveal why the child is stuck, is just struggling in finding the words to describe how they feel or what they remember, or doesn't know how to ask questions about the events in their life. In a traditional setting, this exploration can be frightening beyond words: play is a useful way of removing this fear and encouraging more open discussion.

# References for Introduction and Chapters 1 to 3

Allen, J. (1910) *Above Life's Turmoil*. New York, London, G.P. Putnam's Sons.

Applegate, J.S. and Shapiro, J. R. (2005) *Neurobiology for Clinical Social Work Theory and Practice.* W.W. Norton and Company New York.

Aust, P. H (1981) 'Using the life story book in treatment of children in placement.' *Child Welfare 60*, 8.

Backhaus K A (1984) 'Life books: tool for working with children in placement.' *Social Work 29*, 6.

Ballou, M. (1995) 'Art therapy.' In M. Ballou (ed.), *Psychological Interventions a Guide to Strategies.* Westport, CT: Praeger Publishers.

Barton, S Gonzalez, R and Tomlinson, P. (2012). *Therapeutic Residential Care for Children and Young People.* London: Jessica Kingsley Publishers.

Baum, F. (1900) *The Wonderful Wizard of Oz.* George M Hill Company.

Baynes, P. (2007) Untold Stories: A discussion of life story work. *Adoption and Fostering 32*, 2.

Betts, B. and Ahmad, A. (2003) *My Life Story CD ROM.* London: British Association for Adoption and Fostering BAAF.

Bronfenbrenner, U. (1994) 'Who cares for the children?' in Nuba, H., Searson, M., and Sheiman, D. L. (eds.) *Resources for early childhood: A handbook.* New York: Garland, 113-129 (edited paper from an individual address to UNESCO, Paris, 7 September 1989).

Camis, J (2001) *My Life and Me.* London: BAAF.

Children and Adoption Act (2006) London: HM Government.

Commission for Social Care Inspection (2006) *Supporting Parents, Safeguarding Children.* London.

Connor, T., Sclare, I., Dunbar, D. and Elliffe, J. (1985) 'Making a life story book.' *Adoption & Fostering 92*, 1.

De Pree, M. (1997) *Leading Without Power.* Josey – Bass.

Di Terlizzi, M. (1994) 'Life History: The impact of a changing service provision on an individual with learning disabilities.' *Disability and Society, 9*, 4.

Fahlberg, V (1981) *Helping children when they must move: (Practice series) 2nd edition.* London: British Agencies for Adoption & Fostering.

Fahlberg, V (2008) *A Child's Journey through Placement.* London: BAAF.

Gerhardt, S (2004) *Why Love Matters: How Affection Shapes a Baby's Brain.* Hove: East Sussex: Brunner-Routledge.

Glaser, D (2006) *Understanding Attachment and Attachment Disorders: Theory and Practice*. London: Jessica Kingsley Publishers.

Greenwald, R. (2005) *Child trauma handbook: A guide for helping trauma-exposed children and adolescents*. New York: The Haworth Reference Press.

Hermans, H.J.M. (1992). 'Telling and Retelling One's Self Narrative.' *Human Development, 35*.

Hewitt, H (2008) *Life Story Books for People with Learning Disabilities: A Practical Guide*. British Institute of Learning Disabilities.

Jobs, S. (2005) Stanford Commencement Address.

Lacher, D., Nichols, T. and May, J. (2005) *Connecting with Kids through Stories – Using Narratives to Facilitate Attachment in Adopted Children*. London: Jessica Kingsley Publishers.

Lanyado, M. (2003). *The Presence of the Therapist: Treating Childhood Trauma*. London: Routledge.

Levy, M T and Orlans, M (1998). *Attachment Trauma and Healing: Understanding and Treating Attachment Disorder in Children and Families*. AEI Press.

Levy T M and Orlans M, (2003). 'Creating and repairing attachments in biological, foster and adoptive families.' In Johnson S M and Whiffen V E (Eds), (2003). *Attachment Processes in Couple and Family Therapy*. New York, NY: Guilford Press.

National Institute for Clinical Excellence (2014). *Looked-after children and young people Quality standard [QS31]*. Published date: April 2013.

Nicholls, E (2005). *The New Life Work Model*. Lyme Regis: Russell House Publishing.

Ogden, P, Minton, K and Pain, C (2006). *Trauma and the Body: A Sensorimotor Approach to Psychotherapy: 1st Edition* (Norton Series on Interpersonal Neurobiology). New York, NY: W. W. Norton & Co.

Ogden, P., & Minton, K. (2000). 'Sensorimotor sequencing: One method for processing traumatic memory.' *Traumatology, 8(1)*.

Perry, B.D. (2006). 'Applying principles of neurodevelopment to clinical work with maltreated and traumatized children: the Neurosequential Model of Therapeutics.' In Webb, N.B (Eds.) *Traumatized youth in child welfare*. New York, NY: Guildford Press.

Rees, J (2009) *Life Story Books for Adopted Children: A Family Friendly Approach*. London: Jessica Kingsley Publishers.

Rose, R and Philpot, T (2005) *The Child's Own Story: Life Story Work with Traumatized Children*. London: Jessica Kingsley Publishers.

Rose, R (2012) *Life Story Therapy with Traumatised Children: A Model for Practice*. London: Jessica Kingsley Publishers.

Rushton, A and Dance, C. (2002) *Adoption support services for families in difficulty: A literature review and survey of UK practice*. London: BAAF.

Rymaszewska, J. and Philpot, T. (2006) *Reaching the Vulnerable Child: Therapy with Traumatized Children*. London: Jessica Kingsley Publishers.

Ryan, T. and Walker, R. (1993) *Life Story Work*. BAAF.

Ryan, T. and Walker, R. (2007) *Life Story Work: A practical guide to helping children understand their past (third edition)*. London: BAAF.

Sgroi, S. (Ed.) (1998) *Handbook of Clinical Intervention in Child Sexual Abuse*. Free Press.

Trowell, J. (1992) *Understanding Your Three-Year-Old*. Rosendale Press.

Usher, J (1994). *Life story work: A Therapeutic Tool for Social Work (Social Monographs)*. University of East Anglia.

Vygotsky, L. (1962) *Thought and Language*, Cambridge MA: MIT PressWhite, M. (2007). Maps of narrative practice. New York, NY: W.W. Norton.

White, M (1997) *Narratives of Therapists Lives*. Adelaide, South Australia: Dulwich Centre Publications.

White, M and Epston, D (1990) *Narrative Means to Therapeutic Ends*. New York: W.W. Norton.

Wicks, A. & Whiteford, G. (2003) 'Value of life stories in occupation-based research.' *Australian Occupational Therapy Journal, 50*.

Wrench, K. and Naylor, L. (2013) *Life Story Work with Children Who Are Fostered or Adopted: Creative Ideas and Activities*. Jessica Kingsley Publishers.

Chapter 4

# THE COMPLEXITY OF THE LIFE STORY PRACTITIONER'S ROLE

*Nadine Jay, Play Therapist*

## Introduction by Richard Rose

*I have delivered a therapeutic life story diploma over the last three years in London, and on the first-year course I met Nadine. Nadine has an independent play therapy service based in Peterborough. It was clear from the outset that she had many skills that would lend themselves to the therapeutic life story process and, since qualifying, Nadine has developed her services in the area of therapeutic life story work with children and young people in foster care and adoption placement. She has assisted me in developing more ideas for assessing children and young people, and I am sure this chapter will provide an insight into her approach, but also assistance for anyone interested in developing an independent service to meet the needs of children and their families.*

## My work story

I came in to therapeutic life story work following a background in community building, disability and inclusion and my work as a play therapist, primarily alongside children who are in foster care or have been adopted.

An interest in inclusion saw me utilising person-centred planning tools which focus on strengthening relationships and providing opportunities to empower often very vulnerable and isolated children, young people and their families. This involves listening deeply to an individual's story, acknowledging their very often 'rocky road' and learning what situations have and have not worked for them in the past. There is an overriding belief that much of who we are is down to what we have lived through – our life experiences – and in addition, that listening and planning with and alongside others is nearly always the best way, as it shares responsibility, strengthens relationships and encourages more equal friendships.

As a non-directive play therapist who also practises therapeutic life story work, I strive to do my utmost to provide a space for a child where they feel accepted unconditionally, where I am genuine in my responses and in being alongside them, and where I demonstrate (perhaps most crucially) empathy. In play therapy sessions, the child leads the way, deciding and controlling what happens. I do not suggest things, I do not ask questions and I do not offer praise – all of which direct and can interfere with the child's natural rhythm of what they need to do. This 'taking the stage' is within as few limits as possible – limits which exist to enable the child to feel safe and contained and where they have confidence that it is me as the therapist who has the ultimate control over what is and is not allowed in the session.

I am also trained in filial therapy, a family therapy approach centred on play which was devised by Bernard and Louise Gurney in the 1950s. Here, the principal play therapy skills are passed on to a child's parent or carer with the goal of them having a weekly special play session at home. Filial therapy is a child-centred way of enabling children to feel deeply listened to while very much strengthening the attachment between the child and their primary carer.

I had been interested in life story work with children in the care system for a number of years and had undergone some brief initial training but had not found the opportunity to implement what I really wanted to do. When I happened on the existence of the newly created Diploma in Therapeutic Life Story Work at the Institute for Arts in Therapy and Education in London with Richard Rose as the course leader, providing an opportunity to diversify and expand my knowledge and skills, things finally seemed to feel aligned.

My pull to facilitating the therapeutic life story work model devised by Rose was in the resonance that it has for me for filial therapy. Instrumental in its application is the working in partnership with the child's primary carer – usually the parent, foster carer or significant residential worker. There is a feeling of 'all being in this together', of sharing the process and the journey. More than a side-effect or by-product is the increasing closeness of their relationship with the child. This is because for Rose (2012) it is intentional and of equal importance to enabling the child to further their understanding of their life so far. My investment in enabling that relationship to be better, to be more solid, is what motivates me. The mutual witnessing of and listening to how the child and their primary carer each feel, the questions that they have, the fears and the honesty, is what further cements the relationship.

My approach as a therapeutic life story work practitioner therefore is based on that of Rose's, with the following key characteristics typically in play: direct sessions that involve the child, primary carer and myself being together; the recording of what we do takes place on wallpaper; we meet once a fortnight for an hour; the direct work involves approximately 18 sessions; and the information gathering begins before the sessions start.

# The tripartite approach

Important for me in facilitating therapeutic life story work is trying my hardest to show to a child or young person that they matter. For children who commonly have very low feelings of self-worth as their default position, it is crucial that differing and varied ways are used to support them and give them the message that they absolutely do matter, they are important and they most definitely are worthy.

A ritual that I adopted from the outset was for individual children to have their own art box for therapeutic life story work. I collect together felt pens, shaped sticky notes, scissors, double-sided and normal tape, a collection of different themed stickers and anything else I discover that looks as if it might be useful. This is the child's box and isn't to be used with anyone else; it is left with them and their primary carer wherever possible, unless I am asked to look after it. They are invited to add to the supplies whenever they want and I put additional items in throughout our time together. In my experience, for a child to have completely new and unused items in a personal box that is completely theirs and is not to be shared is often met with disbelief.

I always encourage the unwrapping of new wallpaper to be done by the child as it is their paper and it feels completely right that they open it. It is also their choice as to who looks after it; usually this will be the primary carer but I am on occasion asked to when our sessions take place at school. These touches may seem small and not overly relevant, but they add to the potential opportunities for a child to feel a little more important, special and noticed – children see that they do indeed matter.

To practise therapeutic life story work in this unique way, you have to come from the standpoint that the involvement of both the child and their primary carer is important. It is the child's life story that is the focus, their story that is unravelled, but we need to ensure the presence and participation of the adult they have chosen to share this journey with.

This adds to the complexity of the life story practitioner's role, as there is a responsibility to contain and hold the process for another person and not just the child. I generally keep in touch with the primary carer throughout the work. This obviously varies, but I often share with them what we will be focusing on for the next session. This promotes a heightened feeling of working together and gives me an opportunity to show them that they also matter. This is especially important at the times when we are all trying to make sense of life events for the child, and I will usually make contact after a particularly sensitive session to 'check in' on how they both are.

During the early sessions when we carry out more of the 'getting to know you' exercises like the All About Me book (facts about the child) and Jenga with questions (written on the blocks for all of us to answer), if the child is yet to ask any questions about their history, then it can lead me to wonder if this is truly the right time to be doing this piece of work. Feedback from parents has told me that these primary weeks have felt invaluable in 'setting the stage' and in creating an atmosphere of listening, trust, respecting each other and so on. Questions from the child then commonly follow, but at their pace, where they feel more in control of the process.

Often the physical presence of the primary carer enables the child to listen, to hear information, to ask questions and to be more present in the moment.

One child, aged ten, showed us that when we were looking through and trying to understand the reasons why he was unable to stay with his birth family, he needed to be sat on his carer's lap with her squeezing his arms. This child has a diagnosis of attention deficit hyperactivity disorder (ADHD) and would often need to move around during our sessions. I noticed that, during the times that were trickier to listen to, he needed help to feel more grounded and contained, and he received this from his mum. He was in 'full control' of when he needed this additional support, and it felt completely right that, through having his female carer there and involved, he received this protection from the right person.

I always encourage the child and their primary carer to record, draw, write or doodle on their wallpaper. If this is introduced as soon as possible then it leads to a sense of ownership over the paper, and with that an increased externalisation of thoughts, feelings and behaviour.

## Birth and adoptive parents

I find that some weeks a session feels as if it is more for the primary carer than the child. And, if we are utilising a tripartite approach, then this is absolutely as it should be. With adoptive families, where there have been significant struggles and difficulties along the way, it gives the opportunity for the parent to explain their perspective in a safe space with someone else supporting them.

I often find that, in adoption situations, I mostly present a child's birth family details and their very early beginnings on the wallpaper, and then move to 'handing over' the later story of the child's adoption to the narrative adoptive parent. This can feel like a relinquishing of responsibility whereby the parent 'takes the floor', as they have the most accurate and real experience to share. My role is then more to witness and contain the process for both child and parent, where being an active listener and an empathic witness feels a complete privilege.

My children's past was always 'there' in the background and the worry of how they would cope with their past was always on my mind. When it was suggested that we use a therapeutic approach to go through their past I grabbed the opportunity with both hands! I was always aware that it can be a traumatic experience for many children when they find out about their 'life story', and the reality is sometimes very hard to understand, even for adults. I am currently going through my children's story and am so glad that I can be a part of this, to help and understand why they ended up being adopted. I have learned things about my children that I was not aware of – their fears and loss are part of their very being.

As a mother, I am able to support them and in a strange way it has also alleviated my own fears and loss; having contact with their birth parent(s) via our therapist has left me feeling more confident as a parent. I feel that I no longer have to defend my role as 'mum'. My children have not changed their view of me, if anything it has cemented our relationship. I think a lot of adoptive parents fear losing their children and feel scared about their children's past. Sharing their life story together has strengthened the bond that we have. We will share our lives growing together, just like any family. This has to include the part before we all met, and although for me this was a very small part of their lives it is still a very important part of theirs – one which I have been privileged to have shared. (Liz, adoptive parent, 2016)

It is of paramount importance that (in addition to the child) the parent feels heard and valued. When this happens they also feel more secure and grounded. I find I am afforded an opportunity to take more risks in sharing their own thoughts and feelings. This openness allows for both the child and parent to make sense of their own and each other's history, which is especially important as they were not together to share that.

I consider one of the most significant parts of the process to be when I have permission from a birth parent to speak or meet with them. Their contribution can be central to the shifting of their birth child's understanding and perspective of their life so far. When I have these opportunities, I truly consider that I am there representing the three of us from the direct sessions and with that comes an intense understanding of responsibility.

In my experience, having the option of saying that I am a children's therapist and not a social worker can ease the situation, as many birth parents have painful associations of social workers and the removal of their children. Contributing to their child's life story work does not just offer the sharing of information and answering of questions that their child may have, but it also gives the birth parent a real opportunity (often years later) to tell their story. This frequently includes sharing information about their childhood and reflection on mistakes that they consider they have made. One birth mum, after listening to a brief outline of her two birth sons' lives (provided by their adoptive mum), finally said, 'Thank you so much. Now I know deep down that I never could have given them the lives that they have and it was in their best interest to be adopted.' With this came a feeling of her being more settled and at ease, even though her life had not turned out in the way she had either planned or wanted it to.

Obviously, this is not the experience of all birth parents. Some never accept that their children being adopted was the right thing for either them, their children or the wider family. I am acutely aware that I may be the strongest or sole link for a birth parent with their child and can only try and empathise with how it feels to be with a person who is in physical contact with their child. This exposes the therapeutic life story work practitioner to the extremely real and intense emotions of desperation, loss, longing, regret, hopelessness, anger, remorse and sadness.

Therefore, within life story work with adopted children, there are times when the practitioner may be containing the process of three other individuals – child, birth parent (or family member) and adoptive parent (or foster carer). Again, as a practitioner this feels a privilege to witness, but the managing of these emotions alongside those of happiness, hope, joy and optimism requires regular and thoughtful supervision. This is a vital piece of the process, as containing other people's emotions and experiences is a considerable responsibility and the practitioner requires support with sustaining that.

## From the child's perspective

In utilising a defined approach such as Rose's (2012) model, there are several tasks or activities that complete the process of facilitating a child or young person's life story journey.

I have increasingly come to realise that the most effective way to facilitate therapeutic life story work is to take a child-centred stance and to begin from the perspective of the child. From the outset, it is essential to ascertain, as far as possible, what the child already knows, what they believe happened, what they feel, what questions they may have, what they want to achieve and which parts of their story feel the most 'muddled' to them.

By consistently recording all of these on the wallpaper, these muddles are 'out there', exposed, and are then more able to be dealt with. Finding out as soon as possible what is needed for each individual and unique child means that the sessions can be designed around them rather than purely following a list of exercises. As a practitioner, this comes with experience and confidence, and I have found that most flexibility needs to be had with young people from around 12 years of age upwards as they commonly have more precise questions and prefer a faster pace.

It may be that while I am gathering information from files or meeting with people I am able to answer a lot of questions and fill in many gaps in a child's life. But, if these were not the things that were most important to the child, then they may feel unsatisfied and probably remain preoccupied with unanswered questions, and I will have failed in my role.

Rose considers preoccupation by referring to the use of bar graphs as a way to show the effect of being overwhelmed by past events and so unable to be in the present. This is a straightforward and clear way of graphically representing on the wallpaper what it may feel like to have a head full of worries, questions, gaps and uncertainties. When I describe and draw on the wallpaper two vessels showing where the line sits in a very preoccupied head and where we want to aim for, children commonly take a pen and draw a line right near or on the bottom saying that is where they want it to be – it makes sense to them. It also makes sense to the primary carer. When one child drew the line right at the bottom, the foster carer commented, 'Well if we get to that, I think it would be more than awesome.'

We may not be able to solve all of the uncertainties at that time but voicing and acknowledging them always brings that line down little by little.

I have learnt to 'expect the unexpected'. Going in to a session with a definite plan of what we are going to focus on doesn't necessarily mean that the plan will come to fruition! Sometimes the child is just not up for it that day and we may need to change to playing games, doodling or just talking about whatever the child wants instead. Alternatively, an event or person that we are talking about may spark immediate intense emotions and the child may need the permission and acceptance to cry while we are together. I have had to abandon all plans to make way for essential sobbing that had not happened before for a 13-year-old girl and her foster carer. On another occasion, I wasn't expecting to have unanswered questions from a ten-year-old boy written on paper aeroplanes and launched at me from behind the sofa.

If we talk about times from a child's earlier childhood, especially situations which were neglectful or abusive, this can evoke deep and painful memories. One child I was working with was being supported with her life story work by her foster carer. I had the opportunity to meet with the child's birth mum who was anxious to know if her daughter had remembered an incident where she alleged that a family member had sexually assaulted her. This had been investigated at the time but was unsubstantiated. During the session when I shared with the child and her carer the meeting with the birth mum and we explored the child's own memories of that time in her life, she said, 'I have been living under the cloud of it all my life, I didn't know if it had actually happened until now, and now I do.'

In addition to validating that this painful event did actually take place, we were also able to hear and understand from her mum that she had tried to protect her daughter, as it was she who had informed the police and ensured that her daughter would never visit the family member's house again.

The foster carer and I were overwhelmingly proud of this child; she had felt safe enough in our session to discuss this. As often happens, once I leave a session, the carers and children often process what has been discussed over the following hours and days. In this case, the child told her carer about more memories of that period in time, and these memories were passed to her social worker.

While planning my interventions with the family I was aware in considering the risks of this session that there was a possibility that the child might tell about an abuse she had suffered. I contacted the foster carer and discussed this prior to the session so that we were all ready to protect the child. Practising therapeutic life story work does not just involve finding out information and then facilitating 18 one-hour-long sessions over nine months – it is far more intricate and involves a process of recovery.

In taking an empathic stance, for the practitioner there must be a huge mindfulness of the impact on the child of hearing a parent's experiences, thoughts and reasons as to why certain events happened. It is important that the child understands as far as possible the reasons why hard decisions were made. This is most definitely a balancing act, and caution should be exercised as a vast majority of children who are not with their birth families and have been looked after in the care system can experience intense feelings of shame, self-blame and a lack of self-worth.

If the primary carer is involved in the therapeutic life story process, they can be aware of the information that has been, and will be, discussed, explored and shared. In being part of this discovery, the carer can take a lead on providing opportunities for their child or young person to feel more worthy and good about themselves.

## Conclusion

The process of facilitating life story work is, for me, in essence about belonging. It is about enabling a child or young person to understand more than they did previously and them reaching a position which feels more comfortable, and where they feel more settled with the story of where they have come from and where they are now.

Making sense of where we have come from, especially when we have not been in control of decisions and actions that others have made, is best achieved alongside empathic and caring others. Even better is to travel that journey with a chosen other person as that undoubtedly strengthens and enriches the relationship. It is the relational aspect of therapeutic life story work that for me makes it an exceptional approach.

## References

Guerney. B. G. (1964). 'Filial Therapy: description and rationale.' *Journal of Consulting psychology, 28(4)*, 303-310.

Rose, R. (2012) *Life Story Therapy with Traumatized Children: A Model for Practice.* London: Jessica Kingsley Publishers.

# PART 2

# THERAPEUTIC LIFE STORY WORK IN DIVERSE CONTEXTS

Chapter 5

# KAITIAKITANGA

## SAFEGUARDING THE MEMORIES OF FOSTER CHILDREN'S EXPERIENCES THROUGH THE USE OF THERAPEUTIC LIFE STORY WORK

*Marni Otway, social worker, Aotearoa, New Zealand*

## Introduction by Richard Rose

*I was invited to speak at various conferences in New Zealand in 2013, and then to present for all of the North Island's education psychologists in 2014. In 2015 I was asked to present at a national foster care conference, and it was here that Marni and I spoke of introducing therapeutic life story work to New Zealand. Since this time, Marni and her colleagues have continued to practise and I have supervised them since the spring of 2016.*

*Here, Marni introduces her work and how it attunes to the Māori culture.*

As a social worker working with foster children for over 20 years I came across many children who experienced traumatic situations, including abuse and neglect, and youth who struggled with building trusting healthy relationships. Among the many issues they faced, these children expressed feeling disconnected from their birth roots and complained of having very few photos or other documented experiences of their life. Much of their life experiences were documented from a professional's point of view, with minimal input from the child and caregiver.

In addition to meeting a child's basic needs such as food and shelter, birth parents provide children with a sense of belonging and help them develop into healthy adults (Connolly, de Haan and Crawford 2013). However, in situations where this does not happen, children can end up in the foster care system. The intention of foster care is to provide a safe and stable home for children who are in need of care and attention; however, when children are placed in foster care they are separated from their birth families and whānau (kinship), which results in them being removed from everyone and everything familiar to them (Connolly *et al.* 2013). Often they are separated from their siblings, as many foster families cannot accommodate sibling groups, adding to the child's distress. They may move multiple times, change schools and lose their pets, familiar foods and friendships (Atwool 2010; Johnson, Yoken and Voss 1995), and as a result they may lose connections to their culture and the memories of their experiences. This lack of connection can have a negative impact on the child's sense of belonging and their identity that may jeopardise their ability to form strong, positive, healthy attachments to others.

Children in care have varying experiences depending on where they are placed, the age at the time of placement and the permanency they experience while in care (Sinclair *et al.* 2005). For some children, foster care provides stability, guidance and love; however, for other children foster care is a temporary and unstable place before entering into an uncertain world (Sinclair *et al.* 2005). Unfortunately, the outcome all too often is homelessness, poor educational outcomes, higher levels of unemployment, offending behaviour and an increase in mental health issues (Stein 2006).

## Issues facing foster youth in Aotearoa, New Zealand

New Zealand is a small country of over 4,500,000 people and as of December 2015 there were 5139 documented children in out-of-home care (Child, Youth and Family 2016). New Zealand has one of the worst rates of child abuse in the world, and Māori, Pasifika and European cultures are the most prominent cultures represented within the child youth and family system in New Zealand. There are many different out-of-home care settings in New Zealand, including family foster care, kinship (whānau) care, residential care, family home, independent living and child and family support services (Child, Youth and Family 2016). Depending on the child's legal status, behavioural issues and identified needs, children are placed in the appropriate type of care.

In 1988 the Puao-Te-Ata-Tu report (Ministerial Advisory Committee 1988) was released which raised concerns about Māori children being placed outside the whānau and highlighted the need for them to be placed within their own communities. The Children, Young Persons and their Families Act of 1989 allowed the state to intervene in the lives of families and children if there were care and protection concerns. The specific principles in Section 5 prioritised family involvement in decision making, and Principle 13 mandated that children needed to be placed in a family-like setting close to their birth home to encourage familial ties to remain and to return to family when possible (Atwool 2010). This Act 'radically changed the way in which social workers responded to the care and safety needs of children' (Connolly *et al.* 2013, p.286). Whānau became the first preference for placement to ensure children's links to their family of origin were maintained, and to assist in preserving their sense of belonging (Connolly *et al.* 2013).

Whenever children are placed outside their cultural group and remain disconnected from their culture, we limit their ability to identify with their own community. Unfortunately, for various reasons, children are not able to maintain ties with family, and due to the frequent moves in foster care they may be unable to maintain ties to caregivers. These children begin to ask questions and want answers to help them identify their experiences, but often social workers and caregivers don't have the answers or the resources to facilitate this adequately. Therefore, children are left wondering if and where they belong, which can impact on their ability to connect and feel a sense of belonging. 'All children are concerned with a sense of belonging and the need to know that they are related to and like someone else, an extension of another' (Harper, as cited in Ryburn 1995, p.51).

So why should it be any different for a child in out-of-home care? Many children in care know very little about their lives and often have misconceptions about why they are in foster care. The confusion they may experience in out-of-home care relating to their relationship with their birth families and the lack of clarity regarding their situation can have children feeling lost in the system.

I worked with a little girl very recently who genuinely thought that she was in care because she was a naughty girl. I contacted her family and they wrote a little piece about how they felt when she was going to be born. When I read it to her she said, 'Papa really felt that. They really think that about me – so I am not a naughty girl' (Joanne, social worker).

Many children maintain hope that they will return home to live with their families (Sinclair *et al.* 2005), whereas some children wish to have nothing to do with their birth families (Cashmore 2014). Children who are missing pieces of their lives may find it difficult to integrate those years into their life experience; therefore, social workers, therapists, community workers and caregivers must have the opportunity to help these children make sense of their experiences and understand their relationship to their families of origin.

> I've heard from a woman who is an adult now and she is feeling like she doesn't belong, having trouble feeling a sense of belonging in her own family with her own birth children. She has trouble in her relationship with other adults and her own children. Her children are trying to help her. (Mariana, social worker)

The views of youth regarding their experiences in care are often not validated. Foster children often lack choices and a voice in the system that is meant to protect them (Whiting 2000). Among many, Cashmore (2014) and Whiting (2000) emphasise the value of hearing from children and young people regarding their life experiences, which include providing the social worker with the youth's perspective, providing a youth forum to express themselves and helping youth understand themselves better.

# Kaitiakitanga

In the New Zealand context, there are many cultural considerations that need to be addressed to be sure that children are approached with compassion and their unique culture is honoured in the process. The research supports the need for Māori and Pasifika people being a part of their traditional community and being involved in cultural traditions (Moss 2009). However, in the absence of living together in the same space and participating in cultural gatherings, how are children able to maintain their cultural belonging and identity? Who can provide this knowledge to children who are placed outside the whānau?

For Māori, kaitiakitanga can mean 'a guardian, keeper, preserver, conservator, foster parent or protector' (Marsden and Henare 1992, p.18).

> Kaitiakitanga has a deep meaning spiritually... I was raised with the belief that my ancestors who are not living physically are still living spiritually and they guide me and protect me. My ancestors are my kaitiakitanga... We owe it to the children since we have so much information about them. It is kaitiakitanga... to gather this information – it will be difficult because it is all part of their life experience. (Mariana, social worker)

For Māori and Pasifika cultures, a sense of belonging is not only about belonging to a family or whānau but also about belonging to hapū, iwi and their whakapapa. This is their tūrangawaewae or primary place of belonging whether they live with their whānau or not (Metge and Ruru as cited in Atwool 2010). Māori and Pasifika cultures have a unique ability to connect through genealogy. Often the first question when people meet is: 'Where are you from?' The purpose is to connect through whakapapa.

> If I deal with a Samoan case, the first thing I ask is the family name. We have a Samoan saying: E tele aa ole tagata: lo aa ole laau, which means the root of a tree has less than the roots of a person...so that's the principle for my working with kids. In Samoan, every individual belongs. A sense of belonging in a Samoan sense is a person in his or her family – that's the

belonging...you can't separate that in a Samoan way of life. (Sione, social worker)

However, when a child is placed outside their whānau or their cultural group, they often lack opportunities to reconnect, which can have an impact on their connection to their culture and their continued interest in learning about their culture. The whānau may have broken connections with the child's iwi, but that should not prevent the child from being supported to make connections with their iwi. Social workers and caregivers can offer children an option to approach their iwi elders and reconnect.

Mariana (not her real name), a social worker in New Zealand, raised the issue of approaching birth families for information to include in a life story book and how we do this in a safe way.

Even if there are safety issues, how do we as social workers make sure that children are safe and still active and participating, even if we don't know how to ask the questions of the family. How do we go back to family and find out? (Mariana, social worker)

Atwool (2010) highlights that 'children in care need a person with the appropriate expertise to engage with whānau, hapu and iwi' (p.212). Atwool and Mark (2014) confirm the need for children in care to have a 'guardian of their story', a kaitiakitanga.

As a living being, physical and spiritual, we are valuable and there are some people/families who preserve that value and what I see professionally in my work with foster children through no fault of their own...they don't have someone to protect their knowledge or gather their information or to acknowledge their value. (Mariana, social worker)

According to Māori and Pasifika cultures, it is the responsibility of the cultural group to impart cultural knowledge through the use of storytelling and participation in cultural events (Moss 2009; Tutaki and Tutaki 2014).

For some in Māoridom it would be exposure and connecting... if they are with a new caregiver who is not kin, links can still be maintained. We ask if the caregivers are open to attending family celebrations...they could attend significant events. By keeping themselves aware of what's happening they still have that knowledge. (Mariana, social worker)

Almost all Pacific families in New Zealand will have stories... such stories connect young people with a sense of belonging and identity and to their cultures of origin. (Bush *et al.* 2009, p.143)

The lack of cultural connectedness for Māori and Pasifika people can jeopardise their wellbeing and their ability to trust and can create issues with self-esteem (Cashmore 2014). Additionally, the importance of cultural connection in achieving positive outcomes for children and young people has been identified as one of the protective factors of resilience (Ungar, as cited in Atwool 2010). E. Tutaki (2014) shares that 'even one connection to their culture, is a connection. From that connection, creates another connection.'

In my life my grandparents shared stories with me. I was able to ask family members about similarities and I see where we are similar. Being an important member in my family increased my sense of belonging to the point that family is everything in my world. (Mariana, social worker)

# Current perspective/practice of therapeutic life story work in New Zealand

An important aspect of growth and development is having a coherent life story. Research identifies that a child's lack of knowledge of the reasons they are removed from their families contributes to the problems they experience in foster care (Johnson *et al.* 1995; Shotton 2010), including emotional and behavioural issues (Kraemer, Vetare and Dowling 2005). A life story book has been identified as a way to safeguard the memories and experiences of children while placed in out-of-home care. In the 1970s life story work was identified as a therapeutic tool for children in care in North America (Backhaus 1984). In 1981, the New Zealand

Department of Social Welfare made a statement that 'the creation and maintenance of personal life story books, involving the child, foster parents, social workers and others, is a practice designed to enhance knowledge of personal identity and belonging' (Duffin 1985, p.iv).

International research clearly indicates there are many benefits of life story work with children in care, including a positive impact on the carer–child relationship (Shotton 2013), the provision of assurance, stability and hope (Rose 2012), and a boost in a child's sense of belonging and self-perception (Shotton 2013). Willis and Holland (2009) emphasised the value of the life story process and the positive contributions made to youth's identity and expression of emotions. Many countries are realising the benefit of therapeutic life story work in assisting children to have a coherent picture of their lives. Atwool (2010) confirms that life story work has been identified as an important aspect of a care plan for children in the New Zealand foster care system to ensure they know their identity and background. In light of this research, there appears to be a need to prioritise and safeguard the connections and memories of our foster children to ensure they have a really secure identification with their roots.

In New Zealand, social workers do not receive the training to conduct life story work; therefore social workers may avoid this work with children due to a lack of confidence in the process (Atwool 2010; Watkin and Jones 2016). Watkin and Jones share that social workers in New Zealand are willing to learn and would like to conduct life story work with children in care; however, they recognise that this is a different line of work and they do not have the time to make the commitment necessary to conduct it.

> A child has to have extreme behaviours before life story work is approved in New Zealand. However, we need to have this type of therapeutic intervention provided earlier to avoid the acting out behaviours we see from children in care. (Watkin and Jones 2016)

Watkin and Jones are among the few in New Zealand who conduct this sort of work with children, and unfortunately there is currently no funding to provide the supplies needed to do it effectively, so the money comes out of their own pockets. They further explain that this type of intervention for children must be used as a preventative therapeutic intervention rather than a reactive treatment. The other issue is that, unlike other countries, New Zealand does not have a system that collates all of a child's history in one place, which means there is no access to a chronological picture of a child's life in care. Social workers have to trawl through files and files to obtain this information, which is extremely time consuming (Watkin and Jones 2016). However, Watkin and Jones report that New Zealand has come a long way and social workers are now more aware of the importance of capturing memories and encouraging foster parents to do the same.

> It wasn't until I started working with children, this widened my view of the treatment of children and how valuable it is when a child, young person, adult's life is recorded whether in memory, storytelling or photographs. (Mariana, social worker)

> I only witnessed benefits [of the life story work]. The end result [of life story work] has always been positive. It answers their questions 'who am I?', 'where did I come from?', 'where do I belong?', 'why was I separated?' – those basic questions. (Joanne, social worker)

There are some agencies in New Zealand which are promoting the use of life story tools for children in care. However, Atwool and Mark (2014) express their concern that very few foster children have life books in New Zealand. Ron Mark spoke of his personal experiences in foster care and the lack of information he received about his situation and his family. He shares that he felt misled and that having this information is a critical component of resiliency. Atwool and Mark suggest that kids can only self-actualise when they are healed from their past traumas.

> You have to be in the right place yourself and supervision is really important. If you have a child that is talking about really traumatic experiences in their life, then unless you have that level of self-knowledge or insight this can make you vulnerable.

People don't like talking about horrible things and they want to make kids feel better. There could be a danger that people want to gloss over difficult things that happen to kids in a misguided attempt to think that will cut it. It's helping the child to understand – having those courageous conversations with kids. (Joanne, social worker)

## CASE STUDY: JACOB

*Joanne is a social worker in New Zealand who shares her experience conducting therapeutic life story work with a young boy, Jacob. All of the names in this study have been changed due to confidentiality.*

Jacob was eight when I first met him. He had a difficult start to his life. He and his brother weren't living with their birth parents and were living in a residential placement. They were moved to a small family home and it was in that placement that Jacob started to display difficult behaviours: he ran away overnight and was smoking, hot-wiring cars and not going to school. Jacob went missing for a couple of days and was moved to another facility near his mum. They couldn't handle his behaviour so he was moved into a foster care placement. He set fire to a local church and got an order to take him to a secure setting. All of his behaviours were directed towards himself. He ended up in a residential secure unit but ran away from there with a broken ankle.

He was an engaging child. I was his social worker for six years and I got to know him really well. A guy Jacob had linked with earlier was arrested by police and linked to a child murder. Jacob's behaviour plummeted. He was depressed and he expressed that if he had said something this child would have been alive. He became suicidal and disappeared and we didn't know where he was. I had a feeling he was okay.

Four months later I was sitting at my desk and Jacob called. He was in France and he was picked up and brought back. We wondered what we were going to do with this boy. We found a single male caregiver, Barry, and placed Jacob with him. That placement changed him around. This was the point when life story work was effective. We found out he had gone to find his dad because he wanted to know why he had been removed, why he was not living with his brother and why his youngest sibling was allowed to stay with his mum when the others had been removed. During our first time working together, we had a few stops and starts. He had to feel confident that I was going to look out for his feelings and his emotions. The whole process took 18 months. He wanted to produce a book. It was four pages long and it looked like it had been dragged through the dirt, but it was his book. It was the work. We spent so much time talking it through and letting him know how the decisions were made and helping him to understand his life and why his behaviours in the context of his life made perfect sense. He is 26 years old now and has a family of his own. About nine months ago I got a call from my friend who had worked with me at the local authority. She said, 'Guess who's been in to see you? Jacob! He's doing really well and was asking for you. You'll never guess what he came in for. He wants to be a foster parent!' I burst into tears.

> Encourage the family to commemorate the first time they met and have photos about that and their thoughts around that – they are now a part of that family and it should be celebrated. Foster carers can record something neat the kids did or even their favourite foods, or that they used to laugh with a belly laugh. This documentation will allow these children the opportunity to share their childhood with their own children. (Joanne, social worker)

## Conclusion

The question remains: What stands in the way of this type of intervention being available for children in New Zealand? How can we mobilise those working directly with foster children to direct more energy towards understanding the value of hearing our children's voices and understanding their experiences? Is keeping a child safe enough or do children need someone to be their kaitiakitanga? Children and young people in care need to have that someone who can safeguard and protect them and their experiences. Atwool (2010) suggests that a care plan should have a designated person who has the responsibility to ensure that life story work continues throughout the child/youth's time in care. Thirty-five years ago, the New Zealand Department of Social Welfare made life story work a priority but we are still asking the same questions, exploring the same issues and making the same recommendations. If we are to address the identity needs of children in care in New Zealand, therapeutic life story work is vital as part of our social work best practice and needs to be funded at policy level. Adequately funded and trained life story workers and social workers will ensure that our foster youth are given a secure identity that will prevent them from becoming lost in the system.

## Glossary

Hapū – a division of a Māori people or community

Iwi – a Māori community or people, tribes

Kaitiakitanga – guardianship and protection; guardian, protector

Kaumatua – a Māori elder

Tūrangawaewae – a place where one has the right to stand, a place where one has rights of residence and belonging through kinship and whakapapa

Whakapapa – genealogy, lineage, descent

Whānau – family, extended family

## References

Atwool, N. (2010) *Children in Care: A Report into the Quality of Service Provided to Children in Care.* Office of the Children's Commissioner. Wellington, New Zealand.

Atwool, N. and Mark, R. (2014) 'The importance of life story work with children in care.' Paper presented at the Fostering Kids: Change Makers: The Future of Care Conference. Christchurch, New Zealand.

Backhaus, K.A. (1984) 'Life books: tool for working with children in placement.' *Social Work* 29(6), 551–554.

Bush, A., Chapman, F., Drummond, M. and Fagaloa, T. (2009) 'Development of a child, adolescent and family mental health service for Pacific young people in Aotearoa/New Zealand.' *Pacific Health Dialog* 15(1), 138–146.

Cashmore, J. (2014) 'Children Living Away from Home.' In G.B. Melton *et al.* (eds) *The SAGE Handbook of Child Research.* London: SAGE.

Child, Youth and Family (2014) Key statistics: children in care and foster carers. Available at http://www.msd.govt.nz/about-msd-and-our-work/publications-resources/statistics/cyf/ index.html, accessed on 19 June 2017.

Connolly, M., de Haan, I. and Crawford, J. (2013) 'The safety of young children in care: a New Zealand study.' *Adoption & Fostering* 37(3), 284–296.

Duffin, J.M. (1985) *Growing Up Fostered: Four Young People Present an In-depth View of How it Feels to be Nobody's Child.* Wellington, NZ: Office of Childcare Studies, Department of Social Welfare.

Johnson, P.R., Yoken, C. and Voss, R. (1995) 'Family foster care placement: the child's perspective.' *Child Welfare: Journal of Policy, Practice, and Program* 74(5), 959–974.

Kraemer, S., Vetere, E.A. and Dowling, E. (2005) *Narratives of Fathers and Sons: There is No Such Thing as a Father. Narrative Therapies with Children and their Families: A Practitioner's Guide to Concepts and Approaches.* London: Brunner/Routledge.

Marsden, M. and Henare, T. (1992) *Kaitiakitanga: A Definitive Introduction to the Holistic World View of the Maori.* Wellington, NZ: Ministry for the Environment.

Ministerial Advisory Committee (1988) Puao te ata tu (Day break). Ministerial Advisory Committee on a Māori Perspective for the Department of Social Welfare, Wellington.

Moss, M. (2009) 'Broken circles to a different identity: an exploration of identity for children in out-of-home care in Queensland, Australia.' *Child & Family Social Work* 14(3), 311–321.

Rose, R. (2012) *Life Story Therapy with Traumatized Children: A Model for Practice.* London: Jessica Kingsley Publishers.

Ryburn, Murray. (1995) 'Adopted children's identity and information needs.' *Children & Society* 9.3: 41–64.

Shotton, G. (2010) 'Telling different stories: the experience of foster/adoptive carers in carrying out collaborative memory work with children.' *Adoption & Fostering* 34(4), 61–67.

Shotton, G. (2013) '"Remember when…": Exploring the experiences of looked after children and their carers in engaging in collaborative reminiscence.' *Adoption & Fostering* 37(4), 352–367.

Sinclair, I., Baker, C., Wilson, K. and Gibbs, I. (2005) *Foster Children: Where They Go and How They Get On.* London: Jessica Kingsley Publishers.

Stein, M. (2006) 'Young people aging out of care: the poverty of theory.' *Children and Youth Services Review* 28(4), 422–434.

Tutaki, F. and Tutaki, E. (9 October 2014) Personal communication.

Watkin, D. and Jones, C. (5 April 2016) Personal communication.

Whiting, J.B. (2000) 'The view from down here: foster children's stories.' *Child & Youth Care Forum* 29(2), 79–95.

Willis, R. and Holland, S. (2009) 'Life story work: reflections on the experience by looked after young people.' *Adoption & Fostering* 33(4), 44–52.

Chapter 6

# A DRAMATIC AND NARRATIVE APPROACH TO LIFE STORY THERAPY, FACILITATING ATTACHMENT IN ADOPTION

*Joan Moore, freelance drama therapist, play therapist and adoption support provider*

## Abstract

The knowledge of who we are and where we come from forms the basis of our identity. Gaps in this knowledge cause insecurity, and for children who have been removed from their birth families as consequent to neglect and abuse it almost invariably leaves them with a residual sense of self-blame. Many who are waiting for legal decisions about their future lack any true sense of belonging and on moving to permanence, they often need help to reattach. This chapter describes a therapeutic model called 'Theatre of Attachment' that is carried out in the child's foster and/ or adoptive home, because this is where children usually feel safest. It engages the caregivers in the re-enactment of scenes from the children's past life to bridge gaps in their understanding, enable the children to rebuild their identity and gain a sense of belonging in their family of permanence. It is the backbone of the author's Adopted Child Therapy Service (ACTS), which aims to facilitate secure attachment of children to their adoptive, kinship or long-term foster parents. However, the focus of this chapter is on identity issues arising specifically through adoption.

# Introduction

In the UK, permanence is most often achieved through adoption, which gives children a new family name and rights to inheritance. Adoption is not just about a change of name but involves a change of identity, which for the child is far more profound. Many families who adopt children from care are from a different social milieu and culture and therefore have different expectations to those of children whose earlier lives made them so fearful and anxious that they constantly anticipate disapproval and rejection. Adoptive parents may, for the purpose of keeping the children safe, enforce tighter boundaries than the children had been used to, which some rail against. Confusion may surround the children's loss of identity as a member of their birth family, alongside the coinciding loss of narratives about their past life, because it is on these stories that children depend in order to develop their sense of self and identity (Reese *et al.* 2010). Kenrick (2006) argues that children in adoptive, foster or kinship placements often need help to express themselves and be disabused of wrong assumptions causing self-blame.

Theorists and practitioners such as White and Epston (1990) have long regarded the construction of the life story to be effective in helping children and young people to make sense of their life and realise that their fear and anxiety had been constituted by their relationships and environment rather than by something intrinsically wrong with them. The very composition of the word 'history' being 'his story' symbolises its significance for understanding how the past continues to influence the present.

# Identity formation

We develop our identity initially from our families, the stories we hear from others and those we construct about ourselves. Kelly (1955) observed man to develop constructs according to how he experiences life and relationships; hence the abused individual who anticipates threat and persecution responds accordingly. Indeed, even before the child is born, personality development is influenced by the mother's high stress levels, affecting the brain structure of her foetus and contributing to later mood and anxiety disorders throughout the lifespan (Talge, Neal and Glover 2007), especially when the mothers are anxious during 12–22 weeks of pregnancy (Phillips 2007). Fonagy, Steele and Steele (1991) observed the psychological capacities of the mother to predict how their unborn child would react to separation and stress, a year after birth.

Once babies are born, they discover their right to exist via their interaction with their primary caregivers. Fraiberg (1982) observed infants as young as five months old to become completely immobile in the face of fear. Music (2005) reflects that babies depend on attunement to develop complex skills. Supplementing this attunement is important in therapy with agitated children who struggle to self-calm due to the absence of sensitive caregiving in their family of origin. For this purpose I draw from the model provided by Lave and Wenger (1991) for developing a sense of belonging and allowing people to feel valued for who they are rather than what they do, i.e. 'being' before 'doing' (Moore and Peacock 2007). Their model promotes the construction of identity as a non-conscious process made up of countless experiences of being in the world, seeing one's effect on the world when they participate in it and how we are affected by the world around them. Of course, with traumatised children, the process of life story work can be fraught with risk, and it is essential to be sensitive to the impact it has. A considerable 'balancing act' is required between helping the child recognise what happened that shouldn't have happened, while protecting him/her from becoming overwhelmed. Foster and adoptive carers often worry about the possible harm of 'opening a can of worms' should they attempt to discuss children's life histories with them, and many struggle to access skilled supervision and training. Fortunately, Richard Rose is now providing accredited training in the UK and Australia on life story therapy. Invited to view the past as testimony to their heroic endurance, children start to perceive their pain as a legacy, revealing their strengths.

## Cultural influences

In the first nine months, the primary attachment figure is usually the mother (Prior and Glaser 2006), but from then on it is culturally determined (Crittenden and Claussen 2003), and studies of attachment, globally, describe contrasting patterns in different cultures. For example, LeVine and New (2008) report on variations such as a group of German parents being more 'avoidant', in contrast to children in kibbutz communities, who slept communally away from their mothers and were more 'ambivalent'. As Aldgate *et al.* (2006) note, we react to people according to the environment in which we are raised. Genes and environment interact in multi-faceted ways and children learn language from deciphering adult clues. Indeed, social constructionists have observed each culture to have its own culturally specific understandings and rules for acknowledging emotion (Gergen 2009). In the author's view, the multiple ethnic mix in the UK has brought a greater variation of attachment styles, of which opposites are found in the same family, as described in the case study later in this chapter.

## The significance of play

In pretend play, we are learning scripts for life and 'training for the unexpected' (Spintz, Newberry and Beckoft 2001, p.141). The educationalist Vygostsky (1962) promoted the use of props for helping children to build their knowledge and enhance their skills to plan for the next stage, and thereby develop 'tools of the mind' (Barnett *et al.* 2008). Play can also be a transitional space for giving children practice to cope with comings and goings (Winnicott 1971, 100). To communicate effectively we need to be able to work out another's thoughts and feelings and manage our emotional states, also to be able to put our own feelings into words. Play is found to stimulate aspects of brain organisation – physical capacities and social circuits (Panksepp *et al.* 2007), which helps self-regulation and executive functioning.

## Altering brain structure

As Seigel explains, when someone regularly reflects what is in our mind, we develop a 'witnessing self' (Siegel 2007). Our psychological health is influenced by an increasingly complex interdependence between various brain areas, and Music (2005) warns that, since language is learned from deciphering adult clues, abuse and neglect damage the brain's

'Wernicke's area' (where language is stored). Once an expectation is formed, it remains like water flowing down pre-existing channels. Hence the traumatised child can become stuck in hyperarousal. Joseph Le Doux (1998) advises that therapy helps the cortex to control the amygdala, so that fear-inducing experience can be interpreted in less frightening ways. When strong emotions can be tolerated, brain structure changes. We can't alter the past but we can build new pathways for the future.

## Adolescence

On reaching adolescence a new set of challenges arise, both for the child and their adoptive parents, who may need help to understand and adapt to the changes. Although the developmental tasks of adolescence are conceptualised differently across cultures, class and history, rendering it difficult to generalise, what we do know is that during the teenage years a major pruning of the brain takes place. The increase in myelination allows brain signals to travel 100 times faster, but although the brain becomes more efficient, at this stage it is less adaptable, even though impulsivity and pleasure seeking are more intense than at any other stage, which explains why the 13-year-old may argue, intractably, that the 'the sky isn't blue'. This appears to be because risk-taking lights up the adolescent brain. The swifter reaction of the amygdala (which dictates survival responses), may explain why adolescents react so emotionally and quickly to facial expression and are more likely to read disapproval in adult faces that may merely be expressing sadness or preoccupation. Adolescent bodies are developing ahead of their brains, which are still at an earlier stage (Pine *et al.* 2005). Collishaw *et al.* (2004) found that one in five adolescents in Britain have mental health problems. They recommend building parenting skills to facilitate their children's interactions with their neighbourhood and peer groups.

## Theatre of attachment

Theatre's magnifying of human emotion helps us to feel what others feel and in so doing magnifies interaction in which humans expand on each other's affect, this – the outward expression of emotion – this interaction being the 'theatre of attachment' (Moore 2006, 2009, 2010, 2012). The theoretical orientation of 'theatre of attachment' practice is founded on neurobiological findings (Anda *et al.* 2006; Cozolino 2006) of the impact that abuse and neglect have on child development, particularly social and emotional functioning, which affects the child's capacity for secure attachment and relationships. It also draws on attachment research (Bowlby 1973; Crittenden 2008; Grossman, Grossman and Waters 2006) of humans' ability to adapt to their environment, the most harmful early experience leading to increasingly maladaptive and fixed patterns of behavioural interaction. Most children referred to 'theatre of attachment' intervention have had adverse care and separations, which they experience as further rejection, exacerbating their sense of self-blame and of being unworthy of nurture. In therapeutic play context, this can be addressed by paying close attention to their movements and expression of thoughts and feelings via the dramatic technique of 'mirroring' – a replication of the 'attachment dance' (Hughes 1997; Winnicott 1965) between mothers and infants from which their babies gain vital social and cognitive information. It is these mutual dances of attuned interactive partnership that facilitate joint attention of 'intersubjectivity' (Trevarthen 2010), and are central to therapeutic work with children, to help them develop the more complex social skills. Yet every child and family is different, and for this reason the author has developed, and uses, many different creative techniques and methods in order to address each individual's and family's particular needs.

# A family-oriented approach

Contemporary developments in neurobiological research on the effects of trauma on emotional development have highlighted the importance of facilitating attachment of looked-after children and led to the inclusion of foster and adoptive parents in therapy with their children, the importance of which is emphasised by family therapist Eliana Gill (2012). Dozier *et al.* (2002) found that enabling foster carers to read their children's emotional expression helped the children to master fears and attach more securely. In the author's experience, engaging the child's caregivers as partners in the therapeutic process has proved vital to bring about change. A key purpose of the theatre of attachment model is to enhance parents' understanding and empathy for their child's earlier experience in order that the child feels safe to process anxiety-inducing memories and gains comfort from reciprocal, fulfilling relationships. When children are acting emotionally younger (or older) than their chronological age, I model ways to engage with them at the appropriate level to facilitate parents' recognition of the emotional age being displayed. Informing them of the relevant research on child development helps them to appreciate the source of their children's bewildering, sometimes intimidating behaviour as a mechanism for survival, which can change once they get consistent encouragement and support from their adoptive parents.

## Use of the metaphor

An essential component is the application of drama, story and creative play, this being the most natural way for children to explore their world and relationships. The metaphor and symbols in stories lend the privacy and hope, which encourages children to reframe their identity as brave survivors. Prior to delivering the facts of their history, I often begin with a story, for example about a princess or lion cub encountering adversity and feeling forced to adjust to (unwanted) changes in their circumstances. The purpose is to illustrate feelings and experiences to which the children are likely to relate, and prepare them to explore these feelings. It is also safer practice to use stories, which give metaphoric distance, when working with children who are still seeing their birth parents, prior to the conclusion of legal proceedings.

A conclusion from research by Despert and Potter (1936) is that 'the use of stories appears to be most valuable when the child determines the subject matter of his or her own story' (Brandell 2000, p.4), and for this reason I encourage children to develop their own stories. It is a process that helps bring to consciousness memories which have been suppressed, and I find that these stories frequently illustrate the children's perceptions of their lives. Adoptive and foster parents have also reported that the recording and re-reading of these stories to the children helped to build their self-esteem consolidate learning and enhanced their overall functioning, including their ability to forge more satisfactory, reciprocal relationships (Moore 2012).

When it is agreed that the children are ready to hear their life history, hearing the facts in the presence of committed adults appears to enable the children to feel safer to reattach. With younger children especially, this is achieved via 'small world play', using toys on a life map, illustrating the houses they lived in. I encourage children to add their own drawings to this 'scenery' of their life.

Many children such as Jasmine and Tania in the case study that follows respond well to a costume drama of their life story in which their adoptive or (long-term) foster parents take part. The children are given the choice of watching the play or joining in and taking on roles such as 'birth parents' or the people who tried to help. This gives them new insights into the pressures and choices faced by their birth parents, which clarify why they acted as they did, and alleviates children's self-blame for abuse and rejection. Enactment of the children's history in sequential order helps not only to clarify 'what happened' but enables the children to rewrite endings as they would like them to be, which involves them admitting 'what should have happened'. In 'walking' their story, children discover how the past affects the present and that making sense of this creates more choice for the future. On finding that there are no secrets left to worry about, they become more hopeful. Creative materials used in this context appear to prove effective for directly accessing the sensory, emotional parts of the brain. This may be because the blocking mechanisms of the 'thinking' parts that act on unhelpful assumptions are bypassed, enabling inhibiting pre-verbal experience to be safely processed and reconstructed. Stories and plays that evolve are later typed, illustrated with clip art and placed in the child's life story folder, which contains an age-appropriate account of the child's life history and memories to keep.

# CASE STUDY: JASMINE AND TANIA

*Names and identifying details have been changed to preserve anonymity.*

## History of the children

Two girls, Jasmine, age 11, and Tania, age 14, are white English children, who had been removed a few months earlier from a context of chronic neglect and parental drug and alcohol abuse. They spent six months in local authority foster care until being placed for adoption at the ages of four and six years, with Tony and Sara (also white English). The children's birth mother and maternal aunt had been in and out of psychiatric hospital with drug-related illness, while their father had spent several periods in prison. Most of their birth relatives were involved in criminal behaviour, including their maternal grandmother.

Over the previous two years, during contact with this grandmother, Jasmine and Tania had also been seeing their birth mother, unbeknown to the adoptive parents, who supported the contact. The grandmother undermined the adoptive placement by sending the children text messages saying, 'Your real mum loves you. Your adoptive mum stole you', and that she really wanted to care for them but wasn't allowed to. She also gave them elaborate presents of games consoles and clothes, most of which were stolen goods, and took them to a family wedding, where she got drunk and left the children with strangers.

## Incidents that prompted referral

About a year before the intervention took place, disputes intensified, inflamed by the girls' jealousy of their cousins' relationship with their birth family, despite the reality of the latter's poor material existence. The grandmother enticed Jasmine to 'play up' her adoptive parents, and this culminated in Jasmine making allegations of physical abuse by Sara, of being kicked, pulled by her hair and having her head hit against the wall. While this allegation was being investigated, the girls returned to foster care but did not get on with their foster parents. They felt isolated and picked on. Soon both wanted to return home. Jasmine admitted having exaggerated the injuries alleged against her adoptive mother and confessed that they had actually arisen in play fighting.

The girls returned home to their adoptive parents and the contact with their birth grandmother stopped, but their parents and teachers continued to be concerned about them. Sara requested urgent help for Jasmine and Tania to understand why they were adopted so that they could process their history and recent experience.

*Adoptive parents' history*

The adoptive parents, Tony and Sara, were professionally employed; Tony worked full time, Sara part time. They had a large, modern house and enjoyed a comfortable lifestyle. However, early in their relationship Tony had an affair, from which he contracted a disease and became infertile. Then Sara, too, had an affair. However, the couple stayed together and presented a united front to the girls over Jasmine's allegations. Tony presented as calm, affable and easy going. In contrast, social workers experienced Sara, who was highly critical of their practice, as being 'hot-headed' and aggressively defensive.

*The children*

Tania, age 14, was a slim, quiet, studious girl, described by the social worker as withdrawn and out of her depth regarding her role in the allegations. Sara believed that Tania had supported Jasmine against her inclination, and Tania verified this. Jasmine, age 11, was robustly built, lively, effervescent and keen to please. Described by her adoptive mother as a 'drama queen' who loved attention, Jasmine depended on being at the centre of her peer group, and was easily led. She was often in trouble, not helped by her refusal to back down from arguments. Both girls attended mainstream school and were making progress commensurate to their age.

*Intervention*

Funding was provided for ten sessions, of two-hour duration, some with the whole family, others giving a separate hour to each child. They took place over a period of four months in the family home, at the family's preference. Activities for which the therapist provided the materials included re-enactment of the life history using various techniques, including a life map, costume play and a candle ceremony (Corrigan and Moore 2011; Moore 2012), as well as drawing a family tree, storytelling, painting, clay, collage and icing biscuits.

Having read the files and drawn up the life history, I held a meeting with the adoptive parents to agree the way forward. Tony and Sara were receptive to the proposed plan for intervention, subject to adjustments to my account of the life history, in the interests of making it more accurate and acceptable. I had drawn a life map on canvas to illustrate houses in which the children had lived, and the children chose toy figures to represent the people in their life to re-enact the moves from one house to the next. Jasmine was immediately struck by the sheer quantity of houses they'd lived in and asked a lot of questions about her birth family. Her earliest memory was of strange men entering their birth home to demand money from their parents, an incident that had led to fighting and bloodshed. She drew a prison on the map and asked for more information on which members of her birth family were incarcerated and why. Tania initially asserted that she felt this work had come too late. However, she engaged more enthusiastically in sessions that followed.

Since in my experience children and young people are often far more comfortable with fictional versions (rather than the facts about their real life that can feel harsh and embarrassing), I wrote a story about two tiger cubs in adversity. This prompted Jasmine and her adoptive mother to write their own stories based on their memories. At the following session, we read the (real) life history, a five-page document with large type and illustrations throughout, but Tania experienced it as being too long and more overwhelming than expected, so I wrote a much briefer story about a house with a big heart, to convey the facts in a more manageable length that she preferred. It prompted the children to create a story about a witch who 'uttered evil things in the children's ears', a processing of their perception of their grandmother's malevolent influence.

Four sessions in, we moved into performing the life history, which was titled 'Tears and Fears' and comprised 16 scenes, which the children identified for improvisation. This involved the whole family and gave each the opportunity to try out various roles. It began with scenes from the birth parents' childhood in order to enable the children to recognise and understand how their difficulties had arisen. A narrator introduced scenes, as in the following sample:

Narrator: The education welfare officer (EWO) sees Mary (the birth mum), age 13, with a group, sitting in McDonald's when they should be at school.

EWO: It's Mary isn't it? (Addressing group) Why aren't you lot in school?

Mary: I'm not going.

EWO: It's against the law not to go to school! I'm going to see your mum!

Mary: You can't make me! There's no point anyway. School can't teach me anything that's of use to me!

In the next scene, Mary's mother was rudely dismissive to the EWO. Soon after, the school was burned down and Mary's brother was accused of arson.

Taking turns at the role of 'birth mother' and 'grandmother' prompted Jasmine to demand explanations as to why her birth relatives behaved as they did. The seventh scene was set in the 'hostel' where Mary arrives with her children.

Mary: My partner's locked up and we're homeless.

Worker: There's a room for you but you have to keep it clean.

Narrator: A few days later, other residents at the hostel ring social workers to complain that the children are crying all night.

Health visitor: These children have lots of infections. They must be in awful pain. Mary, you need to get them to the doctor's.

Narrator: But Mary won't take them to the doctor's. The hostel is set on fire. Mary is told she can't stay there any more.

This enactment aroused the girls' empathy for their birth parents, recognising that they too had suffered abuse. It helped Jasmine to release herself from self-blame, reconcile to being adopted and appreciate that these adoptive parents had actually chosen her. Subsequently, we revisited the events that prompted the girls' recent spell in care. Tania talked about her resentment of their foster carer's unkind attitudes towards them. She admitted to having felt in an invidious position – of wishing to be with her adoptive parents but feeling obliged to support her sister, who she felt would otherwise have had no one else.

Jasmine and Tania also enjoyed painting and making collages, illustrating their interests and wishes, which helped to reaffirm their desired identity. In the penultimate session, we made a family tree that they continued to develop in their own time, and they went on to produce more detailed and visually appealing versions. The intervention concluded with a candle ceremony in which the girls candidly spoke their minds to lighted candles representing birth family members. It was a way to say 'goodbye' to the past, deal with 'unfinished business' and also to reflect on and celebrate positive feelings and memories.

### Children's responses

Jasmine and Tania recalled being let down by their birth mother who failed constantly to keep her promises to them. Jasmine spoke of having felt tricked by her grandmother. They were aware that the latter helped herself to goods without seeing any need to pay for them, whereas their adoptive parents had taught them that honesty is the best policy and that items of value had to be earned, saved for and paid for before they could be acquired.

Comparing the different cultures of the families they'd lived in stimulated their interest in the background of their adoptive family, additional members of whom Jasmine and Tania had recently met. Recalling many more happy memories of life in her adoptive family led Jasmine to acknowledge that she now wanted to identify herself as a member of this family.

Tania remembered her early days in her adoptive home when at the age of six she disliked food that was cooked differently from the way she was used to. She remembered acting in Disney stage shows on holidays and eating gaudy ice creams with pirate-shaped cocktail sticks that she'd poked her sister with. Tania spoke about how upset she had been by other children in their foster home, who had wrecked their property and set the girls up to be blamed. She had also been angry with their foster carer for telling Jasmine that she was fat and needed to diet. Tania reflected that in that foster placement she had felt like a number rather than a person. She had also been upset by insensitive comments from a teacher about the girls' adoption breaking down (it hadn't).

*Parents' engagement*

The adoptive father, Tony, attended the introductory session. He also took part in the costume play of the life history and in the final session. The girls clearly enjoyed having him there. Sara was present throughout and joined in the activities, but allowed the girls to talk privately to me about their experience and memories, when they wanted to. She demonstrated her commitment by supporting the girls to ask questions about events where the memories were extremely raw for her. The drama enabled Sara to talk openly about the relationship between Jasmine and herself. Sara found it hard to accept that Jasmine's propensity for getting into trouble indicated struggling self-esteem, but on being given information about brain development in adolescence she recognised that, after disagreements, children can find it hard to forgive their parents and this can affect their relationship for a long time. I gave her a story to share with Jasmine, which illustrated parallel predicaments and demonstrated their resolution. Both parents stated that they found this intervention helped them to put mechanisms into place that would reduce the likelihood of future disruption. They also felt that the girls had used this opportunity to explore their life history to positive effect and had reconstructed their identity as belonging securely with their adoptive parents.

*Reflections on attachment styles*

Opposite attachment styles were observed in this family. Jasmine and Tania had both formed a strong attachment to their adoptive parents; however, their attachment presentation appeared to be strongly influenced by their personalities and family history. Tania being the quieter child proved less of a threat to Sara, whose excitable and volatile personality matched and clashed with Jasmine's. Taking the classifications of Ainsworth (1978) and Crittenden (2008), Tania appeared to be self-possessed and 'secure', although her emotional caretaking of her sister and adoptive mother alongside her defensiveness at the start of the intervention could be classified as 'avoidant-defended'. Jasmine was the middle child in her birth family (the girls' younger siblings were adopted separately) and had probably been the most overlooked. Slow in learning to walk and talk as a consequence of early neglect, she suffered anxiety about separation and demanded attention constantly. She and Sara presented as ambivalent/enmeshed in the way they manufactured dramas and their inability to back down from an argument. Tony's patience in supporting the family indicated a 'secure' style, yet he, like Tania, might classify as 'avoidant-defended', since having initially promised to attend all sessions, he failed to do so, citing work pressure as the reason.

## Conclusion

It appears that there is something especially powerful about dramatic play in being able to step into the space and, from taking on roles, experience other points of view and have the option of changing the ending of their life story, projecting it as they would like it to be. Repetition of the life story combined with continuing awareness of the original experience was observed to prompt the children to create new outcomes and appeared to help cement their learning from the play. The weekly ritual of involving the children in planning the next session created a sense of prediction for them, which also appeared to help them feel safer and more in control of themselves, as did having the intervention in the family home, which allowed them to feel less self-conscious.

Presenting the life history in fictional format as well as the real facts, and processing it in multiple layers, using techniques such as the life map, a fictional representation of their life story, costume play and candle ceremony, enabled both children and parents to assimilate information at a pace they could all tolerate, which softened the impact of painful content and enabled the children to perceive themselves as the 'heroes' of their stories.

The process led the resistance and challenging attitudes displayed by this family to being reframed as positive coping mechanisms, their openness and determination viewed as evidence of their commitment. This was achieved through modelling ways to communicate playfully with the children at the age at which they were presenting, and by providing the parents with information to help them understand where and why their children were stuck (presenting as emotionally younger, due to early neglect and low self-esteem). The modelling, particularly, was instrumental in helping these parents to adjust their reactions and in turn helping the children to adapt and feel more secure in their adoptive parents' emotional availability. Hence an especially important impact was the effect on these parents of having brought about a positive spiral. Another important outcome was the fun and pleasure that the parents and children derived from the experience of joint engagement in creative and imaginative play and, correspondingly, improved relationships.

# References

Ainsworth, M. (1978) *Patterns of Attachment: A Psychological Study of the Strange Situation.* Hillsdale, New Jersey: Erlbaum.

Aldgate, J., Jones, D., Rose, W. and Jeffrey, C. (eds) (2006) *The Developing World of the Child.* London: Jessica Kingsley Publishers.

Anda, R.E., Felitti, V.J., Douglas Bremner, J., Walker, J.D. *et al.* (2006) 'The enduring effects of abuse and related adverse experiences in childhood: a convergence of evidence from neurobiology and epidemiology.' *European Archives Psychiatry Clinical Neuroscience* 256, 174–186.

Barnett, W., Jung, K., Yarosz, D.J., Thomas, J. *et al.* (2008) 'Educational effects of the Tools of the Mind curriculum: a randomized trial.' *Early Childhood Research Quarterly* 23(3), 299–313.

Bowlby, J. (1973) *Attachment and Loss: Separation-Anxiety and Anger, Vol II.* London: Hogarth Press.

Brandell, J.R. (2000) *Of Mice and Metaphors: Therapeutic Storytelling with Children.* New York: Basic Books.

Collishaw, S., Maughan, B., Goodman, R. and Pickles, A. (2004) 'Time trends in adolescent mental health.' *Journal of Psychology and Psychiatry* 45(8), 1350–1362.

Corrigan, M. and Moore, J. (2011) *Listening to Children's Wishes and Feelings.* London: British Association for Adoption and Fostering.

Cozolino, L. (2006) *Neuroscience of Attachment and Human Relationships.* London: Norton.

Crittenden, P. (2008) *Raising Parents: Attachment, Parenting and Child Safety.* Uffculme, Devon: Willan Publishing.

Crittenden, P. and Claussen, A.H. (2003) *The Organisation of Attachment Relationships: Maturation, Culture, and Context.* Cambridge: Cambridge University Press.

Despert, L. and Potter, H.W. (1936) 'Technical approaches in the study and treatment of emotional problems in childhood.' *Psychoanalytic Quarterly* 10, 619–638.

Dozier, M., Highley, E., Albus, K.E. and Nutter, A., (2002) 'Intervening with foster infants' caregivers: targeting three critical needs.' *Infant Mental Health Journal* 23(5), 55–554. Michigan Association for Infant Mental Health.

Fonagy, P., Steele, H. and Steele, M. (1991) 'Maternal representations of attachment during pregnancy predict the organization of infant–mother attachment at one year of age.' *Child Development* 62(5), 891–905.

Fraiberg, V. (1982) 'Pathological defenses in infancy.' *Psychoanalytic Quarterly* 51, 612–635.

Gergen, K.J. (2009) *An Invitation to Social Construction,* second edition. Newbury Park, CA: Sage.

Gill, E. (2012) *Helping Abused and Traumatised Children.* New York: Guildford Press.

Gill, E. (2011) *Working with children to heal interpersonal traumas: The power of play.* New York, Guildford Press.

Grossman, K.E., Grossman, K. and Waters, E. (eds) (2006) *Attachment from Infancy to Adulthood: The Major Longitudinal Studies.* New York: Guilford Press.

Hinde R.A. & Stevenson-Hinde, J. (1991) *Perspectives on Attachment.* In C.M. Parkes, J. Stevenson-Hinde & P, Marris, Attachment across the Life Cycle, pp 52-65, London, Routledge.

Hughes (1997) *Building the bonds of attachment: awakening love in deeply troubled children.* MD: Jason Aronson.

Kelly, G. (1955) *The Psychology of Personal Constructs.* New York: W.W. Norton.

Kenrick, J. (2006) 'Work with Children in Transition.' In J. Kenrick, L. Tollmache and C. Lyndsey, *Creating New Families: Therapeutic Approaches to Fostering, Adoption and Kinship Care.* London: Karnac Books.

Lave, J. and Wenger, E. (1991) *Situated Learning: Legitimate Peripheral Participation.* Cambridge: Cambridge University Press.

Le Doux, J. (1998) *The Emotional Brain.* New York: Simon and Schuster.

LeVine, R.A. and New, R.S. (eds) (2008) *Anthropology and Child Development: A Cross-Cultural Reader.* Oxford: Blackwell Publishing.

Moore, J. (2006) 'Theatre of Attachment: using drama to facilitate attachment in adoption.' *Adoption & Fostering* 30(2), 64–73.

Moore, J. (2009) 'The Theatre of Attachment: Dramatherapy with Adoptive and Foster Families.' In S. Jennings (ed.) *Dramatherapy and Social Theatre: Necessary Dialogues.* London: Routledge.

Moore, J. (2010) 'A story to tell: use of story and drama in work with substitute families.' *Dramatherapy* 31(3), 3–9.

Moore, J. (2012) *Once Upon A Time…Stories and Drama to Use in Direct Work with Adopted and Fostered Children.* London: British Association for Adoption and Fostering.

Moore, J. and Peacock, F. (2007) 'Being before doing: life story work with children with attachment difficulties.' *Dramatherapy* 29(1), 19–21.

Music, G. (2005) 'Surfacing the depths: thoughts on imitation, resonance and growth.' *Journal of Child Psychotherapy* 31(1), 72–90.

Panksepp, J. (2007) 'Can play diminish ADHD and facilitate the construction of the social brain?' *Journal of the Canadian Academy of Child and Adolescent Psychiatry* 16(2), 57–66.

Perry, B. and Szalavitz, M. (2008) *The Boy Who was Raised as a Dog and Other Tales from a Child Psychiatrist's Notebook: What Traumatized Children Can Teach Us about Love, Loss and Healing.* New York: Basic Books.

Phillips, D.I.W. (2007) 'Programming of the stress response: a fundamental mechanism underlying the long-term effects of the fetal environment.' *Journal of Internal Medicine* 261(5), 453.

Pine, D.S., Mogg, K., Bradley, B.P., Montgomery, L. *et al.* (2005) 'Attention bias to threat in maltreated children: implications for vulnerability to stress-related psychopathology.' *American Journal of Psychiatry* 162(2), 291–296.

Prior, V. and Glaser, D. (2006) *Understanding Attachment and Attachment Disorders: Theory, Evidence and Practice.* London: Jessica Kingsley Publishers.

Reese, E., Yan, C., Jack, F. and Hayne, H. (2010) 'Emerging Identities: Narrative and Self from Early Childhood to Early Adolescence.' In K.C. McLean and M. Pasupathi (eds) *Narrative Development in Adolescence: Creating the Storied Self.* New York: Springer.

Siegel, D.J. (2007) *The Mindful Brain: Reflection and Attunement in the Cultivation of Wellbeing.* New York: W.W. Norton.

Spinks, M., Newburry, R.C. and Beckof, M. (2001) 'Mammalian play: training for the unexpected.' *Quarterly Review of Biology* 76(2), 141–168.

Talge, N.M., Neal, C. and Glover, V. (2007) 'Antenatal maternal stress and long-term effects on child neurodevelopment: how and why?' *Journal of Child Psychology and Psychiatry and Allied Disciplines* 48(3–4), 245–261.

Trevarthen, C. (2010) 'What is it like to be a person who knows nothing? Defining the active intersubjective mind of a newborn human being.' *Infant and Child Development*, Special Issue.

Vygotsky, L. (1962) *Thought and Language.* Cambridge, MA: MIT Press.

White, M. and Epston, D. (1990) *Narrative Means to Therapeutic Ends.* New York: W.W. Norton.

Winnicott, D. (1965) *Maturational Processes and the Facilitating Environment: Studies in the Theory of Emotional Development.* London: Hogarth Press.

Winnicott, D. (1971) *Playing and Reality.* New York: Basic Books.

Chapter 7

# THERAPEUTIC LIFE STORY WORK WITH LOOKED-AFTER CHILDREN IN JAPAN

*Shoko Tokunaga PhD, Research Fellow at the Nipon Foundation, Child Welfare Team, Social Innovation Program Division*

*I first met Shoko in Shrewsbury, where we discussed the needs for traumatised children to own and be at peace with their narrative. This meeting was extremely helpful for those who attended, in particular for me, Shoko was pioneering the introduction of life story work for all children in institutions in Osaka and this commitment for her children was infectious. A few years later I was invited to present in Osako on life story work and engage with the universities in the city. Shoko's chapter is an encouraging g account of her journey in therapeutic life story work.*

## Introduction

Life story work is new to Japan, having first been studied and used in practice in the early 2000s. At the same time, life story work is also particularly valuable in Japan because it can help compensate for certain defects in our system for caring for looked-after children.

These defects are: 1) the common belief that looked-after children should be protected from painful information about the abuse or parental failures that led to their institutionalisation; 2) staff rotation practices that weaken relationships between children and their care providers;

and 3) low priority given to sharing information with institutionalised children.

## Becoming aware of the problem

Until recently, I was a care worker in residential schools, which are government-operated boarding schools for looked-after children who have emotional and behavioural issues. Children are identified as having these sorts of issues for a variety of reasons, but one reason is their involvement in criminal activities.

I lived in a group home for boys, along with my husband and two children. In the course of my work, I lived in two different residential schools – one operated by the Japanese government, and one operated by local government (Osaka City Council).

In both schools, my husband and I noticed that many young people knew very little about their own origins. Some did not know where they were born or their parents' names, and some never learned why they were taken from their families and put into institutions.

## Why and how children are deprived of information about their origins

It is a painful truth that children often became wards of the state because their parents were unfit, neglectful or even abusive. Some care workers try to protect children from these painful truths. They feel that it is kinder to tell the child to forget the past and instead start a new life. While they may be right in thinking they do this for the sake of the child, we must recognise that the caregivers themselves also find these conversations painful, and that their silence is not only for the children, but also for themselves.

But often nobody even considers whether or not to discuss children's painful pasts. Often the task of providing information to children is simply overlooked.

It is not uncommon for children to be taken into state care before they can really talk about, much less discuss, adult problems. In the vast majority of cases, a looked-after child is placed into an institution with as many as a hundred other children. Under 2013 guidelines, one adult care worker is required for every five and a half (5.5) elementary school aged children.

Because care workers are responsible for many children, they can only give a small amount of time and attention to each child. A bigger problem, however, is the relatively short time that care workers spend in each job.

By the time the child is old enough to ask how he ended up in the institution, nobody remembers, although somewhere a social worker will have a file, unless the file has been misplaced. The school itself will usually have some sort of record of the child, but the full record for a looked-after child is typically retained in the child guidance centre (what might be called a social work department in other countries).

We should note here that the residential school care workers are not social workers, and in fact it is the social workers in Japan who have truly heavy caseloads – as many as a hundred cases at once. And a social worker considering the various cases he is responsible for will naturally prioritise saving a child in a life-threatening situation over checking in on a child who is already safely in the care of the state.

The final result is that, however well meaning the care workers and social workers might be, the children often end up being deprived of very basic information about themselves.

Some people may argue that the children are better off not knowing, but the United Nations Convention on the Rights of the Child (which Japan ratified in 1994) specifically prohibits intentionally depriving children of information about themselves and their families. Even if the information is withheld *unintentionally*, careless administrative practices create the same result, and therefore the same harm.

# The United Nations Convention on the Rights of the Child includes a right to information

The United Nations Convention on the Rights of the Child (1989) specifies the following (italic emphasis added):

Article 8.1. States Parties undertake to respect the right of the child to preserve his or her identity, including nationality, name and family relations as recognised by law without unlawful interference.

Article 9.3. States Parties shall respect the right of the child who is separated from one or both parents to maintain personal relations and direct contact with both parents on a regular basis, except if it is contrary to the child's best interests.

Article 9.4. *Where such separation results from any action initiated by a State Party,* such as the detention, imprisonment, exile, deportation or death (including death arising from any cause while the person is in the custody of the State) of one or both parents or of the child, *that State Party shall, upon request, provide the parents, the child or, if appropriate, another member of the family with the essential information concerning the whereabouts of the absent member(s) of the family* unless the provision of the information would be detrimental to the well-being of the child. States Parties shall further ensure that the submission of such a request shall of itself entail no adverse consequences for the person(s) concerned.

# Introducing life story work – basic theory and practice: the first decade

As stated above, I recognised the problem of looked-after children not knowing about their origins, and was also aware of the United Nations Convention on the Rights of the Child. Around 2005, I started thinking about how to share basic but important information with young people, and decided to practise life story work by using *My Life and Me* (Camis 2001), which was later translated into Japanese. Some other practitioners had similar ideas and we met to explore the best way to do it. Later that same year a group of practitioners and academic researchers came together and established the Life Story Study Group.

More than ever, local authorities are aware of children's rights and created a Children's Rights Notebook in order to let looked-after children know about their rights.

The UN Convention and the Children's Rights Notebook introduced the idea that children have a right to know both their biological parent(s) and the circumstances which led to them being taken from their parents. Life story work provides a theoretical background and is a practical tool to meet children's need to learn about their own personal histories.

As members of the Life Story Study Group we gather case studies and analyse both the process and effects of life story work, and in cases or parts of cases where it fails we explore the reasons and try to improve it.

In order to prevent life story work from becoming merely another thing for a social worker and a care worker to check off a list, we decided to provide training. We wanted both care workers and social workers to be guided in their actions by the goals and philosophy of life story work, rather than merely following a set of steps. If, hypothetically, a care worker were to simply go through the steps of life story work without regard to the impact and reactions of the child, the work would be wasted or could even be damaging.

From the late 2000s to the early 2010s, we invited some British practitioners to talk in Japan once each year. We also visited them in the UK in order to observe their work. We also translated some English books (for example, Rose 2012; Ryan and Walker 2007; Wrench and Naylor 2013) into Japanese so that Japanese practitioners could always go back to review the theory behind life story work, and study techniques for establishing good relationships with young people that are both creative and child friendly.

## CASE STUDY: TARO (AGE 15)

*This story is a composite of events in several individual case studies, and has been created for illustrative purposes. This is not the record of a specific individual.*

Taro was taken from his mother and put in a children's institution at age three. After his initial institutionalisation, his mother twice took him back, but her problems with money and alcohol prevented her from succeeding as a parent, and both times Taro returned to the institution. As a result, Taro spent most of his childhood in an institution, along with more than 50 boys and girls, aged 2 to 18.

When Taro was 13, his behaviour deteriorated. He missed many days of school and broke the rules of the institution where he was living. He was viewed as a troublemaker and a bad influence on the other children. After police caught him stealing several times he was sent to a residential school.

Once in the residential school, Taro calmed down. Like most other students there, his stay was for one year. He had to start planning for whatever would come after that year.

Taro had never been told why he was taken away from his mother at the age of three. Although his mother visited him once a month, they never talked about the reasons Taro was institutionalised. His parents divorced when he was four years old, and since then Taro had not heard from his father, or even heard anything *about* his father.

Taro had some vague hopes of living with his mother. But when asked about his ideas for the future, and whether he wanted to work or to study, he had no answer. It would not be so bad, he said, if he were homeless.

It occurred to his care worker that Taro did not know anything about his father and therefore did not have an image of what an adult might do for a living. So the care worker suggested that, together, they try to learn more about Taro's father.

The care worker consulted with Taro's social worker, and they decided to begin life story work with Taro. The social worker gathered information about his father, and, when necessary or appropriate, attended life story work sessions with Taro, although most of the sessions were led by the care worker.

The life story work began with the social worker gathering information from the institutions where Taro lived as a small child, including some photographs. Then, the care worker took the case file and met with Taro. The file contained information about Taro's father, including where and when he was born, and what his occupation was. It was on this day that Taro heard his father's name for the first time.

The case worker continued to gather information about Taro's father. There had been no contact for 15 years, but she found his address and Taro wrote him a letter. His father quickly wrote back, and then came to visit him. When they met, Taro noticed that their faces were similar and, interestingly, they had the same kind of hands. But it was not only the appearance of the hands that they shared, but how they used their hands. Taro had always enjoyed making and fixing things, and his father, Taro discovered, was a builder. Until this time, Taro had never had anyone's footsteps to follow. But now he did. Taro decided that, like his father, he would become a builder.

Taro's mother also came to some sessions. She told him how he was born. For the first time, he learned that he was cut from his mother's womb by caesarean section, and that she had been frightened because there was so much blood. And she told him that when he was born and she saw his face for the first time, she was filled with joy.

Taro also learned his true place of birth. He had heard things as a small child, but the facts had become muddled. He had always believed he was born in Tokyo, but that was where his mother had been born. He had been born in another place. (To preserve Taro's privacy, birthplace and identifying details are omitted here.)

There was another question that Taro had always wondered about. He wanted to know why his name was Taro. He asked both his mother and his father this question. They both gave him good explanations. For the first time, Taro was proud of his name.

Life story work changed the way Taro saw himself, and his world. He learned how he had come into the world, and how his parents' marriage ended. His mother and father listened to him, and gave him answers. They told him what they were thinking in the past, and also how they felt now. They felt bad about his situation, and said they would try to support him. It was the first time he had heard something like this from his parents. It was the first time anybody expressed happiness that he had been born.

During this time, Taro and the care worker made a photo album. Once every two or three weeks, they would meet. They collected photos from Taro's past and put notes beside the photos. Looking at the album, Taro could retrace his journey from his birth to the present. Now Taro had a history that he could share with the people who were important to him – a new friend, co-workers or maybe, some day, a girlfriend.

The album continued to grow, with photos from his current home and photos from the day his father visited him.

Life story work helped Taro make sense of his life. He could see that there were reasons for his parents' divorce. And, strange as it may sound, learning that he was put into the institution because of his parents' problems was a relief. It was clear now that it was lack of money that made them give him up, not lack of love.

Also, as Taro looked at his photos taken in the previous institutions, he could see all his friends and the people at the school who cared about him. He could always go back to the institution or to his friends and ask for support. Until then, he had thought that he had no home and no human connections. But the faces in the photographs made him realise he was wrong. He had places he could go. He was not alone.

Another important benefit of the life story work was that Taro gained a more realistic idea about both his own life and his parents' lives. He realised that his mother still had problems; and it was clear that his father already had a new wife. So, after the life story work, Taro gave up his hope of living with his parents and instead decided to live in a group home where teenagers can live and get support.

One year later, Taro left the residential school. He kept in touch with both of his parents and lived with his mother for a year while he took classes at a vocational school to become a builder. Over the next five years, he moved ten times, but he always took the photo album with him.

## Adapting life story work to fit the Japanese social welfare system

The information that Taro learned in the process of life story work were things that he should have been told much earlier, simply as normal social work practice. But Taro's case is not an extreme example. In the past, it was quite common that children who were institutionalised, especially when very young, were not told basic information. This failure to tell children their own histories, as I mentioned before, is a result of flaws in the system.

Some care workers and social workers believe that the misfortunes that led to children being institutionalised should be left in the past. It used to be quite common that looked-after children were told that they were starting 'a new life' when they were placed into institutions, and they should forget about their pasts.

In the mid-2000s, in the first few years after we introduced life story work, the biggest obstacle that we faced was resistance from practitioners, especially at the director level, who did not believe in conducting life story work with children. Some of them simply did not believe that children become healthy adults more easily when they knew their own life stories. Others were worried that if children learned that their parents were in prison – or dead – this news would lead to the children acting out. The information that life story work might dig up was viewed as dangerous.

We tried to persuade them through individual meetings and training. What was ultimately most persuasive, however, was seeing that the new information – which adults defined as 'negative' – actually served to give the children strength (even when they were no longer children). Some children had already guessed the bad news. Other children truly did not know about their pasts, but learning the truth – no matter how bad – helped them give up false hopes of rescue by their birth parents, spurring them to take realistic action to build their own lives by themselves.

Most of the cases which were discussed in the Osaka Life Story Study Group were carefully assessed and provided valuable information to children in a way that helped them. There were, however, a small number of cases where life story work was started but halted out of concern for the child. In cases where a child had been previously severely traumatised or had received insufficient medical support or psychotherapy, the child could become very upset when reminded of the names or places associated with the traumatic incident. Until the trauma is properly treated, life story work is not appropriate.

Another problem with life story work is that it takes time. In some situations, when a social worker recognises that a child needs life story work, there might only be a few months left before the child is scheduled to leave care. In such a case, it is still better to do some life story work with a small and realistic goal.

In Japan, we still have to encourage practitioners to use life story work for all the children who might benefit from it. Once life story work is accepted and used by practitioners, we can consider providing therapeutic life story work. We know that many of the looked-after children have had traumatic experiences, and that they, in particular, would benefit from life story work, but only after their traumas have been treated. The present form of life story work in Japan is considered non-therapeutic, and the therapeutic level of life story work is something that would be administered by only a few professionals.

In order to maximise the positive impact of life story work, we need to adapt it to fit the current Japanese system. At present, the majority of looked-after children in Japan live in institutions. (In 2014, the total number of looked-after children in Japan was 46,000, and of those, 85% were in institutions.) We may have to consider doing life story work as a group, and perhaps include care leavers.

Life story work may help children to see that living in an institution has positive aspects. For example, they may become more aware of the value of their relationships with care workers and other children. They might also see that they should not blame themselves for their parents' divorces or other problems. If care leavers participate, and can be good role models for the looked-after children, all the better.

## Looking ahead to the next ten years

Today, life story work, especially at the basic level, has become well known and is one of the options for social/care work practice in Japan. However, we have some issues to resolve in order to move forward.

The most urgent issue we have to deal with is the establishment of a proper record-keeping system. Records play an important role not only for children but also for adults who left care a long time ago, and yet many local authorities destroy children's records when they become 25 years old.

First, we need laws that require longer preservation of records. The average life expectancy in Japan is about 80 years, and we should consider keeping those records at least until the care leavers die. Second, we need to allocate appropriate professionals to maintain the records.

Once we establish a record-keeping system, we need to advertise widely to make sure that both children and care leavers know that they can access their information whenever needed.

## Conclusion

Life story work has been doing quite well in Japan over the last ten years. In 2012, the Japanese government updated its guidelines, clearly indicating that it is important that looked-after children are able to access information about their personal histories.

In turn, we have more responsibility to maintain good standards of practice in both theory and technique to improve children's rights and wellbeing, because our work influences their entire lives.

I believe life story work can work in the current system. But I also believe that it can be a catalyst for improving the Japanese system, because it reminds us of the need for children to maintain their personal histories and maintain relationships with whomever is charged with caring for them, whether that is their own parents, care workers or foster parents. We need to continue improving the system at both the micro and macro level, from details such as record preservation, to improving support for care leavers, to ways of shifting the care system away from institutionalising children and towards preserving family relationships.

These are all needed to deliver the life story work more safely and effectively, and also to achieve our goal as care workers and social workers, which is to help children overcome difficult times in their lives and grow into socially mature, happy adults.

*I would like to thank my colleagues and my fellow members of the Osaka Life Story Work Study Group. I also wish to thank Matthew Grieder for his careful proofreading of this chapter.*

# References

www.hoyokyo.or.jp/nursing_hyk/reference/27-3s2-3.pdf

Camis, J. (2001) *My Life and Me*. London: British Association for Adoption and Fostering.

Rose, R. (2005) *The Children's Own Story: Life Story Work with Traumatized Children*. London: Jessica Kingsley Publishers.

Ryan, T. and Walker, R. (2007) *Life Story Work: A Practical Guide to Helping Children Understand Their Past*. London: British Association for Adoption and Fostering.

United Nations General Assembly, *Convention on the Rights of the Child*, 20 November 1989, United Nations, Treaty Series, vol 1577, p.3, available at: www.refworld.org/docid/3ae6b38f0.html.

Wrench, K. and Naylor, L. (2013) *Life Story Work with Children Who are Fostered or Adopted*. London: Jessica Kingsley Publishers.

www.mhlw.go.jp/bunya/kodomo/syakaiteki_yougo/dl/yougo_genjou_01.pdf

www.hrw.org/report/2014/05/01/without-dreams/children-alternative-care-japan

www.mhlw.go.jp/bunya/kodomo/syakaiteki_yougo/dl/yougo_genjou_01.pdf

Chapter 8

# WONDERING FROM THE WOMB

## THERAPEUTIC LIFE STORY WORK IN AN EARLY YEARS SERVICE

*Kathy Crouch, Lead Practitioner, Mallee District Aboriginal Service Early Years Service, Mildura, Victoria, Australia*

## About life story work

Life story work has been utilised in many settings from 'reminiscence therapy' with the elderly to the creation of 'life event' artefacts such as All About Me and life story books for children living away from their birth parents. Essentially, such work builds personal narratives and captures meaning in lived experiences, enabling individuals to share information about their past and affirm a nostalgic sense of self (Ryan and Walker 1999). Rose and colleagues have significantly shaped the evolution of meaning making through shared personal narratives over the past decade (Rose 2012; Rose and Philpot 2004). Harnessing trauma-informed practices, adherence to attachment theory and safe relational models, Rose's contemporary formulation of 'therapeutic' life story work delivers beautiful anecdotal evidence of healing and personal mastery in numerous cases of childhood neglect, interpersonal assault, displacement and traumatic experience (Rose 2012).

Considering the benefits of this type of work with individuals who have experienced multiple losses, traumatic insult and dislocation from place, family and self, it is not too great a reach to conceive that it might be well suited to supporting the healing and self-determination of the first peoples of Australia.

Therapeutic life story work shares many methodological similarities with traditional meaning-making systems such as yarning (Robertson, Demosthenous and Demosthenous 2005) and deep listening, giving space and time for 'deep to connect to deep' (Ungunmerr-Baumann 2002) and permission to honour symbols, metaphor and dreaming in the exploration of personal and family identity.

There are many benefits of incorporating the principles of therapeutic life story work within cultural programmes for indigenous families, and as I consider these in my work, I cannot help but feel excited to explore the life and stories of communities in this important area of Victoria. Recognising these opportunities, the following describes how awareness-raising and capacity-building programmes for families and professionals in Aboriginal communities can be enhanced by combining therapeutic life story work concepts, cultural methodologies and powerful antenatal messages.

# A local perspective

As a psychologist working with a talented team of multi-skilled, diversely trained workers in early years services within an Aboriginal community controlled organisation in rural Victoria, I am often encouraging conversations between parents, workers and other service providers around infant development, attachment dynamics and culturally safe practices. These conversations often begin during the antenatal period, when parents and their support systems are just entering the early years service, and continue until their children begin school. While yarning about foetal and infant development is inherent in early years service delivery, a great deal of attention is also given to relational dynamics, safe base interventions, learning enhancement, non-clinical infant mental health supports and family systems functioning. With more than 150 Aboriginal children and families supported each year in Mildura, Swan Hill and surrounding areas, the dedicated staffing body of 20–30 employees provides services ranging from midwifery and maternal and child health to early learning support, play groups, capacity-building groups and in-home case support. Several staff also offer intensive case management and complex care co-ordination for indigenous infants whose caregivers may experience intergenerational patterns of substance dependence, mental illness, suicidality, trauma, insecure housing and poor, sometimes violent, interpersonal behaviour.

Early years staff wrap around these most complex family systems and provide models of safe, regulated care. They encourage teachable moments that shift narratives and perspectives where and when opportunity exists. Frontline workers aim to increase parental reflective capacity, revise parenting styles, skills and values, and enhance cultural and interpersonal safety for the family and community members around the infant.

In several cases, inherited pains affect parenting decisions and behaviours. Few education, clinical health checks and parent training programmes appear to impact some of our most encumbered families, and risk management dominates the care narrative. The threat of child protection looms in many of these instances, with fear, grief and generational, sometimes ancient, wounds hijacking capacities for healing and mastery. Without a non-judgemental curiosity and culturally resonant alternative, the most vulnerable families and their littlest members face repeated traumatic cycles.

## A local possibility

Understanding that the brain develops sequentially and hierarchically from less complex to most complex, from conception through the first three years of life (Perry *et al.* 1995), early years staff at the Mallee District Aboriginal Service (MDAS) wanted to give antenates, infants and children, especially those already facing developmental insults in their relational systems, the best chance of safe, regulated caregiving and experience-dependent development (Mares, Newman and Warren 2011).

Using a trauma-informed lens, the early years team imagined a healing and culturally safe strategy for its antenatal and newborn services which could empower parents, improve health behaviours, increase bonding between parents and their unborn babies and, in the spirit of honouring 'ghosts in the nursery' (Fraiberg, Adelson and Shapiro 1975), allow for past traumas and shame to be honoured without shadowing the process of mentalisation between children and care providers.

Curiosity and wonder would replace any sense of judgement or parental critique. Care providers would have a gentle model for managing their arousal states and minimising threat-response behaviours. Connection and attunement would also have to be a feature in such a strategy, with sensori-motor regulation being encouraged where possible, especially for the pregnant mums who may have embodied toxic stress and traumatic muscle memory (Ogden, Minton and Pain 2006).

Mindful consideration of the baby in the womb would similarly be a central parent-reflection strategy. The ways that a baby's innocence and spirit could be included in dyadic healing opportunities were contemplated, especially in relation to indigenous child-rearing practices. It was vital that observance be paid to 'traditional community lore and the complex and diverse governance, law, health and healing practices which underpinned the resistance, survival and strong culture of Aboriginal and Torres Strait Islander peoples' (Funston 2013). Collective delight in child wisdom would need to champion any new strategy, with narratives and symbols that speak to childhood across generations anchoring shared meaning making. For this to be respectfully captured, the stories of child rearing and growing up in communities as shared by Elders, grandparents, new parents, siblings and community members would need to be honoured.

## Wondering from the Womb: a local labour of love

To explore these ideas, a community action-research process was undertaken throughout 2015, collating the childhood and parenting experiences of Elders, mothers, fathers, siblings, grandparents and professionals living and working along the Murray River across the Loddon Mallee region of Victoria. Over 20 individual yarning sessions were held, explaining wisdom from different perspectives. Themes from these yarns related to sound antenatal care and bonding opportunities for adults caring for infants and children. From these themes, a narrative was written from the perspective of a baby in the womb. Rich in culture, lingo and poetry, the narrative or 'wonder' captured the language, syntax and imagery shared by Elders and interviewees. This 'wonder from the womb' became a personal introduction, with the baby inviting all who listen to connect, feel warmth and consider the ways in which we can support and answer the curiosities of our children waiting to be born. An extract is provided:

> I am here. Full of wonder and potential. All of the dreams and wisdom of our People are with me. I am part of you. I am part of family and future and history. I wonder if we chose each other or if we were just blessed. But we have each other now and I am beginning to take my form with your help and your care and your wisdom... Yes, family. I am Here.

The 'I am Here' narrative was then tested by being read aloud with additional indigenous and non-indigenous members of the community, with responses and experiences recorded and thematically reviewed. An additional eight narratives were created from the feedback offered by participants. These eight narratives, also voiced by the baby in the womb, addressed topics integral to quality antenatal care, including the role of fathers, helping siblings, healthy behaviours, community supports and preparation for birth.

All nine narratives were published in a resource called *Wondering from the Womb*, complete with antenatal care tips, reflection space for writing personal notes and illustrations offered by local indigenous mothers who wanted to explore their baby's questions in visual ways. Although the tangible booklet was in itself a lovely and rich resource of community wisdom, perhaps a more powerful development was the keen sharing of personal life stories, experiences of child rearing and metaphors about traditional ways, past hurts and future possibilities for individuals and families. There was an incredible sense that participants wanted more yarning, more opportunities to talk about babies and stories of childhood. Many interviewees wished that such a resource had been available when they first had children. Most expressed a sense of warmth and connection to their bodies when listening to the narratives, and all urged for more professionals to host yarning and healing sessions.

## Local learning and life story considerations

The creation of the resource, through yarning, storytelling and shared meaning making, was only the beginning. Several requests have been made to use *Wondering from the Womb* in a variety of spaces.

### For healing

The impact of having the baby narrate life stories for pregnant women who have reported difficulties with bonding, coping, emotional regulation and previous parenting experiences is beginning to offer some positive engagement and healing opportunities. While westernised therapy or counselling can be confronting for some indigenous mothers, the chance to learn about their child's world and reflect on their own role in shaping their baby's development appears to be much more appealing. The voice of the baby is initially much more present than that of a therapist, and keeping the baby's wonder central, three participants (mother, baby and therapist) can engage in a triangulation of narration, with curiosity and shared perspective-taking keeping guilt, judgements and blame out of the yarning space. This characteristic is a strength in therapeutic life story work and in incorporating such an approach, similar therapeutic benefits of externalising painful experiences and gestalt processes of triangulating meaning can, so the triangulation of carer, child and life story worker is maintained per session, despite the baby being in the womb. This provision is just beginning in MDAS and will be monitored and reviewed over the next 12 months.

Having baby narratives in family violence settings is another use for *Wondering from the Womb* that MDAS is considering. Incorporating the *Wondering from the Womb* resource in yarning groups for respite and refuge centres is currently being explored, with elements of therapeutic life story work central to this possibility. Rose (2012) describes how wallpaper is a useful resource in collating externalised narratives. The wallpaper is unravelled and adorned with statements, stories, symbols and ideas from shared life narratives. Unlike books, wallpaper is linear and can be viewed as a whole visual scape, showing representations of a person's lived, imagined and externalised identity. The utilisation of wallpaper as a safe container for the shared responses to the baby's narratives in a family violence setting can ensure that the voices of survivors are heard and externalised in a manner that is culturally safe and reduces shame. The information communicated in yarning circles can remain with the participants, their shared experiences creating a unique lived history of their time together as a group during the healing process. Although there is some fine-tuning to be done, the integration of therapeutic life story work and *Wondering from the Womb* is an exciting conversation being held in the MDAS family violence setting.

## For educating parents

Using *Wondering from the Womb* for parenting training sessions to complement other programmes such as Circles of Security has been requested by a number of community members and service providers. The nine narratives can be used as topic generators, with group facilitators encouraging Aboriginal parents to respond to these narratives using their own words, symbols and metaphors to review parenting skills in a culturally responsive yarning circle. Each parent would complete a *Wondering from the Womb* journal and activity log on wallpaper, unravelling it to add their ideas and questions, fears and hopes regarding child rearing and capacity building in their families. This work is expected to be trialled in 2017.

## For training professionals

Interest in *Wondering from the Womb* as a healing and life story resource has generated the need for reflective practice and meaning-making training courses for professionals working with indigenous families. The baby's voice narrating the context for discussion and art making provides a way of moving professional development and case reviews away from traditional planning and performance-oriented learning and gives permission for more reflective processing and deep listening. When frontline workers experience connection and tuning in as part of their ongoing learning, they may also be assisted to retain empathy for even their most challenging of cases.

Furthermore, workers who feel safe and connected throughout the *Wondering from the Womb* experience will ideally have greater capacity to encourage this same phenomenon with families they support, creating a parallel of roles. This replication of 'safe adult connection' can increase the likelihood that attuned, responsive support is always wrapping around the most vulnerable parts of an interpersonal system, be it within families, professional teams or whole communities.

To this end, a pilot trial is underway with invitations to professionals working with indigenous families to experience *Wondering from the Womb* as an extended reflective practice session. Each narrative is linked to an area of best practice enquiry, covering topics like attachment theory, rupture and repair, and intergenerational trauma. Over a day's shared learning, professionals are invited to reflect on the baby's wisdom, the corresponding theory and how they can shape their practice to best accommodate the questions the baby poses. Rather than working on wallpaper, a healing circle or mandala is used to capture symbolic images and messages generated through the exploration of each of the narratives. On completion of the day, participants have a visual summary of their own responses to the nine topics, with nine take-home messages to guide professional practice.

Various professional teams and service agencies have expressed the desire to participate. Two one-day sessions have already been conducted in the community as part of the trial, with the feedback identifying significant benefits in sharing perspectives, building awareness of early intervention in family support and the increased commitment to considering infant development and inner-child wisdom in case management, family-oriented interventions and planning. The need for self-care and honouring personal, lived experience was also reported to be a benefit from the sessions.

Throughout 2017, further sessions will be conducted across the community, with invites to different collegial agencies being extended. Cultural validation will also routinely be considered as this professional development opportunity is more broadly offered. It is hoped, however, that the combination of contemporary theoretical trends and the meaning making, reflection and non-judgemental enquiry so embedded in therapeutic life story work will result in MDAS delivering a culturally respectful way of providing child-centred professional learning for staff on the frontline.

## Conclusion

There is such a lovely synergy between Aboriginal traditions of yarning, deep listening, art making and symbology and the person-centred re-narration of lived experience inherent in therapeutic life story work. Harnessing both to share the wisdom of infants and children in a way that invites reflection rather than shame is an ongoing pursuit for early years professionals. With regular review, evaluation and community consultation, it is hoped that the initiatives described in this chapter will themselves mature out of infancy and become consistent and predictable ways of doing business across the family and health sectors.

Ending on the first page of the resource:

'Wondering From the Womb' invites us into the curiosity and hope that is our unborn babies' world. Created through the yarning experiences of Elders, mothers, fathers, siblings, grandparents and professionals living and working along the Murray River across the Loddon Mallee region of Victoria, this resource shares collective wisdom surrounding the healthy physical, emotional and spiritual development of our future.

Designed and shaped by our Indigenous community and honouring the voice of our littlest members, 'Wondering From the Womb' prompts questions and conversations about how parents, family and community can increase safety and connection with our children, helping them find their place and their identity in our community and culture. It is hoped that through the nine antenatal narratives, the journey that unfolds is a very personal one, rich in hope, permission and, above all, love.

With gratitude, it is important to acknowledge the Loddon Mallee communities for their wisdom and sharing. To the Elders, mothers, fathers, family members and allied professionals across both MDAS and

Njernda Aboriginal Corporation who gave their time and knowledge to support the voice of our future, thank you.

# References

Fraiberg, S., Adelson, E. and Shapiro, V. (1975) 'Ghosts in the nursery: a psychoanalytic approach to the problems of impaired infant–mother relationships.' *Journal of the American Academy of Child Psychiatry* 14(3), 387–421.

Funston, L. (2013) 'Aboriginal and Torres Strait Islander worldviews and cultural safety transforming sexual assault service provision for children and young people.' *International Journal of Environmental Research and Public Health* 10(9), 3818–3833.

Mares, S., Newman, L. and Warren, B. (2005) *Clinical Skills in Infant Mental Health.* Australian Council for Educational Research.

Ogden, P., Minton, K. and Pain, C. (2006) *Trauma and the Body: A Sensorimotor Approach to Psychotherapy* (Norton Series on Interpersonal Neurobiology). New York: W.W. Norton and Company.

Perry, B.D., Pollard, R.A., Blakley, T.L., Baker, W.L. and Vigilante, D. (1995) 'Childhood trauma, the neurobiology of adaptation, and "use-dependent" development of the brain: how "states" become "traits?"' *Infant Mental Health Journal* 16(4), 271–291.

Robertson, B., Demosthenous, C. and Demosthenous, H. (2005) 'Stories from the Aboriginal women of the yarning circle: when cultures collide.' *Hecate* 31(2), 34.

Rose, R. (2012) *Life Story Therapy with Traumatized Children: A Model for Practice.* London: Jessica Kingsley Publishers.

Rose, R. and Philpot, T. (2004) *The Child's Own Story: Life Story Work with Traumatized Children.* London: Jessica Kingsley Publishers.

Ryan, T. and Walker, R. (1999) *Life Story Work.* London: British Association for Adoption and Fostering.

Ungunmerr-Baumann, M.R. (2002) *Dadirri: Inner Deep Listening and Quiet Still Awareness.* St Francis Xavier School, Nauiyu, Daly River, Malak Malak, Northern Territory, Australia.

Walker, M., Fredericks, B., Mills, K. and Anderson, D. (2014) '"Yarning" as a method for community-based health research with indigenous women: the indigenous women's wellness research program.' *Health Care for Women International* 35(10), 1216–1226.

Chapter 9

# THERAPEUTIC LIFE STORY WORK

## A MULTIMODAL THERAPY FOR CHILDREN WITH COMPLEX NEEDS

*Rebecca Wild, Child and Adolescent Psychiatrist,*
*Evolve Therapeutic Services*

Richard Rose's life story therapy has been an increasingly important modality for our team for nearly a decade. We are a small multidisciplinary child psychiatry team working with children in alternative care. All our children are referred by the child protection system. We work in an Australian context with a leadership team based on the Sunshine Coast and clinicians either co-located with us or supported via tele-psychiatry and outreach, in four quite distant regional hub sites. We are one of ten teams in Queensland but the only team with multiple spoke sites, which has meant that we have had to be creative about sustaining team identity and function.

Outcome measures for the statewide programme have been recently published and show significant clinical improvement in our cohort of patients, a group notoriously difficult to achieve this change in (Klag *et al.* 2016).

The initial engagement of our team with Richard's work was based on its accessibility both to our children, who are often difficult to engage, and to community stakeholders, who perhaps find our clinical processes opaque. Clinicians found its flexibility and its use of play and visual art very appealing, as did the kids. Its focus on helping often very avoidant children explore their identity and life narrative and have an opportunity to correct self-blaming or shaming beliefs was valued. The fact that many of our child patients are indigenous and that we strive to offer them a culturally sensitive therapeutic experience meant that life story work offered new opportunities to us, when we could find culturally appropriate partners to work with. The incorporation of a primary attachment figure or other important adult into the therapy complemented work with this patient group, which has a high prevalence of attachment disorganisation. This dyadic format synthesised well with our use of other attachment-informed treatments, such as Dyadic Developmental Therapy (Hughes 2014) and Parallel Parent and Child Therapy (Chambers *et al.* 2006; Amos, Beal and Furber 2007). The fact that life story work has remained a core modality for our team, over a prolonged period, is based on more than these features though. We have become convinced it fits with best practice care for our cohort of patients.

One of my roles as team psychiatrist is to support the development of individualised assessments and treatment plans for our children. Ensuring that treatment plans are both best practice and fit the individual needs of each child is a challenge in our treatment cohort, as it is in most complex populations. The multimodal presentations of our kids – complex trauma, developmental compromise, disrupted attachment, complicated grief and loss, exposure to cumulative harms – within a complex, often fragmented care system, do not lend themselves to simple research models. Large multi-centred, randomised control trials evaluating the impact of one intervention on one outcome measure are not useful for our kids. Funding and ethics approval are not easily accessed either in this population, whose vulnerability quite rightly has led to protections which can make investigation challenging. However, despite the barriers, the vulnerability of this population of children leaves us with an obligation to ensure that the limited resources we have available are being used well, cognisant of the available evidence and the best clinical rationale we can muster.

The team has invested time and resources in developing skills in a number of key therapeutic modalities. We now have a practice of supporting skill development by providing team supervision in these modalities (across our multiple sites, using video link up). We have been very lucky to have access to Richard, initially via workshops and his individual supervision of team therapist Fiona Meredith, and now via regular team supervision. Having Fiona and now a second therapist Sabrina Sandy joining the Diploma in Therapeutic Life Story Work and continuing to offer their enthusiasm and support to other team members has been invaluable. Natalie Crofts and Jodie Waring are both therapists whose use of life story work I have also been privileged to see unfold over the years. All four clinicians were very much in my mind as I attempted to describe our team's use of Richard's model. Peer modelling and support have been crucial in the development of these skills, and the process of whole team supervision in life story work and other therapies has really consolidated our skill base.

We use a number of tools to support our reflection on what represents good practice and which modalities we should use. One of these is a framework we call 'the therapeutic continuum'. We have developed a simple document to use both in treatment planning and ongoing monitoring to check our fidelity to good practice. It draws on Kim Golding's Pyramid (2007) to inform a staged approach to care and incorporate a strong systemic focus.

The concept of the continuum is useful in that it suggests that we are on a journey towards an end point. For our team this hoped-for end point is for each child to be moving forwards on a healthy developmental trajectory. Once this direction looks sustainable without our support we can exit, leaving the rest of the care team to carry on. This is predicated on us having confidence that the care team can complete any outstanding therapeutic work and sustain the developmental gains made.

Each individual child's diagnostic formulation is used to adapt our therapeutic continuum to ensure that they are receiving a best practice, developmentally informed, staged treatment plan which is appropriate for their individual needs. We can monitor our fidelity to the treatment plan over time with a regular review process, adapting it as the child's formulation changes.

It remains important to regularly review and adapt our therapeutic continuum as new evidence or understanding develops for our treatment population. Current mechanisms for doing this include the team's regular professional development and scheduling in time to review it, incorporating feedback from peers and literature review.

The therapeutic continuum supports consideration first of treatment goals and then of the appropriate therapeutic modalities to reach those goals. This informs decisions about which modalities are chosen, whether they need supplementing and how this is staged. It is also useful in identifying which modalities we as a team prioritise for supervision and training. Some modalities quite clearly identify themselves as having characteristics and goals that overlap with those we identify. This is not surprising as they emerge from the work of experienced clinicians who focus on similar treatment cohorts. What has been a delightful surprise is that we can often find potential in some of the modalities we are familiar with, to meet treatment goals that they don't clearly identify themselves. We are also finding a lot of overlap in the skills needed and the frameworks used in the modalities we have focused on. This has meant that sometimes modalities will enhance and complement each other in meeting the goals of the entire treatment continuum. It also means that the skill base of our clinicians is being reinforced and layered by their exposure to modalities that take complementary approaches to building similar skills. Cross-fertilisation via group and peer supervision enhances this.

*Table 9.1 Questions for evaluating treatment against best practice, in complex cohorts with limited evidence base*

- Are there any good quality studies that show positive outcomes in well-matched populations?

  There are very few studies in populations that really matched ours, but early trials from Circle of Security (Hoffman 2006) and Dyadic Developmental Therapy (Becker Weidman and Hughes 2008) came close. This informed our early practice. We look forward to outcomes from upcoming evaluations of life story therapy.

- Is there important evidence in other populations that we can extrapolate from? If so, what modification is needed?

  Trauma-focused cognitive behaviour therapy (CBT) (Cohen *et al.* 2004) has an impressive evidence base in traumatised children. However, we really struggled to make it fit our cohort, who had often had complex trauma, developmental delays and disrupted attachment and lived in alternative care. It wasn't until we looked at the components of trauma-focused CBT and tried to deliver them using modalities that worked for us that we started to see engagement and gains, for example using life story therapy to explore trauma narrative or cognitive distortions.

- Is there a reasonable therapeutic rationale which fits with the research-based schemas (e.g. neurobiological, developmental, trauma and attachment informed) we have available to us?

- Does the treatment plan fit with the relevant guidelines and review documents we have available to us for this population – Rees report (Luke *et al.* 2014), NICE Guidelines (2010) and American Academy of Child and Adolescent Psychiatry practice parameter (Lee, Fouras and Brown 2015)?

- Do we have a good therapeutic rationale for adapting the relevant modalities to meet the specific needs of our patients?

- Is our treatment planning consistent with the practice of credible peers? This includes:

  o our longitudinal cohort experience in the team, shared via multidisciplinary case review, group supervision and training and secondary psychiatric consultation

  o national networks of psychiatrists and other clinicians working with children in care

  o statewide network of teams both in our Evolve Therapeutic Services programme and sister programmes such as Take Two or Australian Childhood Foundation and the National Trauma Conference

  o supervision, training and writings of senior clinicians working in the area.

- Does the modality share some of the features of other credible modalities for this cohort?

- Does it integrate with the other therapeutic work we do?

  Our clinical use of Richard Rose's life story model illustrates both the multimodal nature of useful interventions for this population of children and the capacity they often have to integrate with other interventions. Exposure to a variety of the work of very experienced and thoughtful clinicians gives us the opportunity to look for patterns and overlaps, to draw on the evidence they cite themselves and to match their work to the broader evidence-based principles we are trying to apply.

*Table 9.2 Modalities we have chosen to utilise as part of the therapeutic continuum: which we see as complementing life story therapy and having a framework consistent with it, i.e. strengths based, attachment informed, cognisant of developmental traumatology*

- Kim Golding (2007)
- Dan Hughes's Dyadic Developmental Therapy (2007, 2014)
- Circle of Security (Hoffman *et al.* 2006; Cassidy *et al.* 2011)
- Parallel Parent and Child Therapy (Chambers *et al.* 2006; Amos *et al.* 2007)
- Trauma-focused CBT (Cohen *et al.* 2004)
- Bruce Perry (2006)
- John Briere (2008)

I have chosen a number of treatment goals from our therapeutic continuum and used them to show how our clinicians have used the life story model to meet identified goals. This gives some idea of the potential richness of the model and its capacity to provide a multi-pronged approach to the treatment of children who often have multiple, interwoven, therapeutic needs.

*Table 9.3 Treatment goals for which life story therapy can be utilised*

- Enhancing collaboration
- Cultural connection
- Supporting felt safety and reparative parenting
- Developing a trauma narrative, mourning losses
- Developing a strengths-based narrative of positive intention as per Parallel Parent and Child Therapy (Chambers *et al.* 2006; Amos *et al.* 2007)
- Offering dyadic work where a key adult supports the reflective process:
  - uses PACE principles
  - is relationally based
  - has potential for building mentalisation capacity and empathy
- Weaving in CBT – affect identification, regulation, addressing cognitive distortions or using Parallel Parent and Child Therapy (PACT) conceptualisation (Chambers *et al.* 2006; Amos *et al.* 2007), mistakes of meaning
- Making reparations with family of origin, reducing impact of cumulative harm
- Building resilience
- Exploring identity

Using the case study of Casey, a fictional child with what is I hope a realistic and representative life story process and journey through therapeutic care, below I attempt to illustrate how these goals are met through our use of life story therapy. Casey has been asked to represent a great deal, and because I have used her journey through therapy to illustrate the narrative, it is not always sequential. It is not always clear where Casey is developmentally at each stage of therapy.

My initial impulse was to try and correct this. I finally decided to leave it as written because Casey's journey represents the sometimes fragmented process our life story work becomes, as often we develop therapeutic plans only to discover the child's life circumstance has radically altered again. It also seemed to reflect the uneven development across domains of many of the children we work with. We can be thrown off balance by these children when we pitch our expectations of them at a particular level, only to discover that part of them is much older or younger than we predicted. It didn't seem unreasonable to leave you, the reader, to determine for yourselves how old Casey is.

## Enhancing collaboration

The Sunshine Coast, Wide Bay and South Burnett Evolve Therapeutic Services Team works with children and adolescents referred by our child protection system for support with psychological difficulties. These children have usually experienced complex trauma and attachment disruption with cumulative harm in care, secondary to serial placement breakdown.

We are a multidisciplinary mental health team with a psychiatric clinical lead, and collaboration within the team is important if we are to function. Perhaps even more crucially, one of our primary therapeutic roles is to build a collaborative care team around each child, appropriate collaboration being one of the few interventions with good evidence (Vostanis 2010). This enhances the development of a shared understanding of the child and reduces duplication of resources and the risk of the child being pulled in multiple directions. If we get it right, the hope is that we have a cohesive formulation of the child and a cohesive treatment strategy. The child is therefore having repeated reparative experiences across domains and relationships. 'Injury sustained over multiple occasions across multiple domains requires multiple reparative experiences across multiple domains' (Perry 2009). This team includes a therapist, child protection officer and the foster carer or a key representative from residential care. Representatives from education, youth justice, the police, extended biological family, respite carers and others may also be regular participants.

## CASE STUDY: CASEY

*Supporting collaboration*

Casey's care team was experiencing significant fracture. Recent decisions had been made about Casey's care which resulted in the membership of the care team changing considerably. The therapist remained the only long-term participant. The child's placement had changed; school support was offered by the placement and had also changed; and the child protection officer was new to the case. As months passed there was a polarisation in the positions taken by the therapeutic team and the child protection team, who were the child's guardians.

Representations made by the therapeutic team about the psychological impact of guardianship decisions were not acknowledged. The therapeutic team felt that this had resulted in poor outcomes for Casey. The child protection team felt that the therapeutic team was out of scope in making such recommendations and that they had made decisions in the child's best interests. There were significant tensions around role definition.

The therapist invited the child protection officer to take part in the life story therapy as the most stable person in the current care team. Casey was in residential care without a key worker. There was vigorous discussion in the therapeutic team about whether this was likely to bring the interagency tensions into the therapy.

Casey took to the new placement an All About Me book full of photographs that the therapist had helped her to create with her youth workers and about her journey in the previous placement. This seemed to help the current youth workers see her as a child in need, despite her difficult behaviour, which sometimes led to assaults on them.

The therapist and child protection officer, via a shared connection to Casey and shared narrative about her life, developed a strong working alliance and supported the development of a functional care team around this child. They were able to support the placement and school to adapt to Casey's needs. They appeared much more influential as a dyad, reinforcing consistent messages to the team, than either of them had been individually.

Once the therapy was able to move through the development of the life story narrative, the therapist was able to utilise this preliminary work to help Casey think about the affective experiences in the narrative. How did she feel in thinking about the story? How might the other participants in this story be feeling? With the shared language and therapeutic alliance built into the preliminary work, the therapist and Casey's support person were able to help her think about affects embedded in real-life scenarios meaningful to her and to help her speculate about affect in the minds of others. She could also be co-regulated during the therapy as these affects arose and be gradually supported to self-regulate.

Sharing components of the work with the care team, with Casey's permission and often with her involvement, also helped school staff and residential workers to develop a sense of who she was and an identity as a group invested in her care.

*Supporting felt safety and building a reparative parenting approach: identifying and co-regulating affective states*

Casey's life story process was quite fragmented and there were periods when she was so dysregulated and avoidant that her therapist had to revert to a holding pattern, focusing on sustaining a therapeutic alliance and supporting her to process the present. The more exploratory process of her life narrative was initiated at a time when she appeared to feel quite safe and stable and was held in relationship with a key worker, who supported her team of youth workers' reflection about Casey well. However, there was a long lead-in and repeated intervals when Casey's life circumstances did not offer enough felt safety for her to engage fully in life story therapy.

In the lead-in period Casey's therapist first met and assessed her, supported the residential setting to offer her felt safety and connection, and established an alliance.

Much of the therapist's work was with the residential setting initially, but she was a regular presence for Casey and spent a lot of time just being with her and her key worker. Casey was very mobile and avoidant, so seeing her in an area where she could move around and the therapist could utilise his emerging relationship with his key worker was important. When she was unable to engage they could maintain a curious and kind dialogue, which she could tolerate listening to (intermittently). Dan Hughes's (2008) PACE principles – using a playful, accepting, curious and empathic stance – were very important here.

There was a great deal of bouncing on the trampoline with her, swinging her in hammocks and talking to big piles of cushions from which feet sometimes protruded. Her workers were encouraged to brush her hair, rub her feet, use songs and rhymes, and provide nurturing routines and clear boundaries.

Gradually the therapist was able to help her develop some basic affect identification and regulation skills. Much of this initially involved co-regulation with a trusted, adult but by being curious they were able to build her capacity: 'You are very squirmy today – I wonder if you feel…' 'This dough is very squishy – it makes me feel nice and still inside when I squeeze it…', and by modelling the language for her carers, the therapist was able to support her in having multiple experiences of this in her day. Sensory tools, flow activity (Casey couldn't tolerate mindful or relaxation exercises) and nurturing from her carers were all important. Games were used, such as tracing around her in chalk and drawing all her body cues on the figure. Repeatedly throughout her day her key adults were helping her note and wonder about affective states and the things that triggered and defused them.

When she was ready to return to school Casey's carers initially went with her to support her, and they modelled this for the education staff who were able to use the same language and offer more opportunities for affect identification and regulation in another domain of her life.

The therapist's regular support of the care team members via care team meetings and ad hoc support of individual members helped keep this messaging consistent across relationships and domains.

*Cultural connection*

Supporting meaningful cultural connection for the children we treat is a challenge our care teams struggle with. Casey clearly identified as indigenous and had from birth retained connection to her community and been co-placed with her siblings in kin care. Her aggression and oppositional behaviour increasingly limited her access to kin after her aunt relinquished her care, and the responsibilities the aunt had for Casey's younger siblings became a barrier to her being available for contact. Initially Casey was one of our few primary aged children in residential care – a single placement with rostered youth workers. The task of keeping her safe and contained was prioritised over her cultural connection, and despite the unease of the care team, any opportunities we could identify to connect her again felt tokenistic. She attended indigenous festival days and was taken to see a local indigenous football team play, but none of these opportunities resulted in ongoing relationship or connection.

Fortuitously the therapist was able to co-work with a key youth worker in the residential facility Casey lived in. This worker had strong connections to the local indigenous community and was not only able to bring a lot of cultural content and meaning to the life story process itself, but these connections were able to be built on to enrich her engagement in activities and relationships in the community. Together they produced some beautiful work, which Casey took great pride in sharing with her wider care team. During this period she appeared to flourish, her destructive behaviour reduced significantly and she was able to engage in education and her capacity to let her care team connect and support her. She became 'safer and more containable'.

She also had the opportunity to teach the important adults in her life, mostly white professional authority figures, about something they knew little about, something she had special knowledge and investment in.

I was an infrequent visitor in her life as the team psychiatrist. Her therapist took me to her residential facility when there had been a major incident, or medication needed reviewing. This was often in shame-inducing circumstances, not conducive to rapport building. During the period of life story therapy, however, I remember a visit where, under the umbrella of the rapport built by the therapist and the key worker, a very proud child showed me her life story artwork and gave me a beautiful narrative about its cultural meaning. This resulted in the first really collaborative conversation I had been able to engage her in about her medication.

### Developing a trauma narrative, mourning losses

The development of the life story narrative itself gave Casey the opportunity to meet many of the goals we hoped for her in developing her treatment plan.

In laying out the narrative sequentially using the visual cue of the wallpaper to take her through a past which, in some parts, was held implicitly and in fragments, we hoped to offer her access to a more integrated, less interrupted narrative of her life, scaffolded by both time and place. Because she had limited access to explicit sequentially ordered memories, the research the life story therapist and care team did in finding out what her journey had been was able to give her much more of a coherent sense of her history, of what, when and where.

They were able to use sensory cues to help her hold the story. These were mostly visual: a photograph of the hospital where she was born, a picture of her mother when she was three and drawings of each house she had lived in, which she was able to create and to contribute memories to. We didn't use music (songs her teacher may have sung) or other sensory tools in building the narrative, but with care perhaps we could have. They were certainly used to help her soothe in session, along with the trampoline, hugs from her carer, play doh and so on.

As discussed above, supporting Casey to integrate her affective responses into the narrative was very important. Part of this was the opportunity to mourn losses, and this required some careful 'talking for' and curiosity (Hughes 2008): 'I wonder what Casey missed most when she moved?' 'I wonder where little Casey thought Mum had gone?'

The use of ritual was important in this. The opportunity to light a candle in a small cake as each birthday was reached in the story provided an opportunity to celebrate and have fun with her therapist and carer. It also provided an opportunity to wonder about missed birthdays and lost memories and to share memories that were retained either by Casey or those interviewed for the work.

Looking for positive intentionality and attempts to correct mistakes of meaning like this was first introduced to us via life story work, although we didn't use that terminology. We have found that exposure to PACT and team supervision with Jackie Amos has really deepened this practice for us, and those clinicians who are used to the DDP framework use 'talking for' in a similar manner.

*Addressing cognitive distortions related to trauma, self and relationship, looking for positive intentionality, addressing mistakes of meaning and modulating shame*

Taking a CBT perspective, we can see this part of the work as related to cognitive distortions. We would see this through the lens of PACT in terms of addressing mistakes of meaning and looking for positive intentionality, modulating shame. Again, we find that many of the modalities in which we work share concepts which may be differently framed and labelled but which overlap. We also hope that by doing this work within a therapeutic relationship and while supporting the child's system to offer repeated relationally based reparative experiences, the child's internal working model will alter.

The narrative also provided a rich opportunity to access and address cognitive distortions for Casey. Sometimes these distortions became evident in the placement or at school, and we hypothesised that they were triggered or brought to consciousness and expressed because of the therapeutic process.

For this reason it was very important to educate the adults in her care team about beliefs she might hold and why, as well as how to respond, and the importance of feeding this back to the carer and therapist.

One example was Casey telling the deputy principal, to whose safe haven/office she was used to retreating to after an outburst at school, 'I am so bad, no one likes me.' When she was calm the principal, well informed about therapeutic themes and scripts, could reflect with her, 'You are a great kid, you work really hard with your sad and angry feelings, and today you yelled but you didn't hit and you let your teacher help you. We are pretty proud of you.' This sort of response consistent across relationships helped Casey modulate her shame enough that she started to let the care team help her more.

In therapy, the belief common among traumatised children that they are to blame made itself explicit and could be addressed: 'You weren't a bad baby, you were a tiny little person who needed a lot of loving. Your mum was so unwell she couldn't look after you. She really tried, didn't she? We know she tried hard to stop taking drugs when you were born and we know she asked Grandma to help her care for you.' Life story therapy was our first introduction to exploring family narratives and provided an opportunity to look for authentic positive intentionality in the others in the child's narrative. This is not an attempt to sugarcoat the history but where possible for the child to see evidence that they were valued and that their parent is a person with flaws and strengths.

### Development of empathy and relational repair

It is important to keep in mind that in our work we have the benefit of strong integration with a care team, so the therapeutic work we do is ideally reinforced at school and home. We do this via the inclusion of care team members in the life story therapy (when using DDP, COSI or PACT also). In some circumstances, where we can access an important attachment figure who also directs the milieu of the home, this figure takes the work back into the home. For Casey, this meant that her key worker in the residential setting took the work back to her team so that they were able to support Casey in processing therapy between sessions. They could also parent her in a manner that met her specific needs, for example supporting her to address cognitive distortions about herself and relationships as they came up in placement. As described above, this also translated to the school system. (It is also important to note that we utilise opportunities to provide professional development to schools and other organisations holding our kids to reinforce this.) Regular care team meetings where members could be supported to think about themes that might present and how to support Casey with them were important. The balance between informing the care team and maintaining confidentiality or consent to share is another important focus of our attention.

Our capacity to support Casey in thinking about the minds of others and developing empathy was strengthened considerably by the fact that the reflection in the therapeutic work was reinforced by the rest of the care team. Interestingly, the development of empathy and the capacity for relational repair seemed integral to each other. Perhaps knowing that relational repair was possible modulated Casey's shame and anxiety to the extent that she could be empathic.

The care team went through a period with Casey when she was regularly infringing the rights of others by lashing out at them when she was frightened and angry. The residential staff dealt with this by providing a triangle in which a second worker could support her to think about the impact she had had and help her repair the relationship with some reparative act. Staff helped her bake cakes, write letters and make pictures, and they also supported her to sit with the difficult feelings evoked and separate her behaviour from her identity.

Later in her therapy, after she had worked through her life narrative and been able to consider some of the positive intentionality of her mother, Casey was able to make further connections. Casey's mother was quite hostile when the therapist first contacted her. However, she accepted the therapist's gentle offer to send information about Casey and the process to her. She was never able to engage directly in the work but she did provide information and recollections. Much later, when she was herself further along her own path to recovery, she made overtures to Casey and, supported by her care team, Casey was able to accept these. Eventually there was some share care possible, which proved very important to Casey.

## Conclusion

When Richard offered my team the opportunity to share some of the ways we have used his life story therapy I was eager to do so, as we have found it so useful and have learnt so much both from the model and from the process of making video supervisions across our geographically fragmented team. I was very aware as I wrote this that I wanted to be able to say more, but we are very early in our journey towards effectively treating children in care, and much of what I am suggesting is speculative and incomplete.

There isn't scope in this chapter to discuss the available evidence for the 'evidence-based components' of our treatment approach. I may well have missed other important treatment goals that life story therapy meets. There are overlaps and duplications in many of the theoretical concepts that make up our treatment goals, and these need further exploration. There are other named therapies that also offer avenues for meeting these goals, and the therapies our team has chosen have been in part influenced by the availability of training and supervision. Our team has benefited from the work of practitioners like Richard Rose, who have found their own approach to engaging and treating this complex and vulnerable population of children. I hope we can add a little to the shared clinical experience of those who work therapeutically with kids in care, and contribute to a conversation that formulates hypotheses and research questions.

## References

Amos, J., Beal, S. and Furber, G. (2007) 'Parent and Child Therapy in action: an attachment based intervention for a six-year-old with a dual diagnosis.' *Australian and New Zealand Journal of Family Therapy* 28(2), 61–70.

Becker Weidmann, A. and Hughes, D. (2008) 'Dyadic Developmental Therapy: an evidence based treatment for children with complex trauma and disorders of attachment.' *Child & Family Social Work* 13, 329–337.

Briere, J. and Lanktree, C. (2008) *Integrative Treatment of Complex Trauma for Adolescents: A Guide for the Treatment of Multiply-Traumatized Youth.*

Cassidy, J., Woodhouse, S.S., Sherman, L.J., Stupica, B. and Lejuez, C.W. (2011) 'Enhancing infant attachment security: an examination of treatment efficacy and differential susceptibility.' *Journal of Development and Psychopathology* 23(1), 131–148.

Chambers, H., Amos, J., Allison, S. and Roeger, L. (2006) 'Parent and Child Therapy: an attachment based intervention for children with challenging problems.' *Australian and New Zealand Journal of Family Therapy* Vol 27(2), 68–74.

Cohen, J.A., Deblinger, E., Mannarino, A.P. and Steer, R. (2004) 'A multisite, randomized controlled trial for children with sexual abuse-related PTSD symptoms.' *Journal of the American Academy of Child & Adolescent Psychiatry* 43, 393–402.

Golding, K. (2007) *Meeting the Therapeutic Needs of Looked After and Adopted Children.*

Hoffman, K., Marvin, R.S., Cooper, G. and Powell, B. (2006) 'Changing toddlers' and preschoolers' attachment classifications: the Circle of Security intervention.' *Journal of Consulting and Clinical Psychology* 74(6), 1017–1026.

Hughes, D. (2000) *Facilitating Developmental Attachment: The Road to Emotional Recovery and Behavioural Change in Foster and Adoptive Children.*

Klag, S., Fox, T., Martin, G., Eadie, K. *et al.* (2016) 'Evolve Therapeutic Services 5-year outcome study of children and young people in out of home care with severe and complex behavioural and mental health problems.' *Children and Youth Services Review* 69, 268–274.

Lee, T., Fouras, G. and Brown, R. (2015) 'AACAP practice parameter for youth in child welfare.' *Journal of the American Academy of Child and Adolescent Psychiatry* 54(6), 502–517.

Luke, N., Sinclair, I., Woolgar, M. and Sebba, J. (2014) *What Works in Preventing and Treating Poor Mental Health in Looked After Children?* NSPCC/Rees Centre.

NICE (2010) *Guidelines for Looked After Children and Young People.* National Institute for Health and Care Excellence.

Perry, B. (2006) 'Applying Principles of Neurodevelopment to Clinical Work with Maltreated and Traumatized Children: The Neurosequential Model of Therapeutics.' In N.B. Webb (ed.) *Working with Traumatized Youth in Child Welfare.* New York: Guilford Press.

Vostanis, P. (2010) 'Mental health services for children in public care and other vulnerable groups: implications for international collaboration.' *Clinical Child Psychology and Psychiatry* 15, 555.

Chapter 10

# SEEING MY JOURNEY WITH NEW EYES

## THERAPEUTIC LIFE STORY WORK WITH DEAF PEOPLE

*Goedele A.M. De Clerck, University of Manchester*

Being able to tell your life story is essential for understanding your identity and humanity and for coping with life transitions (Atkinson 1995; McAdams 2006; Bohlmeijer 2007). However, this fundamental aspect of being human is far from evident for deaf adults and young deaf people, who tend to be visually oriented (Hauser, Lukomski and Hillman 2008). For them, the emergence of a secure and healthy identity may be at risk due to limited access to resources for normal language development, whether spoken or signed (Zand and Pierce 2011; Young 2016). Life story work may ameliorate these experiences of exclusion and the negative consequences of barriers to identity-related resources; this work is also in a mutually beneficial symbiosis with the ongoing documentation of deaf communities' emancipation around the world (Mathur and Napoli 2011; Cooper and Rashid 2015; De Clerck 2016).

Thus, as a Marie Curie Fellow at the University of Manchester's Social Research with Deaf People group (EU Horizon 2020, 2015–2017), I am exploring the potential of life story work for enriching the wellbeing of British deaf people and deaf migrants. This exploration aims to tailor this intervention to the unique linguistic-cultural experiences of deaf people, enabling them to strengthen their identities and gain resilience through employing creative and narrative methods.

To introduce the reader to the notion and incipient practice of life story work with deaf people, I will first sketch my personal journey as a deaf scholar who became fascinated by life story work with deaf people, and then describe the interdisciplinary perspective from which I examine this practice. I will also provide examples of recent life story work with the Ugandan deaf community and an ongoing project with British deaf migrants.

## My own journey towards life story work

As an anthropologist, I bring to life story work more than a decade of ethnographic research with deaf communities around the world, a journey that has centred round the cultural practices of signed storytelling. These practices are transmitted intergenerationally and involve both personal life stories and collective storytelling. For my doctoral studies on deaf empowerment, I carried out life story research with deaf community members in Flanders (in the north of Belgium) and international deaf people at Gallaudet University (the world's only university designed expressly for deaf people, located in Washington, DC), reflecting on transitions in their identities. I continued this in my postdoctoral studies, focusing on emancipation with deaf communities in Cameroon and Uganda. My research has encompassed multimedia and produced documentaries in which deaf people in Flanders and Uganda tell their signed stories, and those of their communities, and describe landmark moments in their empowerment (Sign Language Projects n.d.).

I recently wrote a book about this journey, titled *Deaf Epistemologies, Identity, and Learning* (De Clerck 2016), which presents a cross-cultural theoretical framework on deaf identity and the role of storytelling in identity formation. It explores the metaphor of 'deaf flourishing', i.e. deaf people's wellbeing and self-actualisation as it emerges in the variety of cultural practices, in each of the communities mentioned above, in both personal and collective identities. Scholars from various disciplines, such as positive psychology (Seligman 2011), ethics (Sandel 2009) and social justice (Nussbaum 2011), work on the notion of flourishing, which relates to the anthropological view of wellbeing as 'an optimal state for an individual, community, society, and the world as a whole' (Mathews and Izquierdo 2010, p.5). This refers to individual experience and recognises the interconnectivity of humans and interpersonal/ intercultural aspects of wellbeing. It is also supported by theories of learning, which look at the interaction with resources available in the environment, as discussed below.

Looking back on this journey, it was during my work with international deaf people at Gallaudet that I became aware of the potential of therapeutic life story work. There were no life story work courses, but the notion of identity was in the foreground to a much greater extent at Gallaudet than in Flanders because of the university's unparalleled accessibility and intensive transnational contact, which offered the chance to investigate the budding of international deaf identities. I recall an African friend sharing a story that he wrote for a personal development class shortly after my arrival. It was a metaphorical story of his own life, about the necessity of roots and personal growth. It was a common practice for international deaf people to share their stories with each other, to reflect on what had happened in their lives and reframe them from a perspective of strength and possibility. We therefore told our stories frequently, and this practice inspired me to study what was happening within this storytelling, what deaf empowerment was, and how deaf identity formation could be seen as a learning process. This illuminated the roles of an accessible and sign-based learning environment, peer learning, deaf cultural rhetoric, community participation, and learning by doing (De Clerck 2007, 2009, 2016).

During my postdoctoral studies, I became more interested in exploring the relationship between life storytelling and wellbeing, and in 2010–11 I took a postgraduate course called Coaching and Counseling in Existential Wellbeing at Leuven University. It encouraged me to reflect on my personal story, a strength-centred approach in ethnography, and the treasures in life story research (De Clerck 2016); it was during this time that I made the first notes on the proposal for the work I am doing now. The Cameroon context was particularly motivating since many of the deaf community members had never before been able to tell their life stories. They sometimes came to me with heartfelt questions about their lives, wellbeing, family and future, and I noticed the potential for finding answers through the strength that they built in the telling of their story. I wished to be able to support them in this process as well as in dealing with trauma, which is where my research tends at present.

# Deaf life story work at an interdisciplinary crossroads

I am doing this work from a perspective that can be situated at the crossroads of narrative therapy, social work, cross-cultural human development, anthropology and deaf studies. The knowledge from these disciplines can support an emancipatory approach to life story work as an intervention that promotes empowerment and wellbeing by enabling deaf people and communities to tell their own stories and consider their past and future. Here I look briefly at the theoretical justification for this positioning, and then relate some interesting results of communal life story work with the Ugandan deaf community and from ongoing individual work with deaf migrants in the UK. These examples illustrate a practice that draws on these interdisciplinary perspectives.

A cross-cultural perspective on human development looks at learning, identity formation and agency from a socio-cultural approach, understanding it as 'a process of people's changing participation in sociocultural activities of their communities' (Vygotsky 1978). It can illuminate deaf processes of learning, growth and blossoming, which, as in the example of Gallaudet above, may be fostered by interaction with a deaf-friendly environment and peer contact. Centred around stories and autobiographical reflection, narrative therapy (Bohlmeijer 2007) fosters self-reflexive learning and strengthened social, psychological, cultural and linguistic capital in deaf people and communities, while the situated 'knowledges' (Haraway 1991) within deaf life stories may provide alternative pathways for deaf identity (Sheridan 2008).

The exploration of deaf selves and personal knowledge in relation to society and wellbeing is particularly important in the light of socio-political transitions in contemporary deaf communities (De Clerck and Paul 2016), but also in transitions, disempowerment and displacement not associated with being deaf (seen, for example, in the stories of deaf Ugandans and deaf migrants in the UK). For Hannah Arendt (1989), it is in showing who we are, in telling our story, instead of only being able to show our 'whatness' (for example, the physical passport made up by gender and deafness), that we become human and are born for the second time. This subjectivity is always interwoven with the stories of others (for deaf second birth stories, see De Clerck 2016). This process can be supported by life story work in which children and adolescents are able to develop a healthy sense of self in relation to their carers (Rees 2009; Rose 2012; Wrench and Naylor 2013).

Although storytelling has been explored as a linguistic and cultural practice of deaf signers (Metzger 1995; Mindess 2006), my research is the first attempt to harness the deaf life storytelling process as a deliberate and evidence-based means of supporting mental health and wellbeing. I also look at deaf life story work from a human rights angle: Article 24 of the UN Convention on the Rights of Persons with Disabilities (UNCRPD) promotes 'the development by persons with disabilities of their personality, talents and creativity, as well as their mental and physical abilities, to their fullest potential'. Life story work can facilitate this learning, growth and blossoming and contribute to other human rights entitlements such as 'social development skills to facilitate their full and equal participation in education and as members of the community'. As such, life story work could be an essential part of inclusive education and deaf rights, and each deaf person, including young learners and adults in lifelong learning, has the right to tell his or her own story (for further discussion of the UNCRPD and inclusive education, see Jokinen 2016).

# To the beat of our own drum – life story work with the Ugandan deaf community

In 2015, as part of a research project on emancipation processes of the Ugandan deaf community, involving collaboration between the University of Manchester and Kyambogo University (funded by the British Academy), I worked with Dr Sam Lutalo-Kiingi to document Ugandan deaf heritage. This was a process which could be conceptualised as collective life story work in the form of a community profile, a picture that starts from the experiences of community members, is woven through their signed stories and contributes to collective wellbeing. Like individual life story work, a community profile juxtaposes diverse individual narratives with documented information (for example, on historical, demographic and socioeconomic evidence) and aims to raise consciousness and support members in their agency and plans for the future (Dominelli 2006; Ledwith 2012). Around the world, including in Uganda, these members often view their communities as an 'extended family' with whom they share a language, culture and experience of being deaf (Padden and Humphries 1988, 2005; Lutalo-Kiingi and De Clerck in press). From this perspective, communal life story work is as vital as individual work to the wellbeing of deaf people.

This profile consisted of two major parts: 1) a visual timeline of key moments in the emancipation process and significant efforts toward the community's development; and 2) multimedia portraits entitled 'snapshots of the Ugandan deaf community', in which members look back on its early development and reflect on its present status and future perspectives. The timeline and snapshots were presented to the community during an exhibition at Kyambogo on 29 September 2015 and made available on the project website (Sign Language Projects n.d.).

For the video snapshots and the timeline, we worked through regional community meetings in Kampala (central Uganda) and Mbale (eastern Uganda) in which eight deaf Ugandans of diverse ages participated. In Kampala, they were held in the shade of a tree on the site of the Uganda School for the Deaf in Namirembe; in Mbale, members gathered outside on the platform of a large church near the unfinished foundations of what was once supposed to become their own deaf church building. Both sites had symbolic meaning: the former was the first deaf school in Uganda, founded in 1961 (a year before Uganda's independence), and the inception of Ugandan Sign Language (UgSL). It was also where the Ugandan National Association of the Deaf (UNAD) had its first offices and international development partnerships arose. The latter site attests to both the strength and vulnerability of the community, with members steadfastly gathering on Sundays despite the reminder of their shattered dreams of development, symbolised in the unfinished building.

During the four-day meetings, members were invited to explore key moments in their personal and communal lives (such as starting deaf or mainstream school, experiencing the death of a parent, getting married, participating in student strikes and helping to establish the Deaf Association and launch development projects) through signed stories, photographs, performance and film. The meetings were held as signing circles with a drum and began with a discussion of the project's ethics, which continuously balanced an absolute protection of privacy for personal narratives (and confidentiality within the group) with public openness for aspects of community profiles which are intended for a broad audience. The intergenerational dialogue provided opportunities for young deaf people to learn about the history of their community from their elders, and deaf elders in turn had the chance to learn about the perspectives of deaf youth. This is exemplified in this excerpt from a community dialogue in the snapshot entitled 'A fruitful future?' in which a member from Mbale, which is a four-hour drive from Kampala, illustrates the community's vulnerability and restricted means:

> It would be helpful if the UNAD would regularly visit and follow up our work. Then we can develop. If they come to guide us once and then stay in Kampala and forget about us, it discourages the membership. That is partly why the Mbale Deaf Association is declining... We have challenges in our families: our parents are poor and we have spouses and families to take care for. We failed to secure local government funds to run our deaf programmes. That is why deaf people are getting scattered. Some have resorted to farming in the villages and others are weaving. It is deaf elders who keep checking on us rather than the UNAD. It's been five years since the UNAD came here. That's a long time.

The perspectives of members in Kampala, the capital region where deaf people have been able to gain better access to resources, are more hopeful and confident regarding the future, as one young member relates:

> We have had a group of deaf people [involved in establishing the
> Deaf Association and researching UgSL]; they had information
> that I didn't know before; it's been passed on to me now. This
> means that [they] planted a seed from which a tree has grown
> that now bears fruit. [We] youth are the fruit… We can gradually
> take the reins of older leaders…and use our strength to mobilise
> fellow deaf people to advocate for education and UgSL.

This is an example of how the life story of the Ugandan deaf community
is told through a Ugandan metaphor of deaf flourishing, that of the tree.

In the snapshot called 'Ugandan deaf culture: taught as our drum',
members creatively employ a drum motif to weave aspects of deaf and
indigenous Ugandan cultural practices into their exploration of a deaf
engagement ceremony. This topic had organically emerged from the
meetings and illustrates a life transition that relates to both the family of
origin and the 'deaf family'. In a performance, the participants creatively
blended personal experiences and fiction, with the aim of educating
young deaf people about this important time in their lives. Since deaf
Ugandans often grow up with limited communication within their
home environments, vital information on these cultural practices, which
is passed on intergenerationally among families and ethnic groups, may
not reach them. This knowledge is currently not part of curricula in deaf
schools, which makes it difficult for young deaf people to gain access to
it, even at the age of dating. This may become traumatic, for example
when young deaf Ugandans end up unknowingly dating their close
relatives, i.e. members of the same clan. Through co-operating in a video
snapshot on a signed deaf engagement ceremony with representatives
from both their biological family and the deaf community, and adding
a touch of joy and laughter, deaf elders and young deaf people have
been able to draw on their experiences to meet this need and to generate
awareness about communication and cultural transmission among
families of young deaf people.

Moreover, this communal life story work was in many ways a
'road less travelled' (Peck 1990), and required far more pioneering
than we had foreseen. It invited us to explore alternative pathways,

for example due to the scarcity of archives and written resources that could be consulted (in part because of Uganda's civil war from 1973 to 1986). For the timeline, we had gathered over 150 pictures, which were generously shared from personal and non-governmental organisations' collections. We also did life story research with 16 deaf Ugandans in the two regions, to capture more oral/signed historical evidence. We did not necessarily assess impacts on wellbeing, but we could observe how members in Mbale gained resilience and joy throughout the process, which differed from the collective sense of depression and stress at the beginning of the project (expressed as 'not feeling well'). All participants were able to contribute to the intergenerational dialogue and associated pride through beating the drum, sharing pictures, memories and stories, and working together in a filmed performance. The drama also enabled participants in both Kampala and Mbale to relive their experiences of the past while simultaneously reconstructing their communal life story, and taking the role of the audience (Smeysters 2008).

I felt very grateful seeing deaf Ugandans looking at their pictures on the timeline during the Kyambogo exhibition, some of which had survived the war but never seen the light. They were fascinated to see the milestones of their community, recognising themselves in the pictures, and realising their unique place in the collective history. The exhibition also attracted attention from the university, schools, non-governmental organisations and wider society with coverage on national television (UBC and Bukedde TV) and in newspapers (*New Vision* and *The Observer*). Moreover, the timeline and snapshots are to be used as educational materials in the Deaf Studies Diploma Course at Kyambogo, which is particularly oriented towards deaf adults. Securing resources to continue deaf life story work in Uganda, communal as well as individual, is an important goal given how vital this work is for sustainability and wellbeing (see Lutalo-Kiingi and De Clerck in press).

## Deaf life narratives in times of transition: towards a cross-cultural instrument for life storytelling

When I came to the UK for this project, I was very interested in the existing legislation on life story work and associated services for children who are adopted or in foster care, and I was especially eager to partake in the therapeutic life story work training course at the Institute for Arts in Therapy and Education in London. To date there are no life story work services that are tailored to deaf children, youth or adults, and no specialised training for the professionals working with them. I intend for my study with deaf adolescents and adults to advance the development of life story work as a new intervention in deaf wellbeing. The aim is to develop a cross-cultural approach that is sensitive to both British deaf people and deaf migrants in the UK. I focus here on the latter group, which have been my initial focus in the project.

A very large percentage of the world's population today is comprised of migrants, who often face challenges in terms of wellbeing (World Migration Report 2013). In this project I work with deaf signers using various languages (signed and/or written) and participating in multiple communities. Those who have recently arrived may have limited knowledge of British Sign Language and English. The cross-linguistic and cross-cultural skills I acquired around the world help me to ensure that deaf people can access information on this project, and the study also explicitly draws on my own and the participants' multimodal bilingual/multilingual competences, factors described by Quinto-Pozos and Adam (2015) as constituting 'a fertile landscape for the creation of contact phenomena' (p.53). This may include International Sign, a contact language among signers of 'mutually unintelligible language boundaries' (ibid.), and is supported by visual methods of storytelling. A shared basis of language and experience is therefore developed during the life story work process. The motivation for participating in the project varies from simply making a book of their life, to seeking self-esteem and resilience, to being able to share their story with their (future) children.

This project works around three building blocks of present, past and future (Rose 2012; Wrench and Naylor 2013). Starting with the present, in the first session I provide coloured paper, craft materials, glue and pens and ask them to imagine how the first page of their book would look like, for example their name and a list of the important people in their lives, or a drawing of a childhood memory. The page does not necessarily need to end up in the book, but it enables them to make a start. Across the various sessions, the papers are kept in a folder or display book, which helps them to select the documents or pictures they would like to include in the book or share with friends or relatives. It is important that they are able to take this home, and that they have craft materials there with which to continue the creative process. During the first session, participants have mentioned understanding how the life story work guides them (for example, while doing some artwork, a participant said that he suddenly understood how the drawing was like a mental warm-up, helping him to recall memories), and that it equips them with the belief in their own ability and in the value of the process. The initial session also includes establishing a safe place (Wrench and Naylor 2013) for each participant psychologically, and anchoring this place so they can recall it at any time during the life story work, whether in a session or at home.

The project provides iPads on loan to participants, which enables them to build skills in the use of digital devices and make pictures and videos of their life world (for example, their home) and who they are (for example, what they like and dislike, what makes them angry, happy and sad; for more on digital life story work, see Hammond and Cooper 2013). The possibility of telling their story visually and in sign language helps to circumvent language issues and avoid the stress that may be experienced in multilingual communication (for example, what happens when I write in my own language; would you understand it? What does this English word mean?). Participants have mentioned gaining pride in acquiring digital skills that they are able to transfer to other domains (for example, a participant mentioned that the ability to use an iPad combined with increased confidence and assurance about his identity would be helpful in his employment).

Since this digital pathway supplies such advantages, we are devising the first-ever life storytelling app that is tailored to the visual strengths of deaf signers. To contribute towards proof of concept for this app, the project currently provides apps with features similar to those intended for our eventual bespoke app, and participants are encouraged to give feedback on them. These range from travel-related apps on which they can track their journey, to apps for creating timelines with pictures and videos, with an emphasis on deaf-friendly features, including a strongly visual design and minimal written language.

In addition, narrative and culturally sensitive play therapy methods such as working with miniature animals are helpful for participants to reflect on their different selves (sub-personalities) and the important people in their lives (and sometimes the interaction with the different selves of these people) (Riedel Bowers 2013; Gill and Dewes 2015). To support deaf people in visual and symbolic exploration of themes in their lives and compiling family trees and personal trajectories, I also work with puppets (McMahon 2009; also, the method of Marleen Diekmann, titled 'An extra language', which uses duplo puppets and is well known in social and mental care in the Dutch language area, as well as being used with migrant populations and in war-torn areas). In the transitional space of life story work, these methods, as well as visual and digital timelines, enable the participants to gain insight into the relations with their family of origin and their 'deaf family', including movement to different physical and temporal locations in their life journey, and to identify and mobilise resources.

Throughout the life story work, the participants' strengths and resources are consciously recognised, ranging from their own virtues, to people who have supported them, to images or films that have inspired them in difficult moments. In the end, the book that is created might be paper-based or digital, and could be comprised of drawings, collages or paintings, or a mixture of these.

## Conclusion

This chapter described a new intervention which has the potential to enhance deaf people's wellbeing. A cross-cultural approach for life story work is being honed to determine how it may contribute to deaf people's sense of identity, resilience and agency. Contributions toward this endeavour have included my personal journey as well as anthropological life story research on 'deaf flourishing' around the world. I sketched the interdisciplinary crossroads from which I approach this, offering the examples of communal life story work with the Ugandan deaf community and individual work in the UK with deaf migrants. Communal life story work is vital to the wellbeing and empowerment of deaf signers, who participate in multiple communities, including their family of origin and one or more deaf communities with whom they share a signed language and deaf culture. I employ creative and pictorial methods, befitting the visual orientation of deaf signers and the established cultural storytelling practices of sign language communities. The work with deaf migrants also involves an emancipatory stance which fosters self-reflective learning and resilience. The strengths of signers are further exploited through digital storytelling, leading to an ultimate aim of producing a deaf-friendly app which, in concert with the other emerging innovations described here, is intended to contribute sustainably to specialised services and training in deaf life story work.

# References

Arendt, H. (1989) *The Human Condition.* Chicago, IL: University of Chicago Press.

Atkinson, R. (1995) *The Gift of Stories – Practical and Spiritual Applications of Autobiography, Life Stories and Personal Myth Making.* Westport, CT: Bergin & Garvey.

Bohlmeijer, E. (2007) *De verhalen die we leven. Narratieve psychologie als methode* [*The stories we live by. Narrative psychology as method*]. Amsterdam, the Netherlands: Uitgeverij Boom.

Brown, B. (2008) *I Thought It Was Just Me: Telling the Truth About Perfectionism, Inadequacy and Power.* New York: Gotham Books.

Cooper, A.C. and Rashid, K.K. (eds) (2015) *Citizenship, Politics, Difference: Perspectives from Sub--Signed Language Communities.* Washington, DC: Gallaudet University Press.

De Clerck, G. (2007) 'Meeting global deaf peers, visiting ideal deaf places: deaf ways of education leading to empowerment, an exploratory case study.' *American Annals of the Deaf* 152(1), 5–19.

De Clerck, G. (2009) '"I don't worry because I have my education": international deaf people moving toward emancipation.' *Medische Antropologie* [*Health, Care & the Body: International Journal in Medical Anthropology*] 21(1), 131–158.

De Clerck, G. (2016) *Deaf Epistemologies, Identity, and Learning: A Comparative Perspective.* Washington, DC: Gallaudet University Press.

De Clerck, G. and Paul, P.V. (eds) (2016) *Sign Language, Sustainable Development, and Equal Opportunities.* Washington, DC: Gallaudet University Press.

Dominelli, L. (2006) *Women and Community Action.* Bristol: Polity Press.

Gil, E. and Drewes, A. (2015) *Cultural Issues in Play Therapy.* New York, London: Guilford Press.

Hammond, S.P. and Cooper, N.J. (2013) *Digital Life Story Work.* London: British Association for Adoption and Fostering (BAAF).

Haraway, D. (1991) *Simians, Cyborgs, and Women: The Reinvention of Nature.* New York: Routledge.

Hauser, P.C., Lukomski, J. and Hillman, T. (2008) 'Development of Deaf and Hard-of-Hearing Students' Executive Functioning.' In M. Marschark and P. Hauser (eds) *Deaf Cognition: Foundations and Outcomes.* New York: Oxford University Press.

Jokinen, M. (2016) 'Inclusive Education – A Sustainable Approach?' In G. De Clerck and P.V. Paul (eds) *Sign Language, Sustainable Development, and Equal Opportunities.* Washington, DC: Gallaudet University Press.

Ledwith, M. (2012) *Community Development: A Critical Approach.* Bristol, England: Polity Press.

Lutalo-Kiingi, S. and De Clerck, G. (in press) *Developing Sustainably? The Ugandan Deaf Community Looking Back and Forward.* Kampala, Uganda: Fountain Publishers.

Mathews, G. and Izquierdo, C. (2010) 'Anthropology, Happiness, and Well-Being.' In G. Mathews and C. Izquierdo (eds) *Pursuits of Happiness: Well-Being in Anthropological Perspective.* New York: Berghahn.

Mathur, G. and Napoli, D.J. (2011) *Deaf Around the World: The Impact of Language.* Oxford: Oxford University Press.

McAdams, D. (2006) *The Redemptive Self: Stories Americans Live By.* New York: Oxford University Press.

McMahon, L. (2009) *The Handbook of Play Therapy and Therapeutic Play.* London, New York: Routledge.

Metzger, M. (1995) 'Constructed Dialogue and Constructed Action in American Sign Language.' In C. Lucas (ed.) *Sociolinguistics in Deaf Communities.* Washington, DC: Gallaudet University Press.

Mindess, A. (2006) *Reading Between the Signs: Intercultural Communication for Sign Language Interpreters.* Boston, MA: Intercultural Press.

Nussbaum, M. (2011) *Creating Capabilities: The Human Development Approach.* Cambridge, MA: Belknap Press of Harvard University Press.

Padden, C. and Humphries, T. (1998) *Deaf in America: Voices from a Culture.* Boston, MA: Harvard University Press.

Padden, C. and Humphries, T. (2005) *Inside Deaf Culture.* Cambridge, MA: Harvard University Press.

Peck, M. Scott (1990) *The Road Less Travelled: A New Psychology of Love, Traditional Values and Spiritual Growth.* London: Arrow.

Quinto-Pozos, D. and Adam, R. (2015) 'Sign Languages in Contact.' In A. Schembri and C. Lucas (eds) *Sociolinguistics and Deaf Communities.* Cambridge: Cambridge University Press.

Rees, J. (2009) *Life Story Books for Adopted Children: A Family Friendly Approach.* London: Jessica Kingsley Publishers.

Riedel Bowers, N. (ed.) (2013) *Play Therapy with Families: A Collaborative Approach to Healing.* New York: Jason Aronson.

Rose, R. (2012) *Life Story Therapy with Traumatized Children: A Model for Practice.* London: Jessica Kingsley Publishers.

Sandel, M.J. (2009) *The Case Against Perfection: Ethics in the Age of Genetic Engineering.* Cambridge, MA: Harvard University Press.

Seligman, M. (2011) *Flourish: A New Understanding of Happiness and Well-Being and How to Achieve Them.* London: Nicholas Brealey.

Sheridan, M. (2008) *Deaf Adolescents: Inner Lives and Lifeworld Development.* Washington, DC: Gallaudet University Press.

Sign Language Projects (n.d.) Available at www.signlanguageprojects.com/en.

Smeysters, H. (2008) *Handboek Creatieve Therapie* [*Handbook of Creative Therapy*]. Bussum: Coutinho.

Vygotsky, L. (1978) *Mind in Society: The Development of Higher Psychological Processes.* Cambridge, MA: Harvard University Press.

World Migration Report (2013) *Migrant Wellbeing and Development.* Geneva: International Organization for Migration. Available at http://publications.iom.int/system/files/pdf/wmr2013_en.pdf, accessed on 20 June 2017.

Wrench, K. and Naylor, L. (2013) *Life Story Work with Children who are Fostered or Adopted: Creative Ideas and Activities.* London: Jessica Kingsley Publishers.

Young, A. (2016) 'Deaf Children and their Families: Sustainability, Sign Language and Equality.' In G. De Clerck and P.V. Paul (eds) *Sign Language, Sustainable Development, and Equal Opportunities.* Washington, DC: Gallaudet University Press.

Zand, D.H. and Pierce, K.J. (eds) (2011) *Resilience in Deaf Children: Adaptation through Emerging Adulthood.* New York: Springer Press.

# PART 3

# IMPLEMENTING THERAPEUTIC LIFE STORY WORK

Chapter 11

# DISPELLING THE KARMA

*Soula Kontomichalos-Eyre, Elise Saunders, Del Aulich,
Sebastian LaSpina and Anna Fasolo, Melbourne (Inner Eastern
Melbourne) Department of Health and Human Services*

## Introduction by Richard Rose

*Over the last two years I have been engaged with the Inner Eastern Melbourne
Department of Health and Human Services (DHHS) team to consider how best we
can interweave the therapeutic life story work approach into practice. This has led
to numerous workshops and meetings with practitioners, policy makers and senior
managers for the department and for allied professionals, including the police and
education. With the commitment of Soula Kontomichalos, Elise Saunders, Del
Aulich, Sebastian LaSpina and Anna Fasolo, the department agreed to undertake
a unique project involving four workers supporting more than 20 young people in
therapeutic life story work.*

*Having provided supervision and guidance over the last year, I have witnessed
the dedication of the team to deliver the model to very challenged and challenging
young people. This chapter is an account of the programme, and I am in awe
of the outcomes that are now beginning to be researched by Deakin University,
Melbourne.*

## Dispelling the karma

*'It is karma, Miss,' Josh replied resolutely as he slouched back into the
meeting room chair.*

*'What do you mean, Josh? Surely we can do something to help you work through these worries and together get to a better place,' replied the departmental officer authorised to issue a Youth Justice Manager's warning and to support Josh in making positive choices moving forward. 'Karma. It's just with me; I know that bad things will just happen, that's the way it is…' Josh hesitated for a second. 'You don't need to worry about it Miss.'*

This feeling of pessimism was explicitly and implicitly visible in the persona of a number of children and young people who live in the Inner Eastern Melbourne Area of Victoria, Australia, during their interactions with the service system.

This chapter will look at how three government partners attempted to engage with the children and young people living in Inner Eastern Melbourne. In this area, the Department of Health and Human Services, Victoria Police, the Department of Education and Training and local services were equally worried about these children and young people and the relentless number of issues that appeared to plague them.

The area had a range of programmes that were achieving good outcomes for children and young people, but a small group stood out as regularly placing themselves and others in the community at significant risk. These children and young people were coming to the attention of senior practitioners in these government organisations.

Despite good will and commitment for these children and young people, the therapeutic and non-therapeutic interventions were not realising the intended outcomes. Of significant concern was the potential for these young people to offend, their exposure to victimisation and their disengagement from educational programmes. A number of these children and young people were living in out-of-home care, a system for vulnerable children provided by foster carers, kinship carers or residential carers operated by community service organisations and funded through the Department of Health and Human Services.

The partners in the Inner Eastern Melbourne Area committed to regularly coming together and identifying shared concerns, thoughtfully scrutinising the impact of their efforts and collaborating on how to better align their respective investment to realise positive outcomes for the children and young people. These efforts culminated in the development of the initiative called 'Building Resilience of Children and Young People in Inner Eastern Melbourne'. This initiative provided three targeted therapeutic opportunities for a pilot group of children and young people who were exhibiting high-risk behaviours and for the people who care for them. The opportunities were therapeutic life story work developed by Associate Professor Richard Rose, linguistic capacity development and building the capacity of each care team.

This chapter focuses on the Inner Eastern Melbourne Area's experience with one of the interventions: Richard Rose's therapeutic life story work. The area chose this as the approach to help the children and young people unpick the experiences that led them to their current circumstances for the following reasons:

- Its practical methodological approach to safely enable children and young people to explore their personal, family and trauma history with the support of their carers in order to foster an understanding of behaviours, feelings and cognitive processes

- Children and young people being given the opportunity to strengthen existing attachments and form new positive ones with their carers

- Children and young people being able to explore their personal, family and trauma history with their key carer in order to foster a shared understanding of their behaviours and feelings and how these impact on their daily interactions and decisions

- Children and young people being able to develop their abilities to self-regulate their emotions, express their needs, seek support and align their values, beliefs and behaviours in a supported environment

- Children and young people becoming open to positive social, health and wellbeing activities

- Its anticipated 'hope' of sustaining home placements by involving both the child or young person and their carer in considering the child's trauma, personal journey and family history. This approach supports the forming of the relationship and attachment between the carer and the child

- The defined period of time – nine to twelve months – of the intervention.

In addition to these anticipated benefits, the therapeutic life story work approach appeared to align well with contemporary literature on how to best support children who have experienced significant trauma in their lives.

As identified in Shlonsky *et al.* (2013) in a review of the strategies implemented to improve out-of-home care, it was found that a life story intervention in the USA for a group of seven children improved externalising behaviour in the study group. An important component of life story work is the drawing of personal reflection. Therapeutic art and literacy activities can provide healing qualities to children in care. A variety of art, literature, storytelling and writing activities can be used.

Such activities can give children some of the emotional support they need to help them heal and provide an opportunity to maintain healthy cognitive and emotional developmental growth (Thobaben 2013).

## Therapeutic life story work techniques: transition from theory to practice

Throughout the implementation of the therapeutic life story work, the Inner Eastern Melbourne Area's practitioners also used a number of tools to problem solve the following issues faced by the care teams:

- The negative 'internal working model' of the children and young people in residential care

- Carer support

- The 'stuck child and care team'.

## Negative internal working model of the children and young people in residential care

While working with the children and young people, it became evident to the therapeutic life story work practitioners that most, if not all, of the children and young people held a negative internal working model characterised by mistrust, a need for control and underlying feelings of being 'bad'. Their vulnerability to harm by others and self-harm was a significant concern for their care team, family and others.

The application of therapeutic life story work provided examples of how the approach began to heal and restore the bonds of attachment for the children and young people, opening up the ability for keyworkers to have discussions about risk behaviours and concerns.

Where the child or young person was not present, the practitioner would provide a hand-written letter to ensure the child or young person knew the keyworker and therapeutic life story work practitioner's commitment to them. This paved the way for the child or young person to see both the therapeutic life story work practitioner and keyworker as consistent, supportive and caring adults in their life who were committed to helping them understand their world in a supported manner. Several of the children and young people appeared to 'test' the therapeutic life story work practitioner through the relational game playing of Jenga and Uno, yet week by week children and young people became more comfortable and engaged in the relationship.

We believe that this contributed to the safe space created through the focus being on 'play' while building trust and relationship. Allowing the child and young person to have control over when they opened their wallpaper and where the wallpaper was kept was another supportive technique that increased trust in the relationship. The use of the wallpaper during the session was also a huge step forward for the care teams as this approach was contrary to traditional methods. A key enabler of this methodology was the confidence of the therapeutic life story work practitioner in working with the wallpaper. Done well, it enabled exploration of the child or young person's world through activities such as 'Who are the people involved in their life?' and 'What meaning do they hold for this child or young person?'

Additionally, some of the children and young people's internal working model played out with behaviours focused on the need to 'please others'. These children appeared to struggle with significant feelings of rejection and they persistently needed to 'please' others in their world, including the therapeutic life story work practitioner. Through various activities the children and young people began to trust the therapeutic life story work practitioner and feel safe enough to reflect their behaviour.

One of the tools used to assist children and young people understand how feelings of rejection play out in relationships is illustrated in Figures 11.1 and 11.2. Through the use of the 'hula hoops' (Rose 2012) children and young people are able to safely explore alternative points of view. The therapeutic life story work practitioner is able in the first instance to narrate what the child wants others to think about them. In the second hoop, the practitioner narrates what the child is really thinking and how that would make them feel.

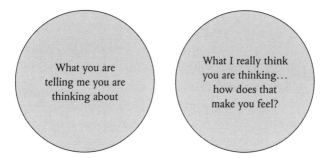

*Figure 11.1 Example of physically using a hula hoop as a reflective activity*

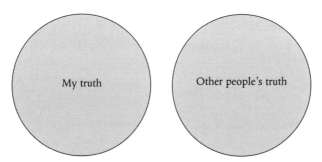

*Figure 11.2 Example of physically using a hula hoop as a reflective activity around how we view the world*

Of significant concern for our children and young people with negative internal working models was their vulnerability to sexual harm, exploitation and lack of consideration of risk to themselves. The age-old question of 'How do we help a young person to see that they are not invincible and to support them in being able to identify risk?' has been explored countless times across generations and communities.

With the children and young people in the initiative who experienced significant trauma, the other layer of complexity observed was low sense of self and self-efficacy. Therapeutic life story work has been a beneficial intervention as practitioners have been able to utilise activities to explore feelings and emotions during sessions. A useful activity is the 'scroll' demonstrated in Figure 11.3. This activity allows the child and young person to explore concerns and discuss risky behaviours.

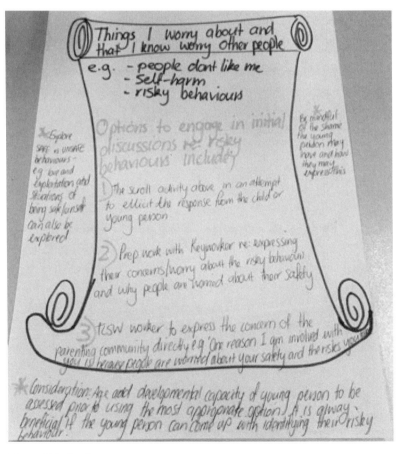

*Figure 11.3: Scroll*

A key piece of practice advice provided by Richard Rose is to ensure that practitioners involved with the child and young person do not confuse the exploration of behaviour as a vehicle for telling the child they were wrong. This may create frustration, anger and confusion – it is important that the therapeutic life story worker narrates thoughts and worries of chosen behaviour and does not dictate behaviour that a child should or should not do. With options and 'could have' conversations, the right pathways can be chosen and followed with the volition of the child or young person as they make strengths-based decisions.

## Carer support

The second intervention of the Building Resilience in Children and Young People initiative is to create a parenting community around the child or young person. This was done by utilising open communication from the beginning of the therapeutic life story work process with members of the care team. The care team essentially delivers 'parenting tasks', and so there was a need to undertake discussion about their roles and functions, and each member of the team needed to reflect on who they were in the child's life. With respect to the therapeutic life story work, keyworkers were encouraged to be mindful of the commitment, reliability and strength required by them to work with the child or young person through their life story and to decide if they wanted to commit to the task. As a result of this transparency within the preparation work, it was refreshing to witness the emergence of solid, engaged and responsive keyworkers and care teams. This alliance provided a strong foundational base for the children and young people involved in the initiative, where successes, challenges and next steps were discussed in a unified way.

Being able to respond in a therapeutic manner to a child or young person can be a difficult task. Many professionals, including keyworkers and care team members, were observed to become nervous or anxious at the beginning of the therapeutic life story work process. Observations included keyworkers who talked consistently during the session or carers who were anxious about the sadness the child or young person might be experiencing during the sessions and did not feel adequate in being able to provide support.

A useful technique we found was having a conversation with the keyworker prior to each session to ensure that they were prepared for what was going to be discussed. In some instances, where keyworkers struggled with the silent spaces, the therapeutic life story work practitioner introduced a 'talking stick' for people to hold when it was their turn to say something.

Keyworker discussions prior to each session allowed for exploration of the keyworker's current emotional capacity and ability to support the young person in the sessions. Often if the observed presentation of the keyworker was acknowledged, this allowed them to engage in an open conversation. This was a therapeutically driven conversation to promote self-reflection and prepare the keyworker for the sessions.

## The stuck child and care team

The initiative also experienced occasions where the therapeutic life story work did not go as planned. The therapeutic life story work practitioner attempted engagement but the child or young person was successful in thwarting them at every corner. The child or young person may not have been ready to contemplate the concept of another worker in their life or perhaps felt the environment they existed in was not stable or secure enough to support and enable the therapeutic life story work process.

In this situation it can take time for the relevant support services to assess and develop effective strategies to address and manage the needs of the child. The therapeutic life story work was put on hold until a more stable time in the child's life to recommence was identified. Throughout this experience the practitioner recognised the importance in attempting some contact with the child and keeping the child informed. After each scheduled session that did not happen due to the child not being available, the practitioner sent a letter to the child letting them know that she was thinking of them. When a decision to place the therapeutic life story work on hold was made, a letter was hand written and posted to the child's residential address informing them of the decision and wishing them well. The aim was to tell the children that they were important and valued and that, although this may not be the right time for life story work, it could be revisited in the future.

If a child was not ready or able to participate in the fortnightly therapeutic life story work sessions, the information-gathering component of the work could still occur in preparation for a time when the child was ready and able. This provided access to invaluable history regarding the child and their family and opened doors to enable positive future opportunities for the child. By interviewing family friends, who had had little contact with the department over the years, a practitioner was able to identify informal supports that could be assessed as safe to be reintroduced into the child's life.

# Considerations for future sustainability of therapeutic life story work and techniques

Through evidence and experience, it has become apparent that new and innovative interventions are required to support our traumatised and at risk children and young people. Considerable thought has been given to the sustainability of the therapeutic life story work model. To date two options have been explored: the use of therapeutic life story work tools in family-led decision-making and therapeutic interventions. Below are the reflections of two practitioners experienced in these interventions.

## *Reflections from a family-led decision-making practice leader*

A family-led decision-making model has been used in the Inner Eastern Melbourne Area since 2008 when it was introduced as part of a demonstration project about how child protection services could do business with families and children, with the hope of better long-term outcomes. The goal was to have families and children and young people involved in creating workable and sustainable case plans that all parties then owned. Since 2008, over 3000 families have participated in the family-led decision-making process. Three common themes that anecdotally appear to be present in most family-led decision-making sessions are:

- unfinished emotional issues, often stemming from some form of familial or childhood trauma

- unresolved grief and loss

- social or medical labels that have not been properly explored and by which the child/family now self-identifies – for example, hyperactive, low functioning, obsessive compulsive.

These issues have impacted on how clients involved with child protection services have been perceived by professionals, which in turn has often affected the way they behave and are assessed and judged. The therapeutic life story work model and its tools can effectively be used by child protection services in working with long-term clients to explore and unravel issues of identity and worth. The result of therapeutic life story work with this cohort of children can then be used, with the child's permission, to help work with their family through the family-led decision-making process. Specific tools like the 'life tree' can also be creatively used in family-led decision making, together with a family tree to map out the issues for the child and young person and how the adults/parents impact on the issues from the child's perspective.

In certain situations, the use of Jenga blocks with key questions would be a valuable tool if used between child and parent(s) or carers facilitated by the family-led decision-making convener, as a way of sensitively exploring issues and solutions between the parent(s) and child. One could imagine the potential for positive impact if both parent(s) and child were given a disposable camera and asked to create a collection of photos together and separately, mapping the issues important to them as individuals and as family members.

With the child's permission and involvement, where suitable, the use of completed therapeutic life story work wallpaper or a book created by the child to commence the family-led decision-making process ensures that the voice of the child is at the centre of decision making and case planning.

By using therapeutic life story work and its tools of communication we may begin to unravel and understand the unfinished business for the child and family so it has less of a chance of evolving within further generations. We may even be able to address some issues of grief and loss by planting the seed in those affected to further address the blockages impacting on their lives and family connections. As professionals, it may improve our understanding about a child or family in terms of 'what really is' and 'what is not' in terms of our assessments, together with working out 'what really can be' and 'what cannot be' in terms of our decision making and planning with children and families.

## Reflections from a therapeutic specialist working with a sibling group

Through the increased sense of safety and security created in the sessions, the therapeutic relationship between four siblings, their discreet residential keyworker and the therapeutic life story work practitioner was strengthened and used as the primary tool in the healing process from their childhood trauma. It is within these relationships that the healing and the magic happened.

Throughout the programme the children were observed becoming more regulated and connected to others, more aware of their bodies and their feelings, and each child has shown an increased and more balanced sense of identity through the integration of both positive and negative information.

Through the games of Jenga, pick-up sticks and balloon popping, rapport and a sense of safety was built between each child, their residential keyworker and the therapeutic life story work practitioner in a playful and non-confrontational way. Through body-scan activities and feeling charades, the children experienced an increased ability in reading and expressing emotions and a stronger connection to their bodies. Through the use of family tree, behaviour tree and timeline activities, a more balanced sense of identity appeared to emerge in the children, as they began to gain a greater understanding into their journey. Through the honest and open sharing of information, the children were able to eliminate 'magical thinking' and the potentially idealised fantasies that this can create.

With this sibling group we have discovered that each child has a different understanding and experience of their past. By addressing all the issues and informing why things happened from the viewpoint of those involved, the child no longer needs to fill the gaps with their own guesses and assumptions and, in many cases, self-blame and shame. This is an exciting piece of work and holds great value for these children in creating an individual narrative for each child but also in creating a collective narrative that they can all share.

## The way forward

The introduction of a therapeutic life story worker into an existing care team changes the dynamics. The focus of all involved will deliver the best outcomes and care, leading to the wellbeing of the child. For therapeutic life story work to be successful, it is imperative that a positive partnership between the practitioner and the care team is established and then maintained. Information sharing, clarity of roles, shared goals and decision making and respect for each other's expertise and knowledge are of paramount importance.

Chapter 12

# THE IMPLEMENTATION OF THERAPEUTIC LIFE STORY WORK

*Dr Jodie Park, private practitioner, Illawarra,*
*New South Wales, Australia*

## Introduction

The goal of this chapter is to discuss the implementation of therapeutic life story work in the Illawarra region on the south coast of New South Wales (NSW). This discussion will provide a statistical summary of the Illawarra with an emphasis on describing the existing out-of-home care (OOHC) service system for the region. The chapter will then present an overview of an informal therapeutic life story work pilot programme, which has been in place since September 2015. The pilot programme involves the practitioner and two different non-government OOHC service providers. This will lead to the presentation of three case studies, which will illustrate therapeutic life story work in action. The case study discussion will critically reflect on the success and the challenges of the implementation and intervention process by considering the intervention from a clinical perspective to determine if the therapeutic life story work intervention has assisted the child and carer to understand, process and explore the child's narrative.

The discussion in this chapter will be presented as a qualitative reflection of the pilot programme. It will also have an emphasis on exploring the practice that has underpinned the implementation process.

## Setting the scene – the out-of-home care context in the Illawarra region

The Illawarra is located approximately 90 kilometres from Sydney and has been commonly described as one of the biggest regional towns in NSW. Statistics from the NSW Department of Family and Community Services (FACS) show that in 2013 the population of the Illawarra was 391,769, which equates to 5.3 per cent of the total population for NSW (NSW Department of Family and Community Services 2016). It must be noted that any statistics provided by FACS include the Shoalhaven region in addition to the Illawarra as both have been combined as one FACS district. For the purpose of the discussion in this chapter, the description of the FACS data will refer only to the Illawarra, as the statistics have been included to provide an overview of the OOHC context for the Illawarra and the inclusion of the Shoalhaven figures does not impact greatly on the context discussion.

There are nine non-government OOHC service providers in the Illawarra region. In addition, OOHC is also provided by Family and Community Services, which are responsible for statutory child protection and the organisation of OOHC for NSW. There is one Aboriginal-specific non-government agency that is funded to provide foster care placements for indigenous children and young people. The FACS data states that 2.9 per cent of the population in the Illawarra identifies as Aboriginal or Torres Strait Islander. The OOHC service provider case manages children and young people residing in foster, kinship and residential care arrangements.

The statistics (NSW Department of Family and Community Services 2016) indicate that (as of June 2015) there are 17,588 children and young people in OOHC in NSW. Of these 17,588 children/young people, 36.8 per cent are identified as being Aboriginal or Torres Strait Islander. For the same time period (June 2015), the statistics demonstrate that there are 5286 foster care and 7876 relative/kinship care households in NSW. In the Illawarra region, there are 1356 children and young people living in a foster or relative/kin OOHC care arrangement. Of these 1356 children/young people, 659 are case managed by a non-government service provider. This means that there are high numbers of children, young people and families in general who require therapeutic intervention to assist in managing the emotional and behavioural consequences of trauma. It is for this reason that the decision was made for my practice to focus on building therapeutic life story work as a viable intervention method.

# Why therapeutic life story work?

I am a social worker who has been working with children and families for the past 17 years. In this time, I have held a number of roles, but predominantly I have always worked with families where there are current child protection risk factors. For nine years I worked as a caseworker and middle manager in a statutory child protection office. I removed children from their parents and placed them in alternative care settings with authorised foster care or kinship carers, in the belief that I was promoting safety and permanency for the children. When I look back at these years, I can see that I promoted safety but I am less convinced about promoting permanency. I have my concerns about a child protection and OOHC system that has an almost resigned view that placement instability is going to occur. We have access to an enormous amount of literature that tells us how to assess foster carers to promote positive outcomes for children (Bromfield and Osborn 2007; Kelly and Salmon 2014; Leahy et al. 1999; Osborn et al. 2008). In addition, we know that children who have experienced abuse and neglect are also at a much higher risk of developing attachment dysregulation (Breidenstine et al. 2011; Barber and Delfabbro 2005; Dallos and Vetere 2014; Rose 2012; Tarren-Sweeny 2013), which is a contributing factor to placement breakdown and instability.

Despite this knowledge, placement breakdowns still occur and placement instability continues. It is my clinical belief that the child protection and OOHC service system has become so enmeshed with discourses of risk aversion and accountability that practitioners specialising in the field have lost the capacity to view difficult behaviours and attachment dysregulation as a relationship and trauma issue rather than an individual pathology. We are working with children who have experienced significant harm, which has fundamentally impacted on their capacity to feel physically and emotionally safe. Because of this, maladaptive coping behaviours have developed to assist the child to manage times of feeling scared, anxious or not in control of themselves or their environment (Kelly and Salmon 2014; Rose 2012). The demonstration of coping behaviours is to be expected. As a service system, we must get better at recognising and understanding that trauma behaviours will occur and that our role as practitioners is not to label these behaviours, but rather to promote a reparative environment that empowers our children and carers to believe that emotional and behavioural change is possible (Collins 2015).

We know that some children who reside in OOHC have developed an internal working model that views relationships as a threat. This generally results in a cycle of internal and external instability, which impacts on the longevity of their placement and the capacity for the child to develop an attached relationship with their caregiver (Breidenstine *et al.* 2011; Barber and Delfabbro 2005; Osborn et al 2008; Rose 2012; Tarren-Sweeny 2013). Building the relationship between a child and their caregiver is paramount to maintaining placement stability so that the child can benefit from a reparative environment. It stands to reason that if a child has been harmed by their relationships, then they require a relationship where they can experience unconditional positive regard, which includes a sense of belonging and connectedness, to help to repair the harm.

This sense of stability is fundamental to the therapeutic life story model, as Richard Rose states: 'Creating an environment that is dependable, boundaries that are strong, explained and visible, creates the opportunity for the child to begin to relate with the external world' (Rose 2012, p.58).

In 2013, I found myself working as a practice specialist for a non-government OOHC service provider. This service provider is a large national organisation that specialises in a myriad of services in different locations but has a core business model based on providing OOHC throughout Australia. For the first time in my career I found myself interacting daily with a local and a state clinical team whose views on the role of trauma differed greatly to my own. The word trauma was being used as a precursor for assessment, intervention, diagnosis and placement support. I had never heard the word trauma being used so much, and I found myself really interested in this. During one day, I counted how many times the word trauma was used; it added up to 242 times in a seven-hour working day.

I began to wonder about trauma and how the use of the word transferred to practice. I read children's files and undertook countless file and practice reviews and yet I couldn't see a link between 'trauma' as a word and 'trauma' as a holistic assessment consideration to help explain the emotional and behavioural functioning of children in their care environment. I found that there was a reliance on 'trauma' without understanding how trauma experiences impacted on the holistic experience of the child in their placement. Placements would break down frequently, and the child's behaviour would be blamed for this. There was seemingly a lack of acknowledgement that the key to placement stability was to build a reparative placement environment for a child. The key to building a reparative environment was by targeting intervention to encourage and promote the development of safety, security and predictability, physically but also emotionally, for a child in their environment. This included the development of realistic expectations about the child's ability to form relational bonds.

> So often the emotional climate in the foster home, particularly empathy for the child, is a core component in effecting positive behavioral change in the child. If the foster parents can truly understand the cause of the child's emotional turmoil, it makes it easier to tolerate and appropriately respond to. This is relevant in any situation involving distressed children. (Single 2005, p.38)

It was around this time that I attended a training session with Richard Rose about therapeutic life story work. This model of practice made sense to me because it mirrored my clinical belief about the role of relationships, attachment and trauma processing. I found myself exploring or revisiting literature about attachment, trauma processing, reparative relationships, treatment models (narrative therapy, play therapy and trauma-focused cognitive behavioural therapy, to name a few) and whatever else I could find about therapy models for children and young people. I started to develop my own treatment models of practice and used these in my direct work with children, foster carers and staff. When the time came for me to start a private social work practice, my experiences in child protection and OOHC, coupled with the model developed by Richard Rose, guided me in making a decision to focus on implementing therapeutic life story work as a practice model.

## The implementation process

The implementation of therapeutic life story work as an accepted practice model was a process. For the model to become an accepted intervention method in the region, there was a need to not only publicise the service to OOHC service providers but also to gather some traction about the service by demonstrating the intervention method in practice.

The first step was to develop a practice framework that could be promoted to the OOHC agencies as a way of educating them about what therapeutic life story work was. During my discussions with service providers I found that there were differing levels of understanding about what constitutes story work, life history work and therapeutic life story work.

In general, OOHC service providers have a sound understanding of the importance of life story work, as this is a requirement for OOHC accreditation. In NSW, life story work in terms of collecting information and documenting a child's journey in OOHC is reviewed by the NSW Office of the Children's Guardian as part of the accreditation process. All OOHC agencies need to demonstrate how they have met the standards of care as outlined in the *NSW Child Safe Standards for Permanent Care, November 2015* (NSW Office of the Children's Guardian). There are 23 standards that are broken up into four separate sections. Section 1 is titled 'Children and young people – care and wellbeing' and covers standards 1–12. Section 2 is titled 'Casework practice to support care' and covers standards 13–17. Section 3 is titled 'People who work with and care for children and young people' and covers standards 18–20. Finally, section 4 covers 'Child safe organisations' and includes standards 21–23. Life story work is discussed primarily in standard 4, which is about promoting a child's identity, and standard 17, which is concerned with the documentation of a child's story in care. The accepted practice for life story work is to provide the child with a life story book in which they can record important aspects of their life. In addition, there is an expectation that the child's carer will collect significant documentation and photos that are kept as memorabilia and presented to the child when they leave the placement. Evidence of life story work is also given to the agency and recorded in the child's file so that they can ensure that they meet their accreditation requirements.

While the above examples of life story work are appropriate and important, they do little to help the child to process and understand their history.

> In essence, life story therapy is not just about the who, what, where, when and why of events – it is also about the consequences of those events, and how they drive the child, and present issues and difficulties. (Rose 2012, p.26)

It is the above definition of therapeutic life story work that was important to promote to the agencies, as a way of ensuring that there was a joint understanding about the intervention and its application with children and their carers. To do this, I developed a practice framework that was very much based on the model. The practice framework is broken into five distinct stages, which will be discussed below.

The initial promotion of the therapeutic practice framework occurred by using my established industry networks. I requested meetings with caseworkers and managers and attended team meetings. I also presented at OOHC practice forums where I discussed trauma experiences for children in OOHC and the impact that these experiences may have on placement and relationship stability. During these meetings I discussed therapeutic life story work and what the benefits of the intervention could be to the child, the placement and the agency.

The next step to the implementation was to provide training about the intervention model to non-government OOHC staff and foster carers. I developed a one-day training package that included information about the life story intervention and the underpinning theories for it, including trauma, attachment, emotional functioning, neurobiology, play therapy and narrative therapy. The training package was successful in promoting the intervention and resulted in a lot of interest from workers and foster carers who wanted to make referrals. It must be noted that the biggest interest came from foster carers. In my conversations with carers about this, they have told me that they liked the fact that the therapeutic practice framework included them and was very much based on promoting placement stability by exploring and processing the child's narrative together. In addition, workers expressed that they liked the practice framework because the carer was part of the process but also because the workers were kept informed about the intervention due to the use of session outcome sheets that were provided to the carer and the agency caseworker after each session. This allowed the workers to track the intervention and encouraged a teamwork approach between the practitioner, the child, the carer and the agency.

The idea of implementing the service as a pilot programme was developed as a way of introducing the intervention into the region. In essence, a pilot programme meant that the service implementation was being trialled to determine if it met the needs of the target population. While the therapeutic life story work model developed by Richard Rose is well regarded and clearly meets the needs of children and carers nationally and internationally, I was concerned about how the model could be enacted in the Illawarra region by a sole practitioner. By calling the intervention a pilot, this allowed me the space to change the practice framework in the future if this was required.

## Practice framework – stages of intervention

The practice framework detailed below was developed to ensure that the intervention had a sound structural basis. The framework is a staged process and helps to ensure that the child's narrative is known to the practitioner so that the intervention can be holistic. In addition, the practitioner can plan intervention strategies that may assist in the trauma processing.

## Stage 1: Prepare the information bank

This is the first step of the model. It is in this stage where I am reading, reviewing and collecting information about the child. This information comes from various sources, including the child's agency OOHC file, meetings with the agency caseworker and manager, and interviews with significant people as identified by the caseworker and manager. This is an interesting step in the process because while I am concerned about ensuring that I have a holistic picture of the child's trauma experiences to date, I am also thinking about what case history information is missing and how I can source this information. In addition, I am also concerned about ensuring that I have information that is more qualitative about the child. This is information that I gather from the children's parents and previous carers. In my conversations with them I am not really concerned about their understanding of the child's care and protection history, but about obtaining nurturing information and stories about the child that can be included in the information bank. For example:

- What was the child's favourite toy?

- What was their favourite book?

- Can you tell me some funny stories about them?

- What are your favourite things about the child?

- What do you most want them to know about you?

- Do you have any photos that I can copy to give the child?

Once I have completed the information gathering, I prepare an information bank, which includes a summary of the above information. The information bank is written in child-appropriate language as it is given to the child.

The information bank covers the following domains in separate boxes:

- Maternal and paternal family members, names, ages, location.

- The current name of the school the child attends and the names of their previous schools. I like to include the names of all the school teachers if this information can be found. For previous schools, I note the dates they attended and a sentence on why they left.

- Previous counselling or emotional support that the child may have interacted with. Again, I note down the name of the counsellor and when they attended.

- The birth family contact arrangements.

- Activities that the child likes to do. I also include names of their friends in this section.

- A description of behaviours.

- 'About…child'. The information included in this section is about where they were born, any previous addresses and who lived with them, and funny stories or information I have gained from their parents or other significant people.

- Placement history – the name of the carer, dates of placement and location.

- What happened at home. This includes a summary of the care and protection concerns.

- Words used to describe the child – these are taken from the file and from my interviews with significant parties.

Each domain has at least two questions listed. These questions form the basis of the initial sessions with the child.

## Stage 2: Psychosocial assessment

An assessment is completed with the child's foster carers prior to meeting the child. The assessment is undertaken over two home visits and is primarily concerned with gauging the carer's motivation and commitment to being part of the process. One of the first questions I ask the carer is about the child's understanding of the process. If I feel that the child is either not ready, or not aware of what is expected, then I will either meet with them or factor this into the assessment analysis and discussion.

The assessment covers the following areas:

- Purpose of the report.

- Terms of reference for the assessment.

- Process of the assessment.

- Limitations to the assessment.

- Child protection and placement history – including a summary of birth family contact and any notable parent–child interactions.

- Demonstrated impact of the child protection history on the child's cognitive and emotional development – including a discussion about the child's internal working model.

- Clinical impressions of the child's internal and external coping skills.

- Nature of the child's current relationships and connections.

- Carer's commitment to the process.

- Recommendations.

The agency and the carer(s) are given a copy of the assessment.

## Stage 3: Session planning

This stage is crucial to ensuring that the intervention flows each week and doesn't become disjointed. This stage is also important as it keeps the practitioner task focused so that the child is not exposed to unnecessary intervention. While the flow of the sessions is somewhat planned for the entire intervention, this does not mean that you remain so focused on each session plan that you do not address issues as they arise. My session planning provides a loose structure only, and the session content and trauma-processing strategies change to reflect the changing needs of the child.

A session outcome is completed after each session and a copy given to the carer and the agency.

## Stage 4: Intervention

The intervention stage is initially planned to include nine sessions at one hour per fortnight. Appointments are made for the same time and day each fortnight to build consistency and predictability for the child. For some children, nine sessions have been enough; for others, I have needed to re-negotiate with the carers and the agency to increase the sessions by an additional six. The intervention occurs in the child's home with the carer. This stage of the framework refers to what Rose has termed the internalisation process (Rose 2012). The internalisation stage is where the narrative unfolds and the trauma processing occurs.

## Stage 5: Closure

This stage involves preparing and presenting the child with their life story book. It also involves the preparation of a brief intervention report that summarises the intervention and makes recommendations for any future support needs.

# The pilot programme

An informal agreement to commence a therapeutic life story pilot programme was formed with two non-government service providers in the Illawarra. The pilot programme commenced in September 2015, and to date six referrals have been received from the services. Of these referrals, the intervention commenced for five children. One child has recently finished the intervention and provided positive feedback about their experience. This will be discussed further below in the case study presentation.

The development of a pilot programme ensured that the intervention would receive referrals, which, as discussed above, assisted in the intervention becoming known in the Illawarra. The pilot programme also allowed the agency and the practitioner to review the intervention to determine if changes were needed to better meet the needs of the target population.

The pilot programme was based on the following agreements:

- The practitioner would prioritise the agency's referrals and provide the intervention at a discounted cost.

- The practitioner could use the case studies to promote the intervention in educational forums. All identifying information about the children would be changed.

- The pilot programme would be qualitatively evaluated after each intervention to determine the following:

  o Did the child and carer feel that the intervention was helpful and useful?

  o Did the agency find the intervention was helpful and useful for the placement?

  o Does the practice framework require amending?

The case studies below will provide an illustration of the therapeutic life story work in action. Please note that names and identifying details have been changed to preserve anonymity.

## CASE STUDY: TONYA

Tonya was the first child referred to the programme. Tonya is nine years old. She lives with her great aunt and uncle and has been in this placement for three years. Prior to this placement, Tonya resided in three short-term care arrangements. She was removed from her parents' care when she was five years old. The child protection concerns for Tonya included:

- Parental drug use

- Neglect including supervisory and educational neglect

- Parental mental health concerns.

Tonya's mother is described in the paperwork as having significant mental health concerns, including paranoia and manic behaviours. Tonya demonstrates external behaviours at home and at school which have resulted in numerous school suspensions. She has a history of being verbally and physically aggressive towards her school teachers and carers. Tonya has numerous behavioural diagnoses including attention deficit disorder and oppositional defiance disorder. She finds it hard to remain settled in one spot for any length of time and demonstrates hypervigilant behaviours and a need to control her environment at all times. This includes needing to know where each of her carers is at any given time of the day.

Tonya's care arrangement has been tenuous at times. Her carers have oscillated between being supportive of her and being overwhelmed about their ability to manage her external behaviours.

A psychosocial assessment was completed for Tonya and a copy was provided to the agency and the carers. The practitioner and Tonya commenced their sessions in November 2015. Tonya presented as interested in the practitioner and enjoyed playing games. She engaged in conversations about herself but refused to discuss her mother. In each session that occurred, Tonya was observed to remain focused for a few minutes more than the previous session. This was positive, and the practitioner could anticipate that, while progress would be slow, just having Tonya engaged for the full hour would be a success. The engagement was centred on mindfulness strategies and specifically on role-modelling a strategy of colouring. The practitioner and Tonya made an agreement that, when Tonya disengaged from the session, the practitioner would remain and colour in a stencil until Tonya returned. Tonya became very interested in the colouring in, so while she disengaged frequently, the time of disengagement became less.

The process of intervention had to be creative as Tonya refused to write or draw on the wallpaper. Each session she would bring the wallpaper out but would be clear that she would not unroll it. The paper was not unrolled until the fourth session. On this session, Tonya refused to engage with the paper but allowed the practitioner to write some words. A pattern was emerging about what were safe topics for Tonya and what would cause her to disengage and escalate in terms of behaviours. Tonya was happy to talk about her strengths, her father and her grandparents, but was unable to discuss her feelings or her mother. There was a significant disconnect between Tonya's thoughts, feelings and behaviours, which was impacted on by her hyperarousal.

The intervention concluded in January 2016. A request to increase the intervention was made by Tonya's carers as they felt that her 'behaviours' were becoming worse. A report was prepared for the agency, which included recommendations for future support.

## CASE STUDY: LISA

Lisa is eight years old and has been in her current placement since she was four. Lisa was removed from her parents' care due to parental mental health concerns, neglect and exposure to domestic violence. She was two years old when she was removed and experienced four previous placements before coming to live with Susan and Greg. On entering OOHC, the sibling group was split and Lisa was always placed with her older brother Simon. Simon is four years older than Lisa. He has a history of demonstrating external behaviours, and a decision was made approximately three years ago to separate Lisa and Simon.

In reading Lisa's files, it became very clear that she did not have an understanding of why she was in OOHC and why she was separated from her brother. Lisa was very comfortable with her foster parents but became emotionally dysregulated easily if her routine was changed and there was no predictability in terms of what she could expect to happen next. Lisa would demonstrate external tantrum behaviours that could last for hours. She had previously experienced psychological intervention with a focus on exploring her life history. This occurred in 2015 and was not therapeutic life story work, but rather counselling with a life history goal.

The sessions with Lisa and her carer, Susan, commenced in February 2016. In total, Lisa participated in ten sessions. In the first few sessions she was very keen to please the practitioner. She participated fully for the whole hour and worked hard on her wallpaper. When asked questions she didn't want to answer, Lisa would start to demonstrate some diversionary behaviour. During the first few sessions these consisted of joking, dancing and using different voices. Lisa was able to articulate and demonstrate her thoughts and feelings about certain topics, although she became overly critical of herself and expressed negative thoughts about her strengths and accomplishments. By the fourth session, Lisa's self-efficacy had become so negative that she could not name anything that she did well. When her carer identified strengths about Lisa, she became overwhelmed and disengaged from the therapy. When she resumed her engagement, Lisa and the practitioner developed a list of affirmations for Lisa to say to herself each day. The list included four points:

- I am Lisa

- I am funny

- I am smart

- I am lovable.

Lisa took ownership over the development of the affirmations and still says the affirmations each day. She was able to express that she thinks her brother Simon doesn't love her any more and that this is upsetting her.

In subsequent sessions, Lisa's engagement in the process wavered considerably. She had become focused on wanting to live with her biological parents, which was unusual for her. The fact, fiction, fantasy, heroism template (Rose 2012, p.120) was used to explore this with her. Lisa was able to identify that living with her parents was a fantasy. By the seventh session, Lisa had told Susan that she did not want to participate in life story work any more because it was hard for her. A decision was made that the seventh session would be about playing. Play doh, Uno cards, Jenga and colouring-in stencils were brought to the home and Lisa was in charge of what was done. This was an important session because it allowed Lisa to take charge, which gave her back a sense of control. A negotiation process occurred at the end of this session between Lisa and the practitioner, and it was decided that time to play as well as time to work would be factored in. The agreement was written on the wallpaper.

This was a turning point in the intervention. In sessions nine and ten, Lisa articulated that she was 'ready to be honest even though it was hard'. Strategies such as the behaviour tree (Rose 2012, p.129) and the preoccupation activity (Rose 2012, p.127) have been instrumental in allowing Lisa to explore her honest feelings about her biological parents. In addition, Lisa's self-efficacy has improved and she is able to verbalise that she is proud of herself for working so hard.

## CASE STUDY: SIMON

Simon is 13 years old. He has been living with his current foster carers since he was nine years old. Simon is the sibling of Lisa (see above) and was removed from his parents' care at the age of six. The child protection risk factors for Simon included parental mental health concerns, neglect and exposure to domestic violence. Simon was his mother's protector and described in detail how he would pull his father away from his mother during times of violence, or he would stand in front of his mother to protect her.

Simon has had eight previous foster care placements. He is able to name each carer and say where his placements were located. His emotional connection to each of these placements was explored as part of the life story work intervention.

Simon has a history of behaviours, which includes being violent and aggressive towards his foster carers, his school teachers and other adults. Simon has previously been diagnosed with anxiety and post-traumatic stress disorder. He was labelled as being emotionally disturbed and was placed in a behavioural unit at school.

Simon and his carers have worked hard at building stability, predictability and routine for him. Simon's instances of external behaviours have reduced considerably in all areas of his life and he was placed back in a mainstream school in Year 6. Simon attends a mainstream high school and is doing well. At the commencement of therapeutic life story work, the practitioner observed that Simon had a good understanding of his emotional and behavioural functioning. His carers had taught him about understanding how his body changes as a response to stress. Simon referred to this a great deal during the intervention.

Simon commenced therapeutic intervention in March 2016 and participated in nine sessions in total. Simon and his carer have provided qualitative feedback about the life story work process. Simon discussed that he now understands how his history has impacted on how he thinks about things. He is now confident and secure in the knowledge that his carers love him. Most importantly, he feels worthy of being loved and knows that he is not responsible for protecting his mother any more and that he can have a life that is different from his parents.

## Practice lessons and challenges – conclusions

The implementation of life story work in the Illawarra region has been an interesting mixture of practice lessons and challenges. These are detailed below:

- As identified in the case studies above, the children who have participated in the programme to date have been similar in some regards but then very different in how they have responded to the intervention. This has meant that I have relied on my practice knowledge to know how to respond to each challenge as it has arisen. It is very important that anyone commencing this work has an established set of practice skills that they can employ quickly.

- The pilot programme has worked very well with the existing two agencies. It remains a challenge that the other OOHC service providers in the region have not sought to implement the intervention for their children and carers. This will impact on therapeutic life story work being seen as a standard model of intervention.

- More assessment is required before initiating the intervention with kinship carers or in placements where internal or external stressors are impacting on the carers' coping mechanisms. As can be seen in the case study of Tonya, the intervention with her was not fully supported by her carers and this impacted on the intervention process.

- The implementation of the pilot is still very much in its infancy. More work is required to evaluate the programme to form a strong evidence base for the intervention in the Illawarra.

# References

Barber, J., and Delfabbro, P. (2005) 'Children's adjustment to long-term foster care.' *Children and Youth Services Review, 27*, 329-340

Breidenstine, A., O'Bailey, L., Zeanah, C. and Larrieu, J. (2011) 'Attachment and trauma in early childhood: A review.' *Journal of Child and Adolescent Trauma 4*, 274–290.

Collins, S. (2015) 'Hope and helping in social work.' *Practice 27, 3*, 197–213.

Dallos, R. and Vetere, A. (2014) 'Systemic therapy and attachment narratives: attachment narrative therapy.' *Clinical Child Psychology 19,4*, 494–502.

Kelly, W. and Salmon, K. (2014) 'Helping foster parents understand the foster child's perspective: a relational learning framework for foster care.' *Clinical Child Psychology 19,4* 535–547.

Leahy, R., Little, C., Mondy, C., and Nixon, D. (1999) 'What makes good outcomes for children in foster care'. *Children Australia 24,2*, 4-9.

NSW Department of Family and Community Services (2016) *District Data and profiles 2013–2014*. Available at www.facs.nsw.gov.au/facs-statistics/facs-districts/illawarra-shoalhaven, accessed on 25 June 2016.

NSW Office of the Children's Guardian (2015) *Child Safe Standards for Permanent Care*. Available at https://www.kidsguardian.nsw.gov.au/ArticleDocuments/449/ChildSafeStandards_PermanentCare, accessed on 25 June 2016.

Osborn, A., and Bromfield, L. (2007) 'Outcomes for children and young people in care'. *Research Brief 3*, 1–15.

Osborn, A., Delfabbro, P. and Barber, J. (2008) 'The psychosocial functioning and family background of children experiencing significant placement instability in Australian out-of-home care.' *Children and Youth Services 30*, 847–860.

Rose, R. (2012) *Life Story Therapy with Traumatized Children: A Model for Practice.* London: Jessica Kingsley Publishers.

Single, T. (2005) *Long Term Foster Care for Abused and Neglected Children: How Foster Parents Can Help in Healing Trauma.* Newcastle, Australia: John Hunter Children's Hospital.

Tarren-Sweeny, M. (2013) 'An investigation of complex attachment and trauma related symptomatology among children in foster care and kinship care.' Child Psychiatry, *Human Development 44,* 727–741.

# Further Reading

Australian Institute of Family Studies (2015) Child Family Community Australia (CFCA) Resource Sheet – June 2015. Available at https://aifs.gov.au/cfca/publications/children-care, accessed on 25 June 2016.

Becker-Weidman, A. (2006) 'Treatment for children with trauma-attachment disorders: dyadic developmental psychotherapy.' *Child and Adolescent Social Work Journal* 23(2), 147–171.

Bowlby, J. (1982) *Attachment.* New York: Basic Books.

Braungart-Rieker, J., Zentall, S., Lickenbrook, D., Ekas, N., Oshio, T. and Planalp, E. (2014) 'Attachment in the making: mother and father sensitivity and infants' responses during the Still-Face Paradigm.' *Journal of Experiential Child Psychology* 125, 63–84.

Center on the Developing Child (2016) Toxic Stress. Available at http://developingchild.harvard.edu/science/key-concepts/toxic-stress, accessed on 4 June 2016.

Chenoweth, L. and McAuliffe, D. (2015) *The Road to Social Work and Human Services Practice.* Victoria: Cengage Learning Australia.

Cohen, J., Mannarino, A. and Deblinger, E. (2012) *Trauma-Focused CBT for Children and Adolescents.* New York: Guilford Press.

Cozolino, L. (2010) *The Neuroscience of Psychotherapy.* New York: W.W. Norton & Company.

Hulbert, C., Jennings, T., Jackson, H. and Chanen, A. (2011) 'Attachment style and schema as predictors of social functioning in youth with borderline features.' *Personality and Mental Health* 5, 209–221.

Kezelman, C. and Stavropoulos, P. (2012) *The Last Frontier: Practice Guidelines for Treatment of Complex Trauma and Trauma-Informed Care and Service Delivery.* Kirribilli: Adults Surviving Child Abuse.

Mares, S. and Torres, M. (2014) 'Young foster children and their carers: an approach to assessing relationships.' *Clinical Child Psychology* 19(3), 367–383.

McDowall, J.J. (2013) *Experiencing Out-of-Home Care in Australia: The Views of Children and Young People* (CREATE Report Card 2013). Sydney: CREATE Foundation.

Osborn, A., Delfabbro, P. and Barber, J. (2008) 'The psychosocial functioning and family background of children experiencing significant placement instability in Australian out-of-home care.' *Children and Youth Services* 30, 847–860.

Price-Robertson, R., Rush, P., Wall, L. and Higgins, D. (2013) 'Rarely an isolated incident: acknowledging the interrelatedness of child maltreatment, victimization and trauma.' *Child Family Community Australia* 15, 1–11.

Riggs, S. (2010) 'Childhood emotional abuse and the attachment system across the life cycle: what theory and research tell us.' *Journal of Aggression, Maltreatment & Trauma* 19(1), 5–51.

Schore, J. (2012) 'Using concepts from interpersonal neurobiology in revisiting psychodynamic theory.' *Smith College Studies in Social Work* 82(1), 90–111.

Schore, J. and Schore, A. (2014) 'Regulation theory and affect regulation psychotherapy: a clinical primer.' *Smith College Studies in Social Work* 84(2–3), 178–195.

Turns, B. and Kimmes, J. (2014) 'I'm not the problem! Externalizing children's problems using play therapy and developmental considerations.' *Contemporary Family Therapy* 36, 135–147.

Chapter 13

# LIFE STORY THERAPY IN A SCHOOL SETTING

*Paula Price, Therapist and Learning Mentor, St Patrick's Catholic Primary School, Liverpool, UK.*

The model of therapeutic life story work as set out by Rose (2012a) can be applied to a range of settings and clients due to the flexible nature of the approach. In this chapter I will look at how life story therapy can be applied within a school setting. To ensure that confidentiality is maintained for children and their families, I have changed the names and randomly assigned genders of those involved, and I have not named the settings that they are based in.

## Schools' perspective

### Context

I am based in a mainstream primary school in Liverpool, and now deliver therapy services to primary and secondary schools across the city, and in social care settings. As I was based in my school when I undertook my training, the majority of my early clients were the pupils attending the school. Following increased interest from other schools and partner agencies about what was happening in my school, it was confirmed that there was a wider need for this work, not just within a social care setting, but also within schools. It was with this knowledge that discussions began around creating a service primarily for other schools, but also for other agencies.

While mainstream schools often look for therapy services, the knowledge of how to access them, or the ability to do so, may be limited. Many schools would say that they do not always know where to look for therapy services, outside the usual child and adolescent mental health services route, or what types of therapy approaches are available. There are currently very few schools that house a therapy service themselves. However, there is an obvious need for this type of support for schools and their pupils. Most schools take a holistic approach to children, and schools increasingly address a vast array of issues beyond their main remit of educating children. Therefore, most schools increasingly see therapy and therapeutic interventions as part of their role in caring for and educating children.

With this need in mind, a proposal was drawn up to outline how a therapy service could be set up and run from my school, offering services to schools and community agencies. In discussion with the headteacher at school, it was agreed that the proposal would be presented to the governing body. The proposal was approved, and the service now operates delivering life story therapy and play therapy to schools and other agencies across the city.

## Workplace culture

Each institution has its own culture, and within that each workplace has its own culture. Large institutions such as education, health and social care will have their own practical and ideological frameworks. With this in mind, there are some obvious variations in working in different settings, and these include the other professionals' understanding or perception of your work, and of the child's needs.

Furthermore, different professionals will have their own agenda depending on the service they work for and the outcomes they are expected to focus on.

Each partner's primary focus is a piece of an overall picture. Ultimately what each agency wants is to support the child to be a functioning, healthy, happy, achieving individual. Life story therapy achieves these various requirements precisely because it is a holistic approach and encompasses all the pieces of the picture.

## *Aims and objectives of a school setting*

Schools who use the therapy service will have a range of requirements, but chiefly their objectives are around supporting the child to function within the school setting and helping the child to be able to access learning. Schools need the child to be able to learn, to get along with others, to comply with routines and boundaries, and to have emotional wellbeing.

Some of the children who are referred for support will only be accessing limited learning, either because they are frequently unable to function in the classroom, are disengaged, being withdrawn from lessons, or at risk of permanent exclusion. Ultimately what schools want as a result of the child attending therapy is not to have to permanently exclude the child, and for the child to be able to stay in class, to work, to co-operate and to progress in their learning.

For many of the children requiring life story therapy, multiple, complex factors are affecting their ability to regulate their emotions and behaviours and to function in a healthy and appropriate way.

In summary, these difficulties may include hypervigilance, attachment difficulties, dissociation, dysregulation, trauma and developmental difficulties. The child may have difficulties understanding social behaviours and relating to others. They may have difficulties with memory, recall and processing, or sensory and somatic difficulties. They may have difficulties of unresolved trauma, or even ongoing trauma.

The impact of these is obvious – a child with such difficulties will struggle to be engaged in learning, to filter out distractions, to deal with being in a room of people for most of the day, and so on. However, there are certain aspects of school that can be beneficial to children with these difficulties, for example relationships with key people can be reassuring, and the routine and consistency of school can provide security.

Supporting the child to explore their history involves helping the child to see how that affects them in the present day and to begin to make changes. Later in this chapter I will explore in more detail how life story therapy addresses these difficulties, and in turn how that impacts on the child and their school.

## Setting up the systems for a school-based life story therapy service

*What shape will the service take?*

In my case I had already set up systems to deliver therapy within my own school and I was developing the service to roll out delivery of therapy to other schools and partners. It may be that others are looking to develop a service solely for their own school and pupils. The systems are largely the same, although you would not need to publicise your work outside your own setting. Assessment and evaluation are essential in either case.

Setting up the system at my school required strategic thinking about the stages of developing the service. What would we offer, how many clients could we cater for, and how many hours a week might be required to deliver this service? Once we had an idea about the shape the service would take, we had to create a referral process and how to measure the impact on individual clients, their carer(s) and their school. There was also a need to publicise the service, to think about the information potential referrers may need to know, and when, how and whom to approach. Finally, we also had to think about how to evaluate the service in relation to our school itself, to measure the impact on the school of delivering this service.

In the publicity information, I felt it was important to include a summary about the therapies on offer, and particularly life story therapy, as it is an emerging discipline and one largely unknown in educational settings. This information was initially shared at meetings for SENCOs (special educational needs co-ordinators), as they are often the people in schools charged with seeking support and commissioning services. I also approached LACES (Looked After Children Education Services) as they co-ordinate services for looked-after children in the education system across the city, and I felt they may have a particular need for life story therapy services.

## What systems will be put in place?

### Assessment and evaluation

Assessment and evaluation should always serve a purpose and truly inform practice. Assessment forms the basis of identifying what the child's needs are and frames how to address them. Reflection should be ongoing as this guides you through the process. Evaluation enables you to measure the impact of what you are doing.

Assessment and evaluation can be summarised as shown in Figure 13.1.

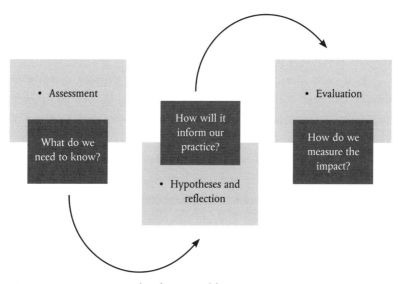

*Figure 13.1 An assessment and evaluation model*

Obviously, life story therapy also requires a very detailed history to be acquired via thorough research. This will also help you to form your hypotheses.

### Building hypotheses

Ann had been referred for therapeutic support. Underlying Ann's behaviours were her experiences of trauma and neglect. The daily uncertainty about the level of care that she would receive due to her parents' inconsistent caregiving and the regular threat of violence had made Ann hypervigilant. Teachers had referred to Ann's restlessness, how she was so easily distracted and her inability to function in class for long. Within the context of her experiences this made perfect sense. I felt that this made Ann vigilant to the actions of others but unable to regulate stress and respond appropriately.

The difficulties she had playing with other children indicated that she found people unreliable and untrustworthy and she could not read their social cues. As such it was simpler and safer to play alone.

When she ran away from people it appeared to suggest a 'fight or flight' response; her parents' care could become so readily unpredictable and aggressive that it was likely she was unable to regulate her response to any potential perceived threat. This would probably lead to her being unable to assess risk accurately, and see even innocuous incidents as high risk and potentially dangerous.

As a baby, Ann would have attuned to her primary caregiver – usually a mother – and as such would have attuned to their stress levels and their hyperarousal, caused by frequent arguments and the threat of violence.

There were possible attachment issues, considering how much parental depression, stress and conflict may have impacted on her mother's availability to care for Ann. Furthermore, her mother's history suggested that she may have insecure attachment patterns herself. I felt it likely that Ann's mother would regularly have been emotionally absent, which would have affected the consistency of Ann's care.

It is a reasonable hypothesis to suppose that where a child has experienced neglect and emotional harm to a degree that eventually causes the removal of the child from their parents, there is an increased likelihood that problems existed at the time of the child's birth, increasing the potential for poor attachment. 'More than 85% of children removed from their parents for abuse or neglect have disturbed attachment capacity' (Carlson *et al.* cited in Perry 2002, p.95).

Key areas to focus on for Ann would be supporting her to regulate her emotions; helping her to better understand people's actions; providing her with the space and opportunity to practise how to judge risk and trust, and begin to practise building relationships; and showing her how to minimise anxiety by learning to assess perceived risk within a less trauma-focused frame of reference and have one more suited to her current everyday life.

The tools for assessment and evaluation are incredibly important, as it is necessary to evidence that the therapy is beneficial and achieving positive outcomes. Evaluation needed to take place at various levels:

1. The impact on the individual child

2. The impact on the carers/parents

3. The impact for the commissioning body and the child's school should this be different

4. The impact on my own school.

Creating documents to assess, review and evaluate the child was my starting point, and in order to do this I had to think about the main elements that I wanted to assess. Inspired by the SHANARRI format of Safe, Healthy, Active, Nurtured, Achieving, Respected, Responsible and Included (Rose 2012a), I devised a tool to measure various elements to gain a holistic view of the child. This framework is described in more detail below. I felt strongly that any assessment and evaluation needed to include the child's own views, so a child-friendly version of this tool was created. I also used some established clinical assessment tools – other people may wish to use those for assessment and evaluation rather than devise their own, depending on how particularly you want to measure specific areas.

In addition, ongoing evaluation is done by discussion and verbal feedback, and a final evaluation form aims to evidence how effective the therapy has been and in what ways.

# Frameworks

## An assessment framework

For my purposes, I chose the following areas to assess and measure (as illustrated in Figure 13.2).

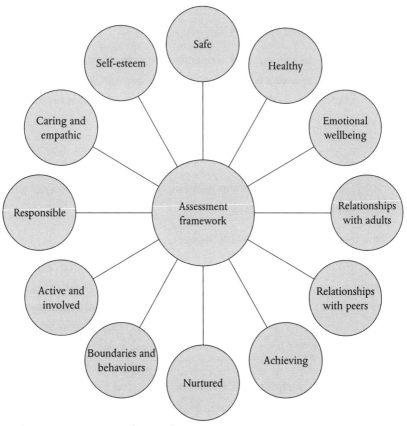

*Figure 13.2 An assessment framework*

- *Safe:* is the child in a secure base; do others keep the child safe; can the child keep themselves safe?

- *Healthy:* does the child have any medical conditions; does the child have any disabilities; does the child have a healthy lifestyle; is the child generally healthy; what are their eating habits; what are their sleeping habits?

- *Emotional wellbeing:* does the child understand their feelings; can the child manage their feelings; does the child express their feelings in a healthy way; are they resilient; do they have healthy coping mechanisms; are they able to be positive in their outlook?

- *Relationships with adults:* does the child have positive relationships with adults; do they have secure attachments; are they able to trust some adults; do they have a sense of belonging, or being part of a family?

- *Relationships with peers:* does the child have positive relationships with peers; do they have social skills; are they able to relate to peers; do they have a sense of belonging, or being part of a group?

- *Achieving:* is the child achieving in any areas, such as academic, sports, music, arts or anything else; even if they are not achieving age-related expectations, is the child making any progress?

- *Nurtured:* is the child supported by adults or peers; is the child cared for; does the child experience warmth and affection; does the child experience love?

- *Boundaries and behaviours:* is the child's behaviour generally positive; is the child able to manage their behaviour; is the child able to modify their behaviour for different situations; can the child accept boundaries; can the child function within boundaries?

- *Active and involved:* does the child participate in any activities; do they do any form of exercise; do they join in with clubs, activities or groups; do they engage in active play, such as skipping and running games, or are they generally sedentary, such as playing computer games?

- *Responsible:* what are the child's basic self-care skills like (i.e. washing, dressing, toileting); is the child able to care for themselves at an age-appropriate level; can the child organise themselves; is the child able to take responsibility for their actions; is the child reliable, or sensible; does the child demonstrate self-awareness?

- *Caring and empathic:* does the child understand that other people have feelings; is the child able to take other people's feelings into account; does the child generally care about others; is the child able to balance their own needs with the needs of others; does the child demonstrate warmth and affection towards others?

- *Self-esteem:* does the child have a sense of identity; does the child have any positive regard for themselves; does the child take any pride in themselves; can the child accept praise and recognise when they have done well?

## A framework for planning, practice and reflection

During the therapy work, ongoing reflection of your own actions will help to plan, deliver and evaluate your work on a session-by-session basis. It is important to reflect on what you did in a session, why you did it, why you chose the methods you used, and the impact this had (see Figure 13.3).

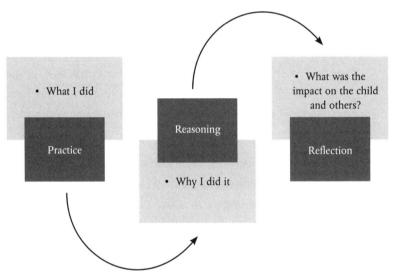

*Figure 13.3 A practice and reflection model*

For example, one of the children I worked with had multiple placement moves. One of the sessions was taking place in the week of her birthday. I decided to demonstrate her moves by drawing a cake for each year of her life and writing where she had lived at the time. The reasons for this included making it relevant to her and helping her to visualise the years that she had lived and the moves she had made. She was only young and the concept of time was difficult for her to understand, so the birthday cakes represented time in a way she could understand, like a long-term version of a child's 'how many sleeps until…' She also needed to see that, after multiple moves, she had now remained in her current placement for more than one birthday. The impact on the child was that she grasped the concept of the passage of time and how much change she had experienced. Most importantly, she could see that her current placement had not changed and she was beginning to understand the idea of what 'permanent' and 'forever' might mean.

However, that is not to suggest that every session adheres meticulously to a plan; it is just as important to be reactive. Sometimes the child brings something to the session and it is important that the therapist works with that. This might not always be dealt with straightaway; often children in their initial sessions ask a lot of questions, or really complex questions, such as, 'Why was I adopted but my brother wasn't?' In these cases it is necessary to explain to the child that as we work together we will try and answer those questions but that we may not have the answers today as they may need more explaining. These situations aside, quite often during your work with the child they will raise something, an incident will have happened, or they will introduce something seemingly innocuous that gives you something to work with. For example, one child wondered why they could remember some things and not others, and this led into a conversation about memory and how it works, and into a simple demonstration with water bottles to help him visualise how the brain cannot remember every moment we have because it would become 'too full', but that often we remember things that are significant in some way. One child came into the session upset following an argument with his friend; by addressing this we were also able to explore his need to manage situations because of his fear of things beyond his control. On another occasion a child came into the session in fancy dress because it was a theme day at school. We talked about the character she had dressed as, and what it was she liked about her. This led into a conversation about the qualities she found reassuring in others, and what she liked about the people she felt safe with.

Taking time to reflect on sessions is important; allow time to write notes and to think about the session and the child. The format of your notes will depend on your own style, but consider including notes on themes and recurring issues, on how the child presents in the sessions, on responses from the child, and the impact of the session.

## *A framework for evaluation*

Using the assessment tools to evaluate allows for comparisons to be drawn. As the assessment tools collect scores and personal statements, it is possible to compare data in the form of both numerical scores and detailed feedback. It is useful to have both sources; on one occasion, for example, I could demonstrate that the numerical data scores showed that the level of concern had reduced by half, and the detailed feedback gave the person's account of what they felt had changed and examples of this.

Using these methods, it is possible to measure the impact on the child, the carers and the host school, as it includes all parties.

I realised that some additional tracking might be pertinent to schools and social care, in order to highlight the impact that could be achieved. This included measuring exclusions, withdrawal from lessons, behaviour sanctions required, attendance and punctuality, and so on. I did this in order to further measure the impact on the school in general; for example, if the individual child's behaviour becomes more positive, this not only affects them, but also the children and adults around them, and the teacher's ability to address the learning needs of the whole class. I added some further measures to gauge the impact of the therapy on social care; for example, the stability of the placement, the quality of contact and the demands on the social worker's time. Ultimately, by having a positive impact on the child, the therapy can also reduce some of the difficulties faced by the carers, teachers and social workers.

Evaluating the impact and benefits for my own school is an evolving process. The systems by which impact is measured are yet to be thoroughly defined. It is certainly the case that the service generates an income for the school, and is providing something unique. Further research into potential benefits will include: professional development, enhancing work in my own school setting; enriching the profile of the school as creative, innovative and collaborative; leading the way in enhanced provision; and working in partnership.

Currently there is discussion nationally about how best to provide mental health services for children and young people, and schools are obviously part of that equation. Few schools can fund their own school therapist, but employing a therapist who delivers services to their own school and others is one way in which they can address this. By doing this, the host school can retain a consistent therapist and secures priority allocation when making referrals.

## Team around the child

When you work with a child you do not truly work with an individual. A child comes with a network of people, both personal and professional. Even the child who may seem isolated or alone will have a range of professionals involved in their life. In a way that an adult is not, a child is the responsibility of someone, be it a parent, a carer or the state. Most children do not self-refer – someone else has referred them – and the therapist will consult with a whole range of people, before, during and after therapy. It is important therefore to have systems to include all of these people while keeping the child at the centre of everything we do.

How this is done will depend on many factors, but generally using existing forums such as looked-after children reviews, core group meetings, EHAT (Early Help Assessment Tool) meetings, team around the child or team around the school meetings will help achieve partnership working. Working collaboratively will help to ensure that the child is best supported and that sustainable support is established by including other key people who will continue to be with the child once the life story therapy has ended.

## Interpreting life story therapy for a school setting

The life story therapy approach differs to some extent depending on the setting in which it is delivered. This is where the flexibility of the approach is one of its strengths and allows for adaptability.

It should be noted that the differences of setting and the cultures within which it is delivered could influence the style of the approach taken. It is this versatility that can lead to new methods innovations.

# How life story therapy may differ in a school setting

The three stages of life story therapy are:

1. The information bank

2. Internalisation

3. The life story book.

In a school setting, stages 1, the research, and 3, the book, are largely the same as in any setting, but stage 2, the direct work, can differ in its approach. I will now look at each stage and examine how it can be interpreted in a school setting.

Regardless of the setting you work in, you will need to have your systems for referral, assessment and evaluation in place. Establish who the lead referrer is in order to have continuity about who you liaise with and who you will report to when you have completed the work. This will be particularly useful in complex cases, or where there are multiple partner agencies involved. It is also worthwhile to have a contract or written agreement in order to ensure that you are supported if necessary.

# The three stages of life story therapy

*Stage 1: The information bank – the research stage*

The research may present some different challenges if you are not based in a social care setting, as potentially accessing records may be more difficult. However, usually meeting with social workers or independent reviewing officers to explain the work you are doing and the need to access records is sufficient to address this. It is also worthwhile having signed permission from parents and carers, especially in the case of adopted children. Some information is difficult to obtain, for example health details, but there are usually ways to find out at least some basic information that the children may want, such as how much they weighed at birth, or what time they were born.

The research stage also differs if the child is based in your own setting and you have more extensive knowledge of them on a daily basis, or have already worked with the family. In this case you may have a wealth of information about the child – recorded, third party anecdotal and personal. It will likely make access to birth family and carers easier, as you will already be known to many of them. However, do not be complacent and rely too heavily on information contained within school; the research should be as broad as if you were conducting it for an unknown client.

When conducting research it is necessary to assess on a case-by-case basis the parties that will be included and the amount of input that is appropriate. Some children's birth parents will want a role in the work and it may be helpful and appropriate that they do this indirectly, sharing memories and information that will not be available from other sources. In some cases, any contact or attempt to contact the birth parents can be unhelpful for all parties and is ill advised.

It may be that ongoing contact with birth parents necessitates their inclusion in the process. Birth parents who are against the life story therapy taking place could potentially undermine it; therefore it is vital that their concerns are explored with them. This does not necessarily mean that they will change their opinion, but at the very least it enables you to have an honest conversation later with the child about why their birth parents may not support what they are doing. In the cases where birth parents are seen to support the therapy, it can be a very powerful message to the child. It can be like the parent giving the child permission to explore and move forward.

In the case of siblings having contact, or living together, careful consideration should be given as to how and when information is shared with each individual and how that will impact on the others.

When you first meet the child, you may ask if there is anything in particular they would like to know. When conducting your research you can make sure you look specifically for this information. For this reason it is helpful to meet the child during the research phase, although you can always search for specific information at any point during the process.

## Stage 2: Internalisation – the direct therapy work

Before you begin there are some things to consider.

### Carer participation

The direct work is the main area in which the approach may differ in a school setting. Probably one of the biggest differences is the level of inclusion of the carers. As most of the sessions take place during the school day it is not always possible to have the carers participating in the sessions. In order to address this, the work has to be set up to include the carers on a regular basis while most of the sessions take place on a one-to-one basis with the child.

What started out primarily as a solution to a practical challenge has actually proved to be a beneficial approach in a therapeutic sense. I have found that working in both ways – one-to-one sessions with the child, and carer and child sessions – has very positive benefits for all involved. Including the carers in the process is incredibly important for supporting their understanding of the child and helping them to reflect on how best to manage and nurture the child. It also helps to strengthen relationships and bonds, and potentially helps challenging or fractured relationships between children and carers.

Conversely, the one-to-one sessions provide the child with an arena to explore issues completely honestly and without fear of the consequences with the carer. Some children will be hiding certain things from their carers, scared that they will upset or repel them. These issues can be dealt with in one-to-one work and the child's fears can be explored, so that when these are shared with the carers it is done in a way that the child finds more manageable.

In the case of one child, he felt a deep sense of shame about his past. This made it very difficult for him to explore his feelings with anyone, as he could not bring himself to discuss memories or experiences that he found shameful. He could not have raised these issues with his carer present because he could not imagine trying to continue with everyday family life knowing that his carer knew these things about him and his birth family. He felt too exposed. However, in the one-to-one sessions with me – an independent person – he was helped to explore this feeling of shame and start to address his experiences, and fundamentally I was able to reinforce that the child was not to blame for any of these experiences.

Initially he was able to address these things in the sessions with me; then he was able to deal with the knowledge that these issues would be shared with the carer in a separate session with me. Eventually he was strong enough to address these issues directly with the carer himself. He needed to work through this in safe, manageable stages, to minimise the anxiety that his carer would reject him. It was important that he did this so that he could reach the stage when he had the confidence to share things with his carer in the knowledge that he was accepted and his carer had a better understanding of him. When his book was complete we held a session; the child then shared the book, and that moment of understanding, with the carer. For the child to talk about it explicitly with his carer was too difficult at first. But, through a process of sharing it indirectly, being accepted and then talking openly, it meant that the child could deal with it.

Furthermore, many children are worried about upsetting carers that they like, and can feel their loyalties divided between birth family and carers. Some children who feel less secure in their placement may be at risk of presenting a false self if they are worried about how the carers will interpret or judge what they say or feel. If children fear upsetting the carers or being rejected by the carers, it will inhibit them. A process which both includes the carers and allows the child one-to-one sessions would appear to meet both needs – the space to bond and the freedom to be honest.

### School-based sessions

Another key way in which the direct work may differ is that the sessions mostly take place within school. There are obvious differences, both practical and ideological, between running a session at home and running it at school.

In a practical sense, if sessions take place at school during the day, it minimises the amount of school time the child misses. In addition, most schools would find it prohibitive if the sessions were to take place at an alternative venue during the school day due to the practicalities of transporting and escorting the child.

In an ideological sense, there are advantages and disadvantages to wherever you conduct the sessions, and for this reason a level of flexibility is required when assessing the needs of individual children. The primary issues when deciding on the setting are whether the child feels secure there, whether the child wants the sessions to take place there, and if the setting will support or destabilise the process. It may also be that more than one venue is used; some children like to have their one-to-one sessions in school and their carer–child sessions at home, and in this way it is as if they are bringing the two spaces together.

There are some elements of school culture that can present a challenge to therapeutic working. For example, schools are communal in their approach; work generally takes place in a shared or open space. Many teacher and child conversations and interventions are not of strictly a confidential nature. Teachers are used to working in a public space; there are a number of practical reasons why this is the case in schools, but the resulting culture appears to mean that confidentiality for children is a vague concept. Therefore, one of the challenges commonly experienced is that school staff do not necessarily understand or respect the need for confidentiality when conducting the therapy sessions. This can result in people walking into the room, for example, and while seemingly a small matter, this can be very significant for the child. One child I was working with visibly froze in this situation; another tried discreetly to obscure their wallpaper. It is important to protect the therapeutic space for the child and to have a range of methods for doing so. A 'do not disturb' type sign can be used, but this needs to be visual so that young children can also interpret it, and be eye-catching (an example is shown in Figure 13.4). It may be necessary to explain to staff why you have this sign and politely ask them to adhere to it. An agreement can also be drawn up before the work starts in the school, stating that one of the requirements is an uninterrupted space. By doing this you will have a key person within the school to address this. If necessary, you may wish to speak at a staff meeting about the importance of confidentiality.

*Figure 13.4 'Do not disturb' sign*

Despite these differences in a school setting, fundamentally life story therapy is the same and the aim is the same. Regardless of the setting, the child is at the heart of the work and their needs should drive the work and the approaches taken.

### The therapy sessions

Life story therapy does offer something additional to life story work. Life story therapy has to be more specific about externalising the internalised hurt and trauma and to intervene. It needs to measure in a more focused way whether the intervention is making a difference to the child's wellbeing. Life story therapy is focused on healing the wounds and overcoming the challenges the child faces. (Rose 2012b)

Therapeutic life story work must be carried out sensitively, within the support network of the child, the therapist and the carer. Although directive, it must be paced carefully in relation to how the individual child is able to manage, and it should be directed gently and with care. However, the very nature of the work means that the child is presented with their history in a way that differs from most other therapies. As Rymaszewska (2012) pointed out in interview, many children will go to great lengths to avoid facing painful memories and difficult feelings. These defensive mechanisms become problematic in themselves, not least because they do not allow the child to process their feelings and experiences and move forward. Life story therapy works to gently counteract this avoidance. The purpose is to enable the child to process their memories and feelings, and to build healthy, positive strategies for the future. One child said to me that 'life story is like the museum of your life', and this was a profound statement on several levels. In simple terms, it is a good summary of what we are doing when we look at our own history. It also implies that precious memories are safe, that they are commemorated, suggesting that difficult or painful memories are also stored and contained somewhere safe. They need not be in the forefront of the mind all the time, preventing us from living in the present. Furthermore, for those who become stuck in the past, unable to focus on the present or think of a future, the statement is symbolic of starting to think of the past as just that – the past. We visit a museum, we do not live in it.

By the time you meet the child you will already have ensured that they have agreed to the therapy, as it is an essential part of the referral. Despite this, in the initial session you should gain their direct agreement to participate in the therapy. Regardless of how much everyone else might want the child to have therapy, it can only proceed with their consent, as they are the one who has to actively participate. I explain to the child how the sessions will work and the aim of the therapy. I also explain that sometimes the sessions can be difficult or upsetting, but that the child will be supported and kept safe. I say that sometimes the sessions are fun, and that in the end the therapy should have helped the child to understand things better.

In my initial session with Helen we talked about what therapeutic life story work entailed and how I hoped it might benefit her. Helen asked if we had to include all the bad memories. I explained to her that therapeutic life story work explores the good, bad and mediocre experiences in her life, and that everyone's life consists of good and bad experiences. This seemed to reassure her. I explained to her that, although I hoped she would enjoy the sessions, sometimes they may be difficult, even painful, but her carers and myself would work to support her through it. I tried to explain the process, saying all the feelings, thoughts and memories that she has are already with her, and therapeutic life story work is a way of making sense of them and organising them in her mind in a safe way, so that they do not have a negative effect on her present and future. I explained that it was her choice whether she undertook life story therapy or not, asking her to think about it and talk to her carers about it before deciding. I felt it was very important that Helen knew she had the choice to engage or not. There would be no value to Helen's involvement in her therapy if she felt obliged to be there. When Helen made her choice to proceed I felt assured that she was ready and willing to engage.

As previously mentioned, I will ask the child if there is anything in particular they want to know or to understand better. In addition to steering me to look for this information, it also gives me some idea as to what is important to the child and what is most difficult or confusing for them to make sense of. For example, a child who wants to know if their birth family are still living may want to know if the world they left is still in existence without them and if they are missed, or they may wonder if they will be returned to their birth family. If you are unable to find the information that the child has asked for, you can still explore with them why you cannot find the information, and why that may have been important to them.

In one of Ryan's sessions we talked about the things he might like to know more about, and that these would be things I would try and find out for him. We wrote his questions down and put them in a decorative tin, a symbol that they were safe.

In the initial sessions, I also used Rose's (2012a) All About Me model. This helps to establish what the child already knows and, importantly, what they do not know. It also affords time to start building the therapeutic alliance with the child.

The first few sessions with Karen involved us spending some time to build a therapeutic alliance. We completed the All About Me book and played some games. We established that at the end of every session we would roll the wallpaper away and finish with a game or similar, to help her to prepare for continuing with the rest of her day. These sessions helped me to form an idea of what Karen knew of her history, and what she thought and felt about her life and relationships. This helped me to form a hypothesis about the themes we might focus on.

When the sessions begin in earnest on a child's life story we start by working on the wallpaper. The fundamental basis of this work remains the same, but the specific methods will be tailored to the individual child. For example, each child might do a family tree on the wallpaper, but how this is presented depends on the child. One child I worked with drew it as a bubble with all the people in their family drawn and labelled around them in the centre; another child wanted a methodical and precise diagram; another represented it literally as a tree with all of her relatives listed on the leaves.

I begin by pre-dating the birth of the child and explaining that our life stories can begin before we are born because the world we are born into influences the life we experience. It is often helpful to explain to children that the difficulties their birth parents experienced pre-dated their own birth by many years. In this way they can begin to understand that they are not to blame. It is also helpful to give the child some information about their birth parents, and some of their history. Many people who live with birth parents will hear stories about them, both before they were parents and after, and this can help to have a sense of their identity. Particularly for younger children who, as is the developmental norm, see everything in relation to themselves, it can be useful to see birth parents as an independent entity.

I felt it was important for John to understand that his parents' problems existed before he did, that he was not the cause of these problems. We began by talking about how all our life stories probably start before we are born; they start with the personal world into which we are born and which, in part, shapes us. I also wanted to be clear with John that this does not mean that we do not shape our own lives and it does not mean that we must live the lives of our parents, or our parents' parents – we are individuals capable of shaping our own future.

Therapeutic life story work can incorporate a range of creative ways of working, and this flexibility enables the therapist to draw on other resources, ideas and observations and to tailor the sessions to the individual. Although reflection on each case will be formed within a theoretical framework, it will also be largely instinctive. This is part of the therapist's role, to be attuned to the child, to have a level of empathy for the child, an understanding of them and their circumstances, to be observant. Something may be felt or observed within the session, and then understood within a theoretical framework. It is important to be proactive and reactive, to notice things and to adjust and accommodate as required. Attunement to the child is key to how you will support them.

One of the children I was working with was interested in magic and magicians, and in one of the sessions they brought their reading book with them, which was a mix and match book of magic spells and potions. This led to a few sessions where we used the idea of magic and spells symbolically to work creatively through challenges and conflict and create spells to problem solve, these spells then being made into 'real-life spells'. In one session, we made 'a potion for being happy when I feel sad' that included things like hugs, playing, telling someone they felt sad, and so on.

One of the children loved role-play and storytelling, and half of his session time involved working this way. These stories were not merely a fabrication, they had a therapeutic element, and they were the child's way of expressing himself. Through these stories and dramas he explored issues and practised responses to challenges.

The work is largely done chronologically – after all we are trying to help the child to gain a sense of order about events, to be able to make sense of the sequence of things, to assemble the jumbled pieces of the picture, and to gain some clarity about the 'who, when, where' questions about their life. However, there will be times when a child may raise an issue or relay a memory that, although chronologically out of sequence, is significant to where we are in the process, or is something that is on their mind at that time. When this happens it can be addressed in a number of ways depending on the nature of the information. We address it fully, record it on the wallpaper, revisit it briefly when we reach the timescale it is pertinent to, and later place it in sequence in the book. We can partially address it and 'park it' on the wallpaper to be explored more fully as further information will help us to make more sense of it. We can 'park it' on the wallpaper to be addressed later and keep checking back that we have addressed any pending issues. I will explain to the child that parking something means storing it until we are ready to use it, like a car in a car park, or a bike in a bike shed.

I will often trace around the outline of the child on the wallpaper, as this has a range of uses. One child wanted to draw and write inside the outline of himself some of the things that he felt made him who he was, for example 'I like football', 'My favourite food is pizza'. Another child had difficulties controlling her feelings, so we used her body outline to show where in her body she felt her emotions in a physical sense – for example, 'When I am angry my heart beats faster' – and what she might do physically when she felt certain emotions: 'I run away when I am scared'. Another child felt guilty and angry at himself that he had not stopped the domestic violence between his father and mother, so we used his body outline to help him visualise his size then, his size now and the size of his father, and to help him to understand that he could not have prevented the attacks.

While the therapy is ongoing, continuous reflection will help you to shape the approach you take, choose the techniques you will use, and phase the therapy. Greenwald (2005) breaks down the treatment of trauma into different phases, which can be summarised as evaluation and planning, building on strengths and safety, trauma resolution and re-evaluation and consolidation. Therefore, the pace at which you work, and the techniques you use, will be individualised, although the aims remain essentially the same.

Some children will have a lot of memories that will be explored; some children will know details that have not been found in any of their files or interviews. One child often relayed memories of experiences that were not recorded anywhere, and this led us to discuss how many of the things they would have experienced would not have been known by social workers, or shared by their birth parents. It also helped to clarify that the official files reflect only a fraction of the reality. This was particularly pertinent to the child regarding the domestic violence that had occurred in the family. When discussing one incident recorded in the files, the child said that such things had happened 'all the time', so we were able to explore the scale of the problem through their experiences as well as from the files.

Some children will have little or no knowledge of why they do not live with their birth parents. In these cases, the sharing of information can be particularly sensitive as it comes as a revelation of new information. Groundwork needs to be achieved before sharing this information with the child so as to ensure that the child and carer have a context in which to frame this new information and to appreciate and cope with these new challenges.

Several of the children I have worked with have little or no knowledge of why they were taken into care, and often carers are conflicted about sharing information and how to do this without appearing to be negative about birth parents. This can lead to children being given vague or misleading information that further confuses or worries them, such as being told their mother was ill, and then becoming very anxious when they or others are ill.

For Melissa the question of 'why?' had become all-consuming. The reasons that her carers gave her did not really answer her questions, and the vagueness of the reasons was making her feel less secure about her position in the world at that point, including wondering 'Could it all happen again?' Her carers did not know how to tell her the reasons and were worried that she would accuse them of 'saying bad things' about her parents.

Many people worry about the sharing of information at this point because it has often been built up as something to be fearful of or that might potentially have devastating consequences. However, as previously explained, the preparation for telling the child is done sensitively within the life story process. Furthermore, the truth can often be reassuring, as in the absence of information, children will often fill in the gaps themselves. Their perception of why they are in care can often be more distressing – chiefly that they are unloved and unlovable. Therefore, finding out the real reason can be liberating, and is essential to the process. From the point in her life story therapy that Melissa learned why her birth parents could not look after her, we could then further explore what this meant for her, how it felt and how she could make sense of it.

An example of preparing for information sharing is when children who were removed from their parents' care due to drug or alcohol misuse need to have some concept of what that means. This entails an age- and experience-appropriate discussion about what drugs and alcohol are, what they can do to affect the way people think and act, and what addiction is. It is also important to discuss the difference between healthy and unhealthy uses of alcohol, as many children will see adults drinking alcohol. It is vital that they can understand the difference between alcohol being a problem for someone, and the reasonable use of alcohol, so as to avoid them becoming fearful whenever they see an adult with alcohol. With one child who was very young I used the analogy of sweets to explore how eating a few sweets was fine and people enjoyed sweets, but if we ate sweets until we were sick all the time, or felt that we had to eat sweets to feel okay, then that would become a problem. With another child who was older and loved watching soap operas, I used one of the storylines at that time about a character who was misusing drugs, as it gave the child a frame of reference as a starting point for more of an in-depth consideration of drug misuse.

Throughout the process of therapeutic life story work the child will be exploring some potentially difficult memories or information, but it is wrong to assume that without this exploration the child will be protected from these difficulties. Some people worry that by talking about things or sharing information it is 'opening a can of worms', inadvertently creating a problem or further complicating it. However, the thoughts, feelings, memories, confusion and challenges already exist for the child. If a child feels unloved, ignoring the feeling does not solve it. Likewise, if a child has been hurt by a birth parent, not talking about it does not make the memories go away. One child said to me that she was worried about bringing up her memories, but as she could not forget them they were there anyway and she had no control over when they popped up in her mind. She later said that by doing life story therapy she did not have to think about things all the time because the therapy sessions gave her a set time to do that, and that also she thought about some things less now that she had explored them and made sense of them.

This is where attunement is so important, to ensure that the pacing and delivering of the sessions engages the child in a way that they feel safe and contained. Attuning takes concentration, to observe gestures, expressions, shifts and changes, to focus just on the child and to be truly present with them.

Throughout my case work I have reflected that many theoretical models support the therapeutic life story work framework. Those that I have often found particularly useful are Herman and Greenwald's treatment phasing, including Greenwald's trauma resolution model:

- Select an order for the memories to be addressed

- Identify upsetting elements of the trauma memory

- Face and master the upsetting elements of the memory

- Repeat with other trauma/loss memories

- Identify trauma-related triggers – reminders that trigger a trauma-related reaction

- Face and master the triggers.

(Greenwald 2005, p.179)

Herman (2001) argues that the phases of trauma recovery are building a healing relationship, reconstructing the story, reconnection to others and commonality with others, and that retelling the story allows the client to process it and transform the story. This argument is supported by the neurodevelopment models of Schore (2003a, 2003b) and Perry (2000, 2001, 2006, 2010) and the trauma theories of van der Kolk, McFarlane and Weisaeth (2007). These theorists argue that neurodevelopment is affected by trauma, that traumatic memory is stored differently in the brain, and that this affects the person's ability to process the trauma. In order to process the trauma, the trauma memories must be accessed. I feel that as life story therapists we build a therapeutic and safe relationship with our clients, providing a safe space for them, and we reconstruct their story, allowing them to tell their story, make sense of it, and challenge it in order to gain mastery.

Loss is obviously a recurring issue in therapeutic life story work, with many children experiencing multiple losses. Many have experienced the loss of their parents, siblings, extended family and multiple carers. Some have lost the life that, although flawed, they knew, and they have been taken out of the context of everything that was familiar. Others have a sense of loss for the family and life they do not remember, a sense of not being affixed to anything. This highlights issues about identity and belonging. What life story therapy can help to do is to give the child a sense of their identity and where they belong, to help them through the grieving process for their loss, and to identify the support network they now have. These children are adrift; life story therapy can provide an anchor to support them to get onto solid ground.

It is essential that the process of therapeutic life story work is carried out in a non-judgemental way, and this includes the child, the carers and the birth parents. It is not about blame, it is about understanding. This is the reason, when it is explained to them this way, why many birth parents will co-operate with the process. It is how carers can be encouraged to fully participate, and to understand that they too are being supported. Most importantly, it allows the child the opportunity to be open and honest in a way that they may not be able to do anywhere else. We all have feelings and thoughts sometimes that we do not freely admit to, and for a child to know that they can explore these difficult feelings and not be judged is very important. To have a safe place where you are accepted and supported allows you to be challenged in a positive way. While always holding the child in positive regard, it is possible to challenge and reframe their thinking in a way that they are more likely to accept and believe.

Dan seemed able to express himself freely because the safe space to do so had been established, largely due to the non-judgemental approach of therapy. He told me that when he expressed his anger about his mother to some people they either dismissed it or disapproved, but that in therapy we could talk about it in a way that made him think about it. I felt it was important that Dan had somewhere where he could just be, where he did not need to try and be what he thought other people wanted him to be: the ideal son, brother, friend or pupil.

As time went on I noticed that Dan continued to present as being at ease in our sessions. Small observations, such as how he would kick off his shoes and get comfy in the sessions, seemed to support his ease at speaking with me, and just being present. By maintaining the consistency in our relationship and our sessions, I was creating a safe relationship. I observed that Dan seemed to present less of a false self in the sessions than in other settings outside the therapy. This also helped me to reflect that ultimately Dan needed support to be able to build safe, yet honest, relationships with other people.

Towards the end of the therapy process I introduce the concept of short-, medium-, long-term and forever relationships. This is done primarily to help the child to understand that not all relationships are lasting, but also that this is a normal part of life changing and progressing and not solely a negative event. It also aims to help them identify relationships they have that are nurturing and enjoyable, and that throughout life they will make new relationships. Furthermore, this incorporates thinking about people who have been in our lives but that we no longer see. This enables the child to explore loss, but also to value the healthy, happy relationships they have enjoyed regardless of whether they are continuing or not. Ultimately, we explore how to build and maintain positive relationships. This can also help to prepare the child for the ending of the life story therapy, as we examine positive endings and coping strategies for change.

In the final sessions we look to the future, recording on the wallpaper the child's hopes, wishes and dreams for the future, and their carers' wishes for them. Finally, we celebrate all the work that they have done and all they have achieved in the life story therapy.

It is an important part of the therapy that the child is prepared for the end of therapy and life afterwards. This is helped by the sessions I have described above. One boy had initially been quite upset at the thought that our sessions would draw to a close; he wondered why I could not just keep coming. We continued to work on this, and to explore the people he had in his life: those who cared for him, those he liked spending time with and those who helped him. He was building relationships with other people – his new teacher and his peers – and beginning to refer to them more frequently in conversation. In his final session I reminded him of such and that I would not be coming back into school, but would see him again when his book was finished. It was clear that the preparation had been effective when he left our final session without any difficulties.

## Stage 3: The life story book

The setting the therapist is working in does not significantly influence the third stage, producing the life story book. Potentially, the method in which the book is shared with the child could differ slightly, depending on how, where and with whom this is done. However, usually this session is done with the child and their carers, and takes place in the home rather than in the school.

The book is something that should continue to support the child in the future. Although produced at the time they participated in the therapy, it can continue to be a resource for them. It has been reported that children I worked with in the past have revisited their book, and that it still has a resonance for them. Also, rather than it being perceived as a book for little children, they make sense of it and explore it further from their viewpoint as older and more emotionally mature young people.

As therapeutic life story work takes place over a number of months, the book helps to consolidate what the child has worked through. It also helps to remind the carers of everything we have done. The fact that the book is a physical object that can be returned to helps to make the therapeutic process sustainable. Just as we all refer back to resources to remind ourselves of things, the book contains important memories, information and messages that the child and the carers can remind themselves of. The book can also be added to if the child and carers wish to continue to document events or maintain some form of diary or journal.

The aim of the session to share the book with Helen and her carers was to talk openly about the work Helen had done in therapy, and to reinforce how it had helped the carers to understand Helen more.

It had enabled them to understand where her challenging behaviour came from, in order to help them manage those behaviours and support her. The security of the placement had previously been deteriorating, and at the epicentre of it was the relationship between Helen and her foster mother. The therapy process had helped them to strengthen their relationship and to understand each other better. The book reminded them of this and enabled them to revisit it.

## After therapy

Even after the life story therapy has finished with the child, its key principles can help the school and the carers to support the child.

Attachment forms a major part of life story therapy and the approach it takes to support the child. Involving the carers in the therapeutic life story work aims to strengthen the attachment between them and the child. They are the people who are likely to be there around the clock for the child, and as such their role is paramount to the sustained progress of the child. Sadly this is not always the case, as some children may not be in a permanent placement when they participate in life story therapy and as such will move on to different carers at some point. However, it is hoped that the work they have done to make sense of their lives and build relationships will help them face the challenges of a new placement.

Attachment is not solely reserved for the placement; schools are a valuable source of relationships, with both adults and peers. There is great potential there to provide the child with opportunities for positive relationships, and that will be particularly key for those children whose placements are likely to change. Many schools will have already informally identified a school attachment figure for the child, without necessarily even realising that they have done so. Often there are particular staff who have a good bond with the child. This is important for the child's ongoing improvement in developing healthy relationships; what has been built and tested in the therapy sessions with the therapist and carers should be extended beyond that into other aspects of the child's life.

Therapeutic life story work aims to help children gain mastery over their feelings and actions; to make sense of themselves and the world; to equip them with the skills to face challenges throughout their life; to build positive relationships and support networks; and to value themselves. If the therapy has made a difference to various aspects of the children's lives, and continues to do so after the process is finished, then we can truly feel that it has had a positive impact.

# References

Greenwald, R. (2005) *Child Trauma Handbook: A Guide for Helping Trauma-Exposed Children and Adolescents.* London: Routledge.

Herman, J.L. (2001) *Trauma and Recovery: From Domestic Abuse to Political Terror.* London: Pandora.

Perry, B.D. (2000) 'Trauma and Terror in Childhood: The Neuropsychiatric Impact of Childhood Trauma' prefinal draft for I. Schulz, S. Carella and D.O. Brady (eds) *Handbook of Psychological Injuries: Evaluation, Treatment and Compensable Damages.* Washington, DC: American Bar Association Publishing.

Perry, B.D. (2001) 'Bonding and Attachment in Maltreated Children' [internet], Child Trauma Academy. Available at www.childTrauma/wp-content/uploads/2014/01Bonding-and-Attachment.pdf, accessed on 19 September 2015.

Perry, B.D. (2002) 'Childhood experience and the expression of genetic potential: what childhood neglect tells us about nature and nurture.' *Brain and Mind* 3, 79–100.

Perry, B.D. (2006) 'Applying the Principles of Neurodevelopment to Clinical Work with Maltreated and Traumatized Children.' In N. Boyd Webb (ed.) *Working with Traumatized Youth in Child Welfare.* New York: Guilford Press. [internet], Child Trauma Academy, 2006.

Perry, B.D. (2010) 'Introduction to the Neurosequential Model of Therapeutics' [internet], Child Trauma Academy. Available at http://cctasi.northwestern.edu/wp-content/uploads/Introduction-to-the-Neurosequential-Model-of-Therapeutics.pdf, accessed on 16 September 2015.

Rose, R. (2012a) *Life Story Therapy with Traumatized Children: A Model for Practice.* London: Jessica Kingsley Publishers.

Rose, R. (2012b) Research interview by Paula Price. Telford, UK, 26 March 2012.

Rymaszewska, J. (2012) Research interview by Paula Price. Shrewsbury, UK, 8 March 2012.

Schore, A.N. (2003a) *Affect Dysregulation and Disorders of the Self.* New York: W.W. Norton & Company.

Schore, A.N. (2003b) *Affect Regulation and the Repair of the Self.* New York: W.W. Norton & Company.

van der Kolk, B.A., McFarlane, A.C. and Weisaeth, L. (eds) (2007) *Traumatic Stress: The Effects of Overwhelming Experience on the Mind, Body and Society.* New York: Guilford Press.

Chapter 14

# SPIN PROJECT – A SOUTHERN APPROACH TO TLSW – PORTUGAL

*Professor Maria Barros and Margarida Marques*

## How did it all start?

One of the many conferences Richard Rose gives, around the world, brought him to Portugal, in 2012. In the audience, was Maria Fernanda Barros, a child and adolescent psychiatrist, responsible for this department in Evora´s district Hospital, that was overwhelmed by the benefits that LSW could bring to her patients and, also, by the enthusiasm of its developer. So, she introduced herself and her work, in the end of the conference, and was very positively surprised by the interest that Richard Rose showed in sharing information, about his work. Two main issues captured his interest, in one hand, the notion of enlarged families, that naturally foster children, and in the other hand, the almost inexistence of foster care families, in the Portuguese protection system.

The communication bond was maintained and Maria, at the time and currently, working with several foster care Institutions, shared LSW information with Margarida Marques, a psychologist that coordinates technical work in one of these Institutions. Together, during 2012, they designed the Project, and named it 'Spin', accordingly to their reality needs, with LSW intervention in two groups: children and adolescents that attended Maria's consultation and lived with informal enlarged families, and children and adolescents that were in foster care Institutions.

Every Project needs partners and 'Spin' was no exception, so 'Fundação Calouste Gulbenkian', one of the most remarkable cultural and social foundations in Portugal, was approached, and LSW was very well received. All through 2013, FCGulbenkian analised the Project and invited two other partners, 'Fundação Montepio', a bank's foundation and 'Coração Delta', a social foundation of the largest trading coffee company in Portugal, located in Alentejo. 'Spin' Project started in February 2014 with a four year duration and supervision sessions with Richard Rose, each semester.

# Demography, Population and Human Resources

Alentejo is the largest region of Portugal - with a total area of 31.551km2 - but, at the same time the region with the lowest population density: 24 inhabitants by km2, living in small villages up to 5.000 inhabitants. The ageing of the population is a reality, for every 100 youngsters, there are 178 elderly people. We find high rates of unemployment, especially among women, as it's essentially a rural area, with almost non existing industry. The dominant type of family is the enlarged one, with different generations living under the same roof or in the neighborhood, and working in the same land.There is a great sense of community, people share their suffering, moments of loss, grief and, also share moments of happiness. These are Communities without undiscovered secrets. We consider that life story work with extended families has its own peculiar aspects. The parenting team has shared, from birth to the present, the child's life, with suffering and losses. They have close and direct family ties, with the children's parents. The deviant behavior of the family members, either their own children or other close relatives, raises the question about its causes. Genetics, birth defects, overprotection, wrong guidance or, simply, bad companies. The parenting team competes with the absent parents, considering themselves the stronger element of the family. They feel poor evaluated in the eyes of the children and they seek to confirm the good job they've done, sometimes sacrificing their own interests. By the opposite, they feel supported by the community.

## Going through Portuguese protection system

Created in 1999, reviewed in 2003 and 2015, the Portuguese child and young person in danger, protection law, is widely considered as updated and modern, despite the challenges of its application.

Initially, focused in downsizing foster care institutions and creating 'temporary' foster care and protection commissions in each county, the main goals were providing basic needs, protecting physical and psychological integrity and promoting global development.

Over the past 10 years, stats of children and young people in foster care has dropped, but that doesn't mean better support of their issues, because their profiles have also changed, being older and more troubled and damaged, when in referral.

In 2015, the aim was on family foster care for children under 6 years old and small 'residential' and specialised care units, up to 18 or 21, emphasizing an ecological overview, sustaining that protection is a social and family matter.

Actual challenges, in Portuguese protection system are, specialised training for teams, therapeutic intent and sustainable interventions, according to individual needs.

Services provided by foster care institutions can be very helpful during and after a family crisis, preparing a child to adoption or providing specialised consulting and therapeutic approaches, among others.

## Spin Project – The Team

With a large experience in psychoanalysis, in the beginning of her career, Maria brought to Évora, a communitarian approach to mental health, engaging other professionals – teachers, social workers, other therapists - in case discussions, highlighting a global overview of the patient.

In 2009, Maria started working as a child and young person psychiatrist, in the general district hospital in Évora – Hospital do Espírito Santo (HESE) - and in 2011 she becomes Head of the Department. In this capacity, she not only attends children and adolescents in her consultation, but she also meets the foster care Institutions staff, that asked her for guidance. That's where she met Margarida and the foster care Institution where she works – Centro Social e Paroquial de Alandroal (CSPA). Founded in 1988, as the social branch of the local parish, CSPA has been developing several relevant social services to its community, like a student's residence, a nursery, psychosocial support for families and foster care to children under 12 years old. With a staff of 23 workers, CSPA is the only social Institution in Alandroal that works with children and families, particularly in what concerns foster care.

Maria and Margarida began working together, around foster care cases at CSPA, when the possibility of a new therapeutic approach – LSW – was discussed and considered very helpful and innovative.

So, the 'Spin Project' first draft was designed and presented to the financial sponsors, in 2012.

## Spin = 'Tailor made' Life Story Work

Spin's first and ultimate challenge was, without any dough, adjusting LSW original methodology to Alentejo's social and institutional reality, maintaining focus on the key issues.

Who is the career and its role in the process, especially in the residential foster care group, was one of the first themes of discussion with Richard Rose and with each partner's team, usually formed by a psychologist and a social worker. Individual profile, the quality of the relationship with the child / adolescent and schedule availability, were thorough fully discussed, in order to make the best choice, in each case.

Afterwards, a training session was held with the career(es), about LSW process and stages, where the main dough's were around being up to expectations. Along the process, often, careers shared daily life events, that happened between sessions, showing that these experiences could improve LSW, and LSW could help the child /adolescent with all the challenges they face, especially in school and in the relationship with their birth families.

Besides working with residential foster care institutions (short and long term foster care), the children and adolescents attending psychiatry consultations in Évora, over the past 6 years, showed that a considerable number of the 'enlarged families', had no biological bonds between them, or were very distantly related, like an informal foster care family.

So, this group became a very particular universe to LSW, although after two years of Spin, families with adopted children or adolescents became, also, a very interesting field of work.

# Some practical examples

The case studies selected reflect the daily challenges of Evora's foster care Institutions, especially in dealing with emergency and multiple placements, management and financial decisions, development threatening health issues and scarce resources, among others. All names have been changed to preserve anonymity.

### RESIDENTIAL FOSTER CARE – CASE STUDY 1: MONICA

Monica is ten years old and had not known that there were six foster care institutions in her life, plus two other shelters for battered women, where she stayed with her mother, until she did therapeutic life story work.

Her mother, not a Portuguese national, had a history of family violence, and came to Portugal trying to find a work opportunity. Alcohol, aggressive and sexually promiscuous behavior and violent relationships, lead her to Monica's pregnancy, not knowing who the child's father was. When Monica was a few months old, complaints of her negligent behavior, took Monica to her first foster care experience. Monica is brought up going in and out of foster care residences, and living with her mother for some periods of time, taking care of her little brother, two years younger, with child protection services and courts giving 'another' chance for her mother to get her life together.

In one of these periods living with her mother, Monica was, again, victim of her mother's violence and neglect, with physical and psychological damage, resulting in a formal criminal complaint and current prison time for her mother. The last time she saw her brother was two years ago, and their life projects are, apparently going in different directions.

When Monica started 'Spin', she presented herself as a very lively and talkative girl, that likes to write and draw with vivid colours, and to control everything that happens around her. Her life project was, up until last November, staying in foster care up to adulthood, when suddenly, through a lawyer that had been previously in her legal process, she found out that she has some relatives in Portugal, whose existence she didn´t know of.

These relatives are, currently, very interested in being part of her life, assuming legal guardianship. This amazing turnover happened in the middle of 'Spin', resulting in adjusting timings and inviting her new family to participate, by doing all together, the 'Life Story Book'.

Also quite remarkable, is the opportunity that 'Spin' provides of reflecting and elaborating all the thoughts and doubts that Monica might have, such as 'Am I going to like them?', 'Are they going to like and accept me? ', 'Am I going to be happy with this new family?'

*First assessment: after 3 months*
Monica's least scored areas were identity, attachment and emotional intelligence, that also affect her learning skills, although Monica is quite capable in her social relationships and communication.

*Third assessment: after 9 months*
In spite of all the changes that occurred in her life, Monica's results are sustainable, even after the follow-up assessment. (See Comparison Results Grid.)

## RESIDENTIAL FOSTER CARE – CASE STUDY 2: PETER

Peter is ten years old and, when he started 'Spin,' was for the second time in his life, in residential foster care, together with an older brother. Peter is a very imaginative and musical child who likes to draw and play charades.

He had no memories of his first foster care experience, because it happened when he was less than three years old. This reality, alongside the knowledge that his parents had also been in long -term foster care up to their adulthood, due, among other reasons, to the tragic deaths of their mothers, was a revelation to Peter. However, these events helped him to understand where he came from, and realising he was repeating, up to a point, his family's story.

In 'Spin''s last three months, unexpectedly he had to be placed in another residential foster care institution, due to the sudden closing of the unit he was in. Peter had to go through his third change of environment carers, school, teachers, classmates, etc. Although he was compelled to change everything in his life one more time, Peter didn't show signs of distress in the diagram assessments, and was able to complete LSW, with another career. The follow up assessments, six months after completing 'Spin', sustain the positive achievements, especially in what concerns emotional and social issues.

Although contact with his parents, currently separated as a couple, and spending short periods of time with his mother is possible, returning to one of his parent's home, definitely, is not in the agenda. Peter showed himself to be a very resilient child, being integrated in a class that combines the learning of music with the learning of formal school matters.

## INFORMAL FAMILIES – CASE STUDY 3: THOMAS

Thomas is 11 years old and lives with his working grandmother, Ann, a widow and his sister Jane, who is nine years old and has some learning disabilities.

His mother, Rose, was addicted to alcohol and drugs and he doesn't know who his father is. Rose is described as violent and unstable, finding new partners, having little attachment to her children.

Rose left the house and the village, with a drug dealer when Thomas was four years old. Social services traced her and considered she'd be able to take care of her children.

The grandmother recalls the moment, when the children, upset and crying, with a little bag of personal belongings, entered the social services car.

The court allows Ann to visit them, 200 km away, on Sundays for 2 hours in a public place, near their new home.

Two years later, the police contacts Ann, informing her that her daughter has abandoned the children at the local railway station. Evidence of neglect transpired, with Thomas reporting episodes of severe violence, like his stepfather keeping guns at home.

In the meantime, two twins brothers were born and Thomas had to take care of them and his younger sister. Rose is nowhere to be found and Thomas and Jane stay with their grandmother. The twins are given for adoption and the social services department closes the case.

*First assessment: After three months*

Thomas functions as a much younger boy. He expresses his anger with tantrums, and frustration with tears. Thomas is emotionally dependent, and he cannot share his feelings about his mother with his grandmother, because he thinks she will be angry. His attachments are insecure and Thomas feels unsafe, has difficulties sleeping and nightmares, crying out loud and remembering the time he spent with his mother and her partner. He has witnessed severe domestic violence between them, and remembers being alone with Jane and the baby twins, feeding them and changing their diapers.

At school, he enjoys playing with his schoolmates, and his teacher defines him as a nice, shy boy, with difficulties in abstract thinking.

The grandmother centers her thoughts and speech in the past. She expresses rage towards the social services that evaluated positively, the mother's ability to up bring the children.

Ann understands Thomas fragilities, but she fears the role of genetics in his development and keeps alert to signs in Thomas behavior, that reminds her of Rose, the mother.

*Third assessment: After 9 months*

Thomas is now able to express his feelings of sadness about the absence of his twin brothers, of anger about his unknown father and of neglect, about his mother.

He is able to cope with multiple relationships, although he finds it difficult to manage two relationships at the same time. He gets jealous, when he perceives his grandmother gives more attention to his sister.

His relationships with adults are essentially based on trust. He perceives the world as a safe, warm place, but also has the ability to threaten and hurt him, reflecting his story.

At school Thomas has a behavior consistent with his age, is well integrated, socializing with pleasure, both with adults and peers.

He feels confident and proud about his new independence, he travels everyday one hour by bus from his village with some schoolmates and stays away from home all day long. He has his own pocket money, has lunch at school and entered the football team of the school.

The grandmother is proud of Thomas achievements and her fears about the power of bad genetic inheritance are fading away. She talks more about the future than about the past. She considers the possibility of moving to town and invest in the future of her grandchildren. She no longer needs the enveloping protection of the community where she and the children grew up.

## INFORMAL FAMILIES – CASE STUDY 4: JULIE

Julie is 15 years old and lives with her maternal aunt and brother Matthew, 13 years old. They live in the second largest village of Alentejo, with 8456 inhabitants, where the main industry is coffee roasting and packaging, a market leader in Portugal.

They both lived with their parents until Julie was four years old, when the parents drowned their two-week old sister.

The parents were taken into custody and several months later the mother, Marianne, is released and the father, Peter, is found guilty. He'll stay in prison for several years.

Marianne comes back home, under heavy psychiatric medication. She doesn't show signs of improved stability and is supported by social services. By the time Julie was ten, Marianne commits suicide by overdose of medication.

The children are taken in foster care in a town nearby where they stay for two years. Afterwards, they begin to live with aunt Helen, Marianne's sister, and a 25-year-old cousin.

Aunt Helen, 45 years old, divorced, is a cold and very strict woman. For her, the custody of the siblings is viewed as a social obligation, as the only and ultimate solution. The remaining members of the family are younger and in the beginning of the construction of their own lives, so they don't present themselves as a solution.

Aunt Helen tells that her childhood has been difficult, and that there was poor attachment between herself and her mother. Her father was alcoholic and violent.

She married very young, and after four years of an immature relationship, her husband left her with three little children. She cared for them alone.

Julie's aunt complained about her difficult behaviour to social services. Verbal abuse, self harm and sexualised behavior were reported.

*First assessment: after three months*
Julie mostly uses anger to express her feelings towards her aunt and her cousin. She considers her aunt doesn't really love her. Julie describes physical punishment, verbal aggression and humiliation.

Julie doesn't feel grateful or guilty towards others. She thinks she deserves full attention after being deprived from her mother.

Julie lacks emotional regulation and she can experience a wide range of feelings from rage to pure joy, in a very short time. She shows sexualised behaviour and easily 'falls in love'.

Her absent father is described as a monster, responsible for all the bad things that had happened.

She often bursts into tears, when it comes down to talk about her present life and feels locked into her idealised relationship with her deceased mother. She writes poems to her and her diaries are filled with drawings of portraits of her mother.

*Third assessment: after nine months*
Julie is more able to control her rage and to understand this feeling. She has difficulty in identifying another person's feelings.

Julie admits she is dependent on the approval of others and considers the concern of adults as a sign of protection instead of control. Since the beginning of Life Story Work, she has developed trust and mutual understanding, as a key to establishing secure relationships.

Julie needs support to learn how to manage several relationships at the same time.

Julie has to seek out adult guidance when she needs to make a personal or social choice.

# 'Spin's' update, November 2016

After two years of LSW, several new paths have been opened. Maria's work, has one of the very few child and adolescent psychiatrist, working in Portugal, took her outside Évora's region, where she met professionals from foster care Institutions, that saw LSW has a powerful tool, in their daily work with difficult children and adolescent mothers. So, Maria started a 'Spin's' new goal, training these teams in LSW, and offering monthly supervision, so they can apply it themselves. Attending seminars as partners and bringing LSW to other professionals, in the region, has been very rewarding to 'Spins' team, and has considerably enlarged the number of children and adolescents that can benefit from this work.

Another very exciting branch of 'Spins' work, has been working with children and adolescents in adoptive families, because going through LSW with an adopted child is still a 'tabu' in Portugal and, a very stressful situation for most adoptive parents.

## The Future...

Richard Rose's conference in November 2014, at the FCGulbenkian, in Lisbon, presenting LSW and 'Spin', brought a new group of large Social Institutions, located outside Évora district, particularly in the Lisbon area, very much interested in training their teams.

Richard Rose's presence in Portugal in early June of 2016 has provided the ground rules of LSW training, being up to 'Spin', the development of consultancy and supervision for a considerable number of professionals, working in residential foster care units, that range from emergency to autonomy apartments, going through young children, adolescents and adoption.

'Spin' is also partnered with other projects that work with families where there are murder victims, being LSW able to make a difference, in accepting the past.

Some of these projects and professionals are, also, very well placed in terms of decision makers, concerning the protection system, in Portugal. So, 'Spin' and LSW have a lot of ground to cover, but also a great chance of becoming, in the future, a fundamental work tool to all those that give their time, skills and know-how to the success of the Portuguese protection system.

## References

Rose, R. (2012) Life Story Therapy with Traumatized Children: A Model for Practice. London: Jessica Kingsley Publishers.

Rose, R. and Philpot, T. (2004) The Child's Own Story: Life Story Work with Traumatized Children. London: Jessica Kingsley Publishers.

Rees, J. (2009) Life Story Books for Adopted Children: A Family Friendly Approach. London: Jessica Kingsley Publishers.

Wrench, K. and Naylor, L. (2013) Life Story Work with Children who are Fostered or Adopted: Creative Ideas and Activities. London: Jessica Kingsley Publishers.

# Chapter 15

# PROJECT LOGIC – PROVIDING SERVICES AND SUPPORT FOR THE PROVISION OF THERAPEUTIC LIFE STORY WORK

*Amanda Jones, Senior Manager, Evaluation, Policy and Research, Berry Street, Melbourne, Australia*

## Introduction by Richard Rose

*In 2010, I met with Berry Street's amazing Annette Jackson in Melbourne, Australia. Dr Bruce Perry suggested that I should meet with Annette, then the Director of the well-respected therapy service Take Two. Annette is a Fellow of Perry's Child Trauma Academy and the lead for the Neurosequential Model of Therapeutics (NMT) in Australia. Annette and I discussed the effective use of the therapeutic life story approach. With her support, I was asked to present on the intervention in the State of Victoria the following year. I had already begun to present as a guest of Evolve Therapy, part of Queensland Mental Health Services, and with Laurel Downey, then a member of the Cairns Institute in Far North Queensland, where I was appointed as a visiting scholar for a month at the James Cook University.*

*Over the following years I have become more and more involved with Berry Street and became a Fellow of their Childhood Institute in 2014. In 2015, Amanda Jones and Julian Pocock, alongside Marg Hamley, Pam Miranda and senior board members, committed to adopting my life story model within Berry Street. Amanda Jones was tasked with undertaking an implementation evaluation of the model designed to improve the program prior to evaluation of its impact and generate learning about how best to support its integration and replication within Berry Street's out of home care contexts.*

*For those interested in understanding how program logic can be used to inform both the implementation and evaluation of an intervention, the following chapter should prove helpful.*

## About Berry Street

Berry Street was established in 1877 as the Victorian Asylum, and since then its core activity has been protecting children in need and strengthening families so they can provide better care for their children. Berry Street is now the largest independent child and family services organisation in Victoria.

Berry Street provides a range of services for children, young people and adults in a number of different locations. Services include: foster and kinship care; residential and reception care; youth support services including case management, outreach, employment and training, and accommodation; family support and counselling; education and employment programmes and a school with three campuses; family and domestic violence services; financial counselling; a heritage information service and Open Place, the support service for Forgotten Australians; three children's contact services; community development and support programmes; and a state wide intensive therapeutic service for children and young people (Take Two).

Berry Street works across Victoria, from 35 offices and another 25 worksites, with the majority of services in the Grampians, Gippsland, Hume, and Northern and South Eastern metropolitan regions. Berry Street employs over 1000 staff, has 245 carer households, and has the support of over 600 volunteers and mentors.

Take Two is an innovative therapeutic service for children and young people who have experienced trauma and disrupted attachment, most of whom are involved with the child protection system. The programme commenced in 2004 and is now well established and embedded in the service system. In 2016, Take Two comprised a partnership of child and family welfare services, mental health, academic and Aboriginal and Torres Strait Islander services as follows: Berry Street, La Trobe

University School of Social Work and Social Policy, Mindful and the Victorian Aboriginal Child Care Agency.

Since its establishment, the Take Two programme has featured the dual objectives of providing a high quality clinical programme and contributing to service system improvement. In addition, it has a clear mandate and dedicated budget for the provision of practice development, training and research in relation to the Take Two client group. The Take Two approach emphasises the need to understand the children and young people's experience of trauma and disrupted attachment within their context, including cultural identity. Take Two aims to intervene at multiple levels to harness resources available to the children and young people and to build on their strengths. In addition to tailoring interventions to the child or young person, Take Two seeks to develop a culture in which staff engage in knowledge development and dissemination (Jackson *et al.* 2009).

## Background to the trial

From late 2014 to the end of 2015, Berry Street undertook a 14-month trial of therapeutic life story work, based on the model developed by Richard Rose. Berry Street secured trust funding to support programme delivery for this period, including the cost of employing a therapeutic life story work practitioner. Berry Street also negotiated with Richard Rose, as founder of the model and practice expert in its delivery, that he would provide progressive secondary consultation to the therapeutic life story practitioner on a monthly basis for the life of the trial. Berry Street thus had a unique opportunity to resource such a trial at this time.

The objective of the trial was threefold:

1. To articulate its programme logic as a basis for clarifying both model implementation and design of an evaluation.

2. To undertake a process and formative evaluation of the therapeutic life story work intervention model, designed to improve the programme prior to a second phase evaluation of programme effects, or an outcome evaluation.

3.  To generate learning about how best to support therapeutic life story work's subsequent integration within Berry Street's home-based care and therapeutic residential care contexts.

From Berry Street's point of view, therapeutic life story work was effectively an innovation: it employs strategies and processes that are unique in terms of how they seek to address the identified issues. Therapeutic life story work had not yet been tried out in our specific context – in a regional, organisational and out-of-home care service system sense. A trial would therefore serve to build understanding about the model intent between partners (out-of-home care, mental health, life story programme and child protection), 'work out the bugs' or operational practicalities as it proceeded, and identify implementation requirements for its broader take-up within Berry Street.

The focus of this chapter is the first trial objective, i.e. a description of the programme logic developed for Berry Street's therapeutic life story work model.

## The therapeutic life story work conceptual model

Berry Street set out to implement Rose's task-oriented and time-limited model in the following three phases:

-  18–20 hours over two to three months of information gathering and assessment of the young person's past life history, prior to direct work with the child (the 'information bank').

-  Planning and delivery of a minimum of 20 two-hour (fortnightly) direct sessions with the young person, together with their carer/keyworker ('internalisation'), over nine months.

-  20 hours over two months of co-producing with the young person a comprehensive life story book ('externalisation').

The Berry Street model (see Figure 15.1) was also predicated on the 'triangular relationship' between the carer/keyworker, therapeutic life story worker and Take Two therapist, as introduced to stakeholders by

Richard Rose in the planning phase, based on his own model, the Ring of Confidentiality (Philpot and Rose 2005).

Take Two therapist/clinician

Therapeutic parent (carer/keyworker)

*Figure 15.1 The therapeutic life story work model within Berry Street*

# The programme logic approach

Programme logic is one major approach within the Clarificative Form of evaluation (Owen 2007). At its heart is a model of an intervention showing how an identifiable set of inputs and activities logically link to an identifiable set of outcomes (Patton 2008). The linkages should make explicit the intended or hypothesised cause and effect, with each step logically preceding the next in order for each to be accomplished or achieved. Hence, the 'If–Then' structuring of this basic original model. Importantly, these linkages should be logical and testable (Patton 2008). Traditional logic models based on this linear sequential causal concept will typically consist of some variation on the five components shown in Figure 15.2 in the form of a schematised graphic (Funnell and Rogers 2011, p.17).

The purpose of programme logic is first and foremost descriptive and explanatory. It serves to make explicit the causal linkages or relationships among the elements necessary to operate an intervention (Knowleton and Phillips 2009). The hypothesised linkages of the logic model should be subject to empirical testing (Patton 2008), which only becomes possible when it is articulated. In fact, as Patton (2008) notes, the idea of theory of change and programme logic emerged in the 1970s out of the realisation among evaluators that programmes could not be readily evaluated as they frequently lacked an adequately conceptualised theory of change that could be critiqued, i.e. evaluability readiness was poor. Several benefits have been identified with the use of programme logic, and there is strong convergence among theorists and evolution practitioners about these. Funnell and Rogers (2011) have helpfully provided four clusters as a way to organise thinking about these benefits.

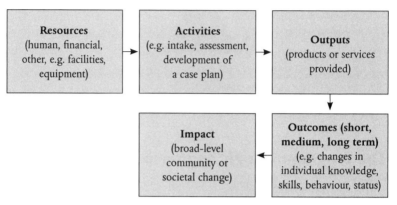

*Figure 15.2 Typical template for the traditional linear programme logic model (adapted from Furnell and Rogers: W.K.Kellogg Foundation)*

## Designing and planning intervention

The logic model approach supports programme managers in answering basic questions as to what the problem is, the programme rationale (there are usually a number of different interventions for a given problem, so choice should be defensible), and the likelihood of success (for example, are resources sufficient for the programme to be effective; are the activities appropriate?). It guides what the programme manager needs to plan for in putting the programme into operation, for example resources to secure and allocate, and setting objectives and goals. Patton (2008) notes that programme logic has in this regard served to bring evaluation forward as integral to programme design and planning, rather than as a back end last-thing-done activity.

## Engagement and communication

Programme logic modelling has the benefit of bringing key stakeholders together in a (it is hoped) safe facilitated way to determine the extent to which views about the programme rationale, intent and operational detail are divergent or aligned. This is not always explicitly voiced or known, and yet can nevertheless create dissonance within teams and between teams and external stakeholders. The process can allow these views to be aired, and a shared understanding to be fostered. Additionally, the process can serve to affirm and validate practitioners' efforts and contributions to the whole, thereby boosting morale and enhancing team cohesion. Programme logic is also a strong tool for promoting communication about the programme intent, rationale and importance to external stakeholders. It also empowers through recognising the knowledge practitioners hold and their capacity to influence programme design, planning, implementation and improvement.

## Monitoring and evaluation

As already noted, programme logic is strongly articulated with evaluation. It can be thought of as a map for scoping evaluation planning. It can inform choice of performance measures, it can guide understanding about success and it can be used to monitor the progress of implementation (Patton 2008). All of this feeds into more informed management decision making about the programme, including whether it is working and no action is required, or whether it needs to be redesigned, needs work on implementation fidelity, or is ready for impact evaluation.

## Contributing to knowledge generation and translation

Programme logic can inform the scaling up of successful programmes, serving to identify which elements are important to replicate or adapt for other conditions or other target populations (Funnell and Rogers 2011).

There are limitations to programme logic, essentially associated with how complicated or complex the intervention is that is being represented. Its main problems, according to Funnell and Rogers (2011), are that it does not explain the causal mechanisms that lead to the intended outcomes; it implies that service activities apply only at the start; and it fails to reflect the existence of different causal strands that could operate. Complexity theory and systems theory together have advanced understanding here. Complicated interventions involve multiple components, including levels of operation, number of objectives, and number of implementing agencies. Complex interventions are recursive in their causality, and emergent, i.e. the specific outcomes and causal processes are unpredictable and expected to evolve and adapt during implementation. The notion of complex adaptive open systems also applies here: a dynamic web-like network of many interacting parts in which change in one part can mean all parts change at the same time, and where small changes can lead to disproportionate change. In such an environment, applying the linear model is likely to misrepresent what an intervention does and can achieve (Patton 2008).

Notwithstanding this critique of the traditional linear model, this was the form adopted and reviewed as a basis for building understanding and informing the first phase of evaluation for the Berry Street therapeutic life story work trial. This version builds in a set of assumptions and evidence (where it exists) as a way to begin to understand causal mechanisms.

## Programme logic for therapeutic life story work

The key elements of the logic developed for therapeutic life story work within Berry Street are outlined in turn below.

Typically, separate programme logic is developed wherever there is a discrete target/client group that receives a distinct service. In the case of therapeutic life story work, the participating children are seen as the client, but the foster carers and residential care keyworkers who enable and support the process are nevertheless explicitly recognised within the programme logic in terms of the short-, medium- and long-term outcomes they also receive in parallel.

*A note on outcomes:* These can be thought of as more proximal (short term to medium term) or more distal (medium term to long term). The logic works in such a way that each outcome is a precondition for a subsequent outcome, and if credible and robust, earlier outcomes can be presumed to contribute to later outcomes even if it becomes more difficult to evidence those later outcomes.

## *Assumptions and evidence*

- Children and young people in out-of-home care have frequently experienced trauma and disrupted attachment as a result of abuse and neglect. A key part of this experience for many of these children is the lack of a coherent understanding of the narrative of their life and history, including understanding about the reasons why they are in care. Their story is often fragmented, discontinuous and characterised by confusion, misconceptions, blame and shame about what went wrong and why; simultaneously, they tend to have strong coping defences against efforts to explore and make sense of this experience. The persistence of this incoherent and incomplete personal life narrative can put the child or young person at risk neurodevelopmentally (Perry, in Rose 2012).

- This fragmented understanding can often lead to confusion about identity and belonging, and is thought to lead to or compound preoccupation with the past, inattention, poor impulse control and restlessness (hyperactivity), poor memory, poor engagement in learning, poor mood (anxiety, depression), dysregulation, challenging behaviours, difficulties interacting and connecting in the here and now with current carer(s), and lack of hope about the future.

- This preoccupation and dysregulation typically result in significantly reduced capacity to engage in positive aspects of the child's life, including forging rewarding attachments with carers and participating in formal learning.

- Carers and keyworkers, in turn, frequently have inadequate information about the child's history, background and beliefs and attributions about this. The child protection and out-of-home care systems currently do not facilitate sufficient sharing of information to support the child in the 'reconstruction' of their life narrative. In fact, there can be as many versions of the child's history and experience as there are or have been carers and keyworkers in the child's life, and the absence of a thorough systematic effort to make sense of this holistically for and with the child can perpetuate their sense of a fragmented life.

- Therapeutic life story work is complex and intensive. It is a targeted intervention, which is task-driven and staged over nine months, i.e. it is time oriented and time limited. It typically requires an extended period of information gathering and assessment; planning and delivery of a minimum of 18 direct sessions with the child and carer/keyworker; and production with the child of a comprehensive life story book. Given both the time and extra skill level requirements, it is not possible for this intervention to be absorbed into existing worker roles within therapeutic home-based and residential care without significant backfill or allocation of skilled dedicated roles, in combination with ongoing tailored group supervision. Likewise, therapeutic out-of-home care clinicians typically do not have the time within their current caseloads to undertake the extended and intensive work required for therapeutic life story work to be done well.

- Therapeutic life story work extends and enhances therapeutic out-of-home care through a more comprehensive and intentional focus on creating an integrated life narrative in partnership with the child and their carer/keyworker. This work, if successful, contributes to the child's healing and the quality of the carer–child attachment.

- Therapeutic life story work works with 'the placement', i.e. not with the child only, but rather with the child and their carer/keyworker. It requires skill to enhance the relationship between the child and the third person (carer/keyworker). In this way it could be seen as similar to dyadic clinical work; however, it is therapeutically informed work, not therapy.

- Narrative therapy is not new and is recognised as valuable and utilised by many therapists who provide regular direct therapy for traumatised children within out-of-home care. However, while therapeutic life story work is informed by narrative theory and practice, its time-limited and time-oriented nature makes it a distinctly different, but related, intervention.

- 'Scrapbooking' and 'story booking' are related activities that are currently being done with and for children within the out-of-home care system in Victoria. These are not, however, equivalent to therapeutic life story work. They don't address any difficulties the child has had with their birth family and life journey since removal, and engage in the healing process of co-authoring a holistic narrative; rather, they tend to focus on the 'highlights' only. Therapeutic life story work is designed to be more intentionally therapeutic than either of these activities.

- The existing models of out-of-home care within Victoria are not able to pay enough attention to the child or young person's story, and exponents of the therapeutic life story model hypothesise that this reduces its overall effectiveness. Therapeutic life story work, a 'cortically mediated coherent personal narrative' (Perry, in Rose 2012, p.10), is believed to enhance out-of-home care.

## Client group

Therapeutic life story work targets children who:

- are 5–17 years old, anywhere in Victoria

- live in therapeutic residential care or foster care

- have an assessed potential to benefit from the intervention in terms of degree of emotional regulation, learning capacity and suitability of placement environment

- have been in their placement for a minimum of three months, and who are likely to be in a longer-term placement.

## Resources

Therapeutic life story work requires:

- a trained therapeutic life story worker (1.0FTE per caseload of 12 clients)

- ICT tools of the trade (mobile phone, laptop)

- a resources/materials budget (games, stationery, camera, storage, book production)

- access to a car for outreach work

- access to regular line supervision and monthly group reflective supervision (one hour).

## Service activities

Therapeutic life story work includes the following processes and functions:

- initial assessment and intake

- assessment of readiness (clinically supported where appropriate)

- provision of therapeutic life story work welcome books to each child and carer/keyworker, and an introduction to therapeutic life story work

- provision of an All About Me book

- development of a comprehensive understanding of the child's own history and that of their family (three-month information-gathering phase)

- development of an understanding of the child's internal working models

- assessment of current developmental presentation

- assessment of the child's current and past care environment

- planning of direct sessions, and ongoing assessment

- rapport – building and engagement with the child and carer/ keyworker through play-based activities, then moving into a directed, staged exploration of the child's life story, with support to make sense of their experience

- role-modelling for the carer in how to interact in a more nurturing, trauma-informed way

- production of a visual record in the form of 'wallpaper' in partnership with the child and carer/keyworker, which supports the creation of a coherent life story narrative

- creation, in partnership with the child and carer/keyworker, of a life story book reflecting their co-authored narrative.

## Participatory benefits

While engaged in therapeutic life story work children should feel:

- heard

- supported

- accepted

- safe

- not judged

- not isolated or alone

- respected

- culturally understood.

## Direct benefits/short-term outcomes

In the short term (12+ sessions), children will have:

- an All About Me book

- opportunities to explore and understand their birth family history more fully, including having gaps filled and misattributions and assumptions supportively and safely challenged

- opportunities for 'play' time

- validation of their emotions

- a dedicated witness to the re-authoring of their life story

- opportunities for mediated family contact where appropriate in relation to building or completing the child's life narrative.

In the short term, carers/keyworkers will have:

- access to an enhanced information bank about the child, their history, internal working models, developmental presentation and care environment for a more holistic understanding

- opportunities to better understand the benefits of creating an integrated life narrative

- support to practise the child's self-expression and meaning making as they develop their life story.

## *Medium-term outcomes*

In the medium term (from 12+ sessions to exit from the therapeutic life story work), children will have:

- improved insight into the meaning of their life history

- reduced preoccupation with past life history

- improved affect regulation and arousal, for example mood, emotions, behaviours

- a more positive perception of self

- improved relationship with carers

- improved capacity to trust others and to form rewarding, pro-social friendships

- improved capacity for executive functioning, i.e. cause-and-effect and strategic thinking and future thinking

- improved engagement in formal learning

- improved connections with birth family, where appropriate

- stronger connections to culture and a stronger sense of cultural identity.

In the medium term, carers/keyworkers will have:

- improved insight into the meaning of the child's life history and how this has impacted on their internal working models, thinking and behaviours

- enhanced attunement to the child's needs and enhanced nurturing style

- more rewarding interactions with the child.

## Long-term outcomes

In the longer term (post-exit), children will have:

- a more integrated narrative of their life history

- a more congruent internal and external sense of self

- a sense of identity that is no longer led by the past

- ongoing capacity for self-regulation

- ongoing positive relationship with their carers

- ongoing involvement in education (or training/employment)

- ongoing positive friendships

- increased potential for family reunification or strengthened connections where achievable

- a life story book that documents a new, more integrated life narrative.

In the longer term, carers/keyworkers will have:

- an ongoing commitment to therapeutic life story work

- reduced 'alienation' of role, i.e. an ongoing sense of self-efficacy and rewards in the role.

## Social change

The therapeutic life story work will contribute to the following broader changes at the community level:

- improved life chances for children in out-of-home care

- reduction in cycles of intergenerational trauma

- improved stability of out-of-home care placements

- improved retention of carers.

# Testing the logic of therapeutic life story work

The programme logic was reviewed by key stakeholders at the end of the trial, in light of operational experience. Overall, stakeholders considered that it held up well – all programme logic domains were broadly endorsed as reasonable by the end of the trial, with the exception of the 'client group' for whom the eligibility criteria were underdeveloped/ underspecified. The evaluation, including a review of the original programme logic, served to identify a clearer, more elaborated set of eligibility criteria, which are documented below. The programme logic has now been revised accordingly to reflect these criteria (and to support the development of more robust referral and assessment processes).

The therapeutic life story work intervention targets children who:

- have expressed interest in or curiosity about their past ('What happened to me?' 'I want to know more about my family'). The therapeutic life story work practitioner and/or the child's case manager should be really clear about what therapeutic life story work is, and they should talk about readiness/level of interest with the child and provide many opportunities for the child to not proceed or to pull out, or to resume at a later stage if desired

- have a level of internal regulation, resources that enable them to think about and tolerate uncomfortable thoughts and feelings and delayed gratification and be co-regulated by the carer as part of their emotional safety to engage in the intervention

- are over five years of age and developmentally ready to engage in a language/talking-based therapeutic intervention

- are not experiencing serious mental health issues, and not engaged in serious self-harming (this requires careful assessment)

- are settled in their placement, with an established carer relationship. An unstable out-of-home care system can render therapeutic life story work potentially unsafe. It can be difficult or protracted to engage a new carer in the process

- typically have a history of care from a young age that has created instability, multiple placements, gaps and transience, such that we know they have an incomplete picture that is likely to give rise to confusion, and misattributions about where they have been, with whom and why – for example, the children have never known their father's family, or cultural background

- have no court activity that is contesting the placement

- have carer(s) with the capacity to support the process, i.e. how integrated they are in their own life story/how vulnerable they themselves might be to being triggered by the process in which they might be subject to a dysregulated child; what supports they have in place to support the child's process

- for whom other – traditional – therapies are not helping.

In terms of the hypothesised outcomes of the programme logic, the therapeutic life story work intervention clearly did align with the short-term outcomes. It was shown to provide an opportunity for children to find out entirely new facts about the context of being in care, to uncover previously unknown extensive family and, notably, previously unknown Aboriginal family background, to think and feel differently about their family history, to engage with family, and have opportunities for 'play' time. Available findings consistent with the short-term outcomes of therapeutic life story work hypothesised in the original programme logic include the following:

- Children generally enjoyed the life story process, including learning about themselves and/or their family background, and the associated drawing and games.

- Children generally expressed the view that life story work helped them to feel or think differently about their family or family background.

- Carers regarded therapeutic life story work as helpful for the children in learning about their family, and better understanding their family of origin and the situation of them being in care.

- Carers were also of the view that therapeutic life story work did help them in their role as carer. Benefits identified included the following:

  ○ Improved understanding of the life history of the child/young person in their care ('Things made much more sense to me, which helped in supporting the young person').

  ○ Improved confidence and comfort in supporting the child/young person in their new understanding about family, and sharing in further exploration of that.

  ○ Assisting both child and carer to 'understand their own journey together'.

There was also promising observation of some medium-term outcomes for some children that could reasonably be attributed to therapeutic life story work, including:

- Improved insight into their family history and behaviours.

- Improved relationship between the child and their carer.

- Meaningful new connection to and involvement with their birth family's Aboriginal culture.

Therapeutic life story work also seemed to enable some carers to 'step up in their role', i.e. it seemed to contribute to their own sense of efficacy in and commitment to the caring role. There was also one unintended positive of the therapeutic life story work process identified for some carers: the fact that the intervention enabled them to talk more with case managers about plans seemed to strengthen their commitment to working more actively with services.

## Conclusion

The development of a programme logic for Berry Street's trial of therapeutic life story work did generally prove useful when considered in terms of the four functions that Funnell and Rogers (2011) have identified. However, it needs to be used intentionally to advance each of these, and, obviously, a range of other project management and governance factors will inevitably mediate how well each of those functions is achieved. The therapeutic life story work programme logic did, for instance, support critical front-end preparation for operationalising the intervention in Berry Street's specific context, but it did not push this enough in terms of target group criteria. It did serve to bring together key stakeholders early to facilitate discussion of their respective understandings about programme rationale, design and intent, but there was still considerable shared learning that needed to be fostered that only surfaced once everyone was in the 'thick of' the trial. It did inform evaluation planning and choice of performance measures, but strong project management and governance are required to ensure that the evaluation plan itself is implemented as intended.

# References

Funnell, S.C. and Rogers, P.J. (2011) *Purposeful Program Theory: Effective Use of Theories of Change and Logic Models.* San Francisco, California: John Wiley & Sons.

Jackson, A., Frederico, M., Tanti, C. and Black, C.M. (2009) 'Exploring outcomes in a therapeutic service response to the emotional and mental health needs of children who have experienced abuse and neglect in Victoria, Australia.' *Child & Family Social Work* 14, 198–212.

W.K. Kellogg Foundation (2004) *Logic Model Development Guide.* Michigan, W.K. Kellogg.

Knowlton, L.W. and Phillips, C.C. (2009) *The Logic Model Guidebook: Better Strategies for Great Results.* Thousand Oaks, California: SAGE.

Owen, J.M. (2007) *Program Evaluation: Forms and Approaches* (3rd edition). New York: Guilford Press.

Patton, M.Q. (2008) *Utilization-Focused Evaluation* (4th edition). Thousand Oaks, California: SAGE.

Rogers, P.J. (2008) 'Using programme theory to evaluate complicated and complex aspects of interventions.' *Evaluation* 14, 29–48.

Rose, R. (2012) *Life Story Therapy with Traumatized Children.* London: Jessica Kingsley Publishers.

Rose, R. and Philpot, T. (2005) *The Child's Own Story: Work with Traumatized Children.* London: Jessica Kingsley Publishers.

Chapter 16

# LEARNING TO UNDERSTAND – LIFE STORY WORK AT METRO INTENSIVE SUPPORT SERVICES IN NEW SOUTH WALES

*Melissa Stokes, Anna-Elizabeth Mattiuzzo and Natalia O'Keefe*

Working with children and young people who experience the ongoing effects of childhood trauma is a challenging, yet ultimately rewarding, experience. In a very busy casework office, often amid the crisis-driven nature of work with children and young people with complex needs, we know that healing is important. For over ten years, Metro Intensive Support Services (Metro ISS) within the New South Wales (NSW) Department of Family and Community Services (FACS) has been working with children who have complex needs, seeking ways to help them make sense of their past and to provide opportunities for healing. This chapter will outline the therapeutic life story work model as it has been implemented by Metro ISS in Sydney, Australia, over 12 months and the benefits that we have seen this model bring.

## Child protection and out-of-home care in New South Wales

Child protection services in NSW are provided by Community Services, a division within the NSW Department of FACS. As at 30 June 2015 there were 17,585 children and young people in out-of-home care in NSW (FACS 2014–15). The majority of children in out-of-home care live in family-based care, and one in two children is placed with a relative or kinship carer. Children in out-of-home care are supported directly by Community Services, a non-government organisation, or a combination of the two.

## Metro Intensive Support Services

Metro ISS is a team within Community Services providing intensive, specialist case management for children in long-term, statutory out-of-home care. Metro ISS sits within the broader Intensive Support Services system, which was 'developed to provide dedicated resources and expertise within Community Services to obtain quality outcomes for children and young people with high and complex needs' (Intensive Support Services 2011, p.3).

Metro ISS is concerned with approximately 80–100 children at any time. The caseworkers have a limited caseload of around six clients to allow them to provide intensive, long-term support and service co-ordination for the children, their carers and family. The caseworkers generally have face-to-face contact with children weekly or fortnightly, with the focus being on achieving positive outcomes across all domains of the Community Services case plan, including health, education, placement stability and family contact.

Metro ISS has a team of psychologists who provide consultation, assessment and therapeutic intervention for the children. There is also a leaving care caseworker who provides specialist knowledge for caseworkers about the support and resources available to a child leaving care, as well as remaining a contact and referral point for our clients into adulthood. Strong partnerships with other government and non-government agencies are also an important part of the ISS system.

Children can be living anywhere across the Sydney metropolitan area when they are referred to Metro ISS by other Community Services centres, and their caseworker remains the same regardless of transitions across the area (and outside the area where practical). The extended nature of the work allows for the child to develop a long-term supportive relationship with their caseworker.

Metro ISS primarily works with children and adolescents between 10 and 18 years who live in a range of placement settings. They may have experienced family placement breakdown, multiple foster care placements as well as moves within the residential care system.

Although the majority of children in out-of-home care in NSW live in home-based care, the majority of Metro ISS children live in residential care and often experience significant placement disruption. During a review of Australian research on short-term outcomes for children in out-of-home care, Osborn and Bromfield (2007) noted that although many children obtain a stable out-of-home care placement there appears to be a small subgroup for whom ongoing and severe placement disruption occurs. For those children, they also identified the concurrence of significant early trauma and abuse.

## Children with the experience of complex trauma

The children referred to Metro ISS present with high and complex support needs. Many of this group have experienced multiple traumatic events – often within their early attachment relationships – have had placement disruptions within the care system and present with a range of social, emotional and behavioural difficulties.

These children have been impacted by the experience of 'complex trauma', a term which encompasses both the exposure to traumatic events and the impact of that exposure over the short and long term (NTCSN White Paper 2003). The children we support have generally experienced multiple types of abuse, whether this is physical abuse, sexual abuse, emotional abuse, neglect or being witness to domestic violence, or a combination of these. Their experience of abuse usually begins in early childhood, sometimes prenatally, and often within early attachment relationships.

The children we work with often arrive at our team with a variety of diagnoses such as attention deficit hyperactivity disorder, oppositional defiant disorder, post-traumatic stress disorder, pervasive developmental disorder, disruptive behaviour disorder, anxiety disorders and depressive disorders, although we know that 'no single current psychiatric diagnosis accounts for the cluster of symptoms that research has shown frequently to occur in children exposed to interpersonal trauma' (D'andrea *et al.* 2012, p.188).

It is well documented that early adverse experiences, especially those involving trauma and abuse, impact on brain development in structural and functional ways (van der Kolk 2003; Perry 2004; Delima and Vimpani 2011; Gaskill and Perry 2012). Cook *et al.* (2005) outline the seven domains of impairment resulting from complex trauma as: i) Attachment; ii) Biology; iii) Affect regulation; iv) Dissociation; v) Behavioural control; vi) Cognition; and vii) Self-concept. In practice these can be seen as children who have:

- difficulty trusting others and feeling safe

- few friends or social supports

- difficulty accepting help from others

- complex physical health needs such as unexplained stomach pains, skin problems, pseudo seizures and related help-seeking behaviours such as calling ambulances and attending hospitals

- difficulty labelling their own emotions and expressing how they feel

- difficulty regulating emotions which may cause them to lash out or react in a way that seems disproportionate to the current concern

- self-injurious behaviour

- impulsive or risk-taking behaviour that places them at immediate risk of harm

- substance use/abuse issues

- speech and language delay

- difficulty coping with change, for example changes to daily routine

- difficulty at school, including problems with attention and learning

- low self-esteem, high levels of self-blame and a poor sense of self.

A diagnosed intellectual disability is also apparent for about 30 per cent of children referred to Metro ISS, which is significantly more than the general population. In a 2012 survey by the Australian Bureau of Statistics (2012), 2.9 per cent of the overall population and 4 per cent of all children aged 0–14 years identified as having an intellectual disability. Not only does exposure to abuse increase the likelihood of developmental disability, but children with an intellectual disability are more vulnerable to abuse in childhood, are more likely to experience ongoing victimisation and may experience greater difficulty accessing appropriate help (NTCSN 2004). This means we need to be aware of the impact of disability and further vulnerability for these children when they enter the out-of-home care system.

The children we support often come from vulnerable families who have experienced social and economic disadvantage. Finally, it is recognised in NSW and across Australia that Aboriginal children are disproportionately represented in child protection and out-of-home care services.

## Context for life story work and the beginning of the team

In NSW, there is a strong legislative and policy imperative to ensure that when children enter out-of-home care they have access to life story books and work which helps them understand who they are, their family of origin, their history and their time in care.

At Metro ISS we found ourselves working with children who had missed out on their story. These children had experienced considerable change, and were disconnected from family, past carers and from people who held their history. Moreover, in practice it can be difficult for a caseworker to afford the time and resources to do life story work when day-to-day energy is often focused on managing crises, placement issues, educational challenges and supporting family relationships, especially when working with clients with complex needs. Humphreys and Kertesz (2015) identified the quality of life story work to be variable in Victoria, and similarly in NSW, the Office of the Children's Guardian (2015) has recently released a 'Snapshot of Trends in Practice across the Out-of-Home Care Sector', noting inconsistent practice in this area.

We realised that the complexity of their history meant these children needed help understanding their past and required support to know their story. We saw a need for a dedicated resource to do this work, away from the day-to-day complexity of casework. Following a workshop with Richard Rose in November 2014, the Metro ISS life story team began. The team consists of a part-time manager casework and two part-time caseworkers. There is also a full-time casework position which is a 12-month rotating position and is filled by other Metro ISS caseworkers who indicate an interest in this area.

## Understanding why children in care don't know their story

We all have stories about our life. These stories have often been told to us by family, have been shared over time and are stories that help us learn who we are (Rose 2012; Swain and Musgrove 2012; Humphreys and Kertesz 2015). Often children in care have not had the opportunity to hear their stories, to share memories with those close to them or to make sense of who they are. Within their home environment, when parents aren't safe and children need to focus on protecting themselves from harm, they have little opportunity to develop or explore their sense of self (Barton *et al.* 2012).

When children enter out-of-home care they may lose connection with family or have contact that varies in quality and frequency (Mendes, Johnson and Moslehuddin 2012; Swain and Musgrove 2012). This means that opportunities for learning about family history directly from family can be limited.

Children may rely on their foster family to provide them with information about who they are. However, foster carers are not always provided with information about a child's early history. There may be concerns about providing sensitive family information, sometimes workers lack the time to compile historical information or are unclear what should remain private (Humphreys and Kertesz 2015), and sometimes workers are concerned that a child's past may influence the way that a foster carer sees a child.

As each placement ends, the child risks losing more of their 'story'. Ongoing placement disruption, moving between carers and often between agencies, can lead to information and stories becoming disjointed or lost. In recognition of the difficulties experienced by children in out-of-home care in relation to family and identity, several jurisdictions have considered how to improve their practice. The work of the Who am I? research project in Victoria, Australia, is one such project. During interviews with out-of-home care staff, Humphreys and Kertesz (2015) found that school reports, medical information, life story material and sometimes birth certificates remained on an agency file instead of being passed on with the child, even when the child changed agencies. This led to information being 'scattered across many organisations, people, and service systems' (Humphreys and Kertesz 2015, p.511). For Metro ISS children, who may have experienced numerous placements over a relatively short period of time, it becomes apparent why neither they nor those around them know their stories.

It may be through their files that care leavers search to replace the stories most of us receive from our families (Humphreys and Kertesz 2015). The significance of access to records and information about their past for children who live or have lived in out-of-home care is becoming better understood. The Who am I? research project looked at a range of areas related to care leavers' records, including access to historical records, consideration of how records being prepared now can be improved to increase their meaning, and how to support care leavers who are likely to be searching for information to piece together their own story and have questions about their identity (Swain and Musgrove 2012; Humphreys et al. 2014; Humphreys and Kertesz 2015).

Murray and Humphreys (2014) found that care leavers were often looking to records to provide them with information about family they had not known and to understand why they had gone into care. Care leavers were glad when records could provide new information or confirm uncertainties; however, it was disappointing and even maddening when they realised records were sometimes judgemental, missing crucial information or when they failed to tell the whole story of the child (Murray and Humphreys 2014).

The type of records that are kept by agencies can impact on children and those around them having a clear understanding of their story. Records may include case notes, court documents, professional reports, case plans, cultural plans and school reports. While these are useful and necessary records to be held for children in out-of-home care, they are not written to provide a life narrative for the child and their purpose is not about helping a child to develop their identity (Swain and Musgrove 2012; Hollingworth 2015).

Finally, when a child has been in care for an extended period of time, it might be assumed that they know information about their family and their history. A previous caseworker or carer surely would have provided information or answered the child's questions? However, sometimes, no one has asked the child what questions they have or what information they would like to know. During the first year of the Metro ISS therapeutic life story work programme we were often surprised and sometimes saddened by the questions that children had at the beginning of the life story work process. Some of those questions were:

- Is my mum alive?

- Why can't I live with my mum?

- Does my mum/dad have a job?

- How did mum and dad feel when I came into care?

- Why was I sent to live with my Aunt Helen and not my Uncle Jeff?

- Why is it okay for my sister to live at home and not me?

- What do my parents look like? What do my siblings look like?

- Why did I have to leave the placement with Bill and Jane?

- Where do my brothers and sisters live?

- What do my brothers and sisters like doing?

- How do I pronounce my brother's name?

## Our experience with therapeutic life story work

When we first started the life story team at ISS we were not entirely sure how the process would unfold or what the benefits would be. Our work has become an important and powerful first step for children who know little about their background to explore and begin to develop their identity. We realised the importance of clarifying information and stories that children may have heard, especially where they have not been available or have been inaccurate (Rose 2012).

Also, because we make time to explore who is in a family and because life story work can decrease the anxiety of those working with children about their responses to family contact, there has been an opportunity for children to reconnect to family. Barriers that we may have thought existed, such as very complex histories or intellectual disability, can be overcome to allow all children an opportunity to know their story.

Since the establishment of our team we have encountered many challenges, which have dictated that our practice be flexible and that we continue to evolve our work through our experiences. For example, new procedures are put in place as we learn from issues that arise. When doing background work with families there have been times when we are not successful in tracing family members, or those that we do find may be reluctant or unwilling to speak to us. We have found it best to be honest and sensitive about this with children. Sometimes, sessions do not occur, or the aim of the work has been modified due to the changing circumstances for children. The case studies below demonstrate some of our learning. Please note that the names and details of the children referred to in the case studies have been changed to protect their confidentiality and some children's stories have been merged into the same case study.

### CASE STUDY: SKYE

Skye, aged 16, was referred to the life story team. The initial referral advised that Skye had a diagnosis of depression and anxiety. She had a history of physical aggression and high risk-taking behaviours such as spending significant periods of time away from placements and self-harming. Over the past year, with the support of her care team, Skye's presentation had stabilised significantly and she was now attending school part time. The focus of Skye's case plan was to support her to develop the relationship with her mother Debra, a relationship which over the years had been extremely challenging.

At the time of the referral, Skye was living in a residential care placement with other young people. Prior to her placement in residential care, Skye had experienced over 15 foster care placements. The majority of her placements ended due to her carers being unable to meet Skye's high-level support needs. The referral information also noted that Skye experienced challenges in forming and maintaining relationships.

Skye's care team recommended that Skye's mother should be involved in the sessions. This was the first time that a life story worker in our office had undertaken joint work with a child and family member. Prior to beginning sessions, the worker spent some time meeting with Debra and discussing the purpose of life story work and how this might support Skye. These meetings also provided an opportunity to speak with Debra about how she might manage challenging discussions during sessions and what support she required to meet her own emotional needs. Despite this background work, the life story worker still had some concerns around how the sessions would proceed. For instance, how would it unfold having the mother present when talking about Skye's entry into care? Would Skye be able to speak openly about her thoughts and feelings during sessions?

Skye articulated to her worker that she wanted to understand the challenges her mother faced raising her as a sole parent; she also wanted to understand why she was removed and why her two half siblings, who her mother gave birth to after Skye's removal, continue to live at home. These issues were extremely contentious for Skye and had for a long time been a source of anxiety and confusion.

Several sessions were dedicated to discussing these issues. In session Skye spoke about her apprehension around exploring her entry into care. She said that she did not want to ask her mother any questions that may hurt or upset her. Skye was clearly invested in building her relationship with her mother and did not want to jeopardise this. Skye was encouraged by her mother to ask questions and share her thoughts, and this put Skye at ease. Time was spent discussing with Skye and Debra how children in care often hear various stories from different people about how they come into care and how this can be very confusing. Skye agreed and explained that over the years she had heard different versions of her care entry from caseworkers, various carers and family members.

In order to help Skye make sense of the information that she was holding, and why she entered care, her life story worker wrote three headings on the wallpaper:

- What I know

- What mum says

- Community Services records.

Time was spent sorting through the information with Skye and Debra. Skye wrote down her understanding of her entry into care. This included:

- Mum used to hit me

- I was left at home alone

- Mum used drugs.

In one particular example Skye gave, she said that she heard that when she was little her mother had refused to take her to the doctor's after she had an accident. This accident resulted in Skye receiving scarring to her forearm, which is still visible.

Debra was then given the opportunity to respond and tell Skye her version. Debra spoke about the challenges she faced as a young mother raising Skye with minimal support. Debra spoke about her own upbringing and how she struggled with her own relationship with her mother; this, Debra explained, meant that she found it difficult to show affection and emotion to Skye. Debra also spoke about not having much money and moving around. Debra explained that she was also suffering from depression, but she denied using drugs as a means to cope. Debra told Skye that she did not have the accident when Skye was in her care. On the wallpaper the life story worker wrote:

- Money problems

- No stable accommodation

- Mum was young with little support

- Mum was having trouble managing her emotions

- Mum says that she did not use drugs or hit me

- Mum says the accident did not happen when I was with her.

The life story worker spoke about Community Services' reasons for the removal. On the wallpaper the life story worker wrote:

- Mum was not always around to watch Skye

- Worries about mum using drugs

- There was no stable accommodation

- Worries about how mum was coping

- Skye was not attending school.

Time was spent during the session discussing how these issues would impact on Debra's ability to keep Skye safe in the home.

The life story worker had found a report in the file that stated that the accident Skye referred to happened in one of Skye's early foster care placements. The report confirmed that the carer did seek medical treatment. Skye was initially angry, stating that she had been lied to about her accident and her mother's involvement.

Skye expressed confusion about the differences in the three versions. The life story worker reminded Skye that it was unlikely that her mum and Community Services would agree entirely and this was an area that was still very hard for her mother to discuss. By this stage Skye was feeling more at ease in asking some difficult questions of her mother. She asked her mother about how she felt when she (Skye) was removed. Debra also spoke to Skye about what had changed in her life to enable her to keep Skye's two younger siblings in her care.

At the end of these sessions Skye spoke about feeling 'relieved' and as though she felt a 'huge weight' had been lifted now that she had been able to address some of the information she was holding with her mum. Likewise, Debra also spoke about feeling proud and happy that her daughter was able to speak openly and honestly with her.

One exercise done in the session was to plot each of Skye's placements on her wallpaper. Skye had in excess of 15 placements during her time in care. When the wallpaper was rolled out it was quite visually striking for both mother and daughter to see the multiple placements listed. The life story worker helped Skye to talk about what it was like for her to move from place to place and the pressure she felt to 'fit into' each new family she moved to and how she found it difficult to bond and trust each new carer. This was important because Skye was actually describing her own struggles with attachment, and the enormous expectation around this was able to be discussed. Her mother was then able to better understand their relationship in the context of the challenges her daughter faced.

## *My Journey*

Our team has worked with several children who have an intellectual disability. Because of the complexities surrounding their disability, some of these children were unable to participate in the full wallpaper work due to writing, language and comprehension difficulties. Instead a different format was used called 'My Journey'.

My Journey aims to give a brief and clear outline of significant events in a child's life including family structure, important relationships and placement changes. It includes photos, pictures, positive stories and simple statements about safety, along with a basic narrative of the child's history.

During the information-gathering phase, stories and memories are collected, for example memories of the child's favourite foods and places they liked to visit. Pictures related to these stories are then included in the child's Journey (see Figure 16.1). When children see their Journey it often prompts them to share their own memories.

| | | |
|---|---|---|
| Jason was born in June 1999. At home he lived with his mum, dad and brother. |  | Jason went to his local public school. Sometimes Jason didn't have any lunch or go to school. |
| Jason loved to sing to all kinds of music, and roast was his favourite dinner. |  | Sometimes when Jason's mum and dad weren't well he would stay with his grandma. |

*Figure 16.1 Example of My Journey*

## CASE STUDY: KIRI

Kiri was referred to the life story team when she was aged 15. Kiri was diagnosed with oppositional defiant disorder and had a significant history of engaging in high risk-taking behaviour such as drug and alcohol use, running away, sexualised behaviours and criminal activity. Kiri had lived with the same residential care provider for the past two years and had formed some positive relationships with her care staff.

Kiri's referral explained that she was born in New Zealand and had moved to Australia with her father and step-mother when she was 10 years old. Kiri was removed from her father's care when she was 12 years old due to concerns about her escalating behaviours and her family's ability to manage these behaviours and keep her safe in the home. Kiri had not had contact with her birth mother since her parents separated when she was two years old. It was believed that her birth mother was still residing in New Zealand, and information obtained at the time of Kiri's removal indicated that Kiri had a half-sister in New Zealand, also in out-of-home care.

At the referral meeting Kiri's caseworker spoke about Kiri being interested in learning more about her maternal family. The caseworker explained that Kiri's father was extremely reluctant to share any information about Kiri's mother, and when he did speak about her, this was quite negative. It was thought that Kiri's birth mother may be of Maori or Islander descent, but this had not been confirmed. When meeting with her life story worker Kiri explained that she would like to know what her birth mum looked like, if she had a job and what hobbies she enjoyed. Kiri said that she was keen to have contact with her mother. She also wanted to know more about her sister.

During the information-gathering phase the life story worker contacted New Zealand Child Protection Services and the agency confirmed that Kiri did have a half-sister, Reka, who was three years younger and was in kinship care with her paternal family. The agency also confirmed that the girl's mother, Riana, was of Maori descent. The life story worker began liaising with Reka's caseworker. After much planning and preparation with both girls, they commenced having email contact, which then gradually progressed to regular Skype sessions.

The caseworker in New Zealand was able to provide information about Riana. The caseworker explained that Riana had battled drug dependency for many years and has significant mental health issues, which had resulted in her spending large periods of her life homeless, in jail or in mental health facilities. The caseworker advised that Riana had recently declined to have contact with Reka.

The life story worker made contact with Riana's social worker. It was relayed via the social worker that Riana did not wish to participate in a life story work interview and did not wish to have photos or contact with Kiri. During life story work sessions, the life story worker supported Kiri to understand information about her mother's illness and spent time talking about her mother's decision.

Despite this setback, Kiri continued to invest in her relationship with her sister and wanted to learn about her Maori heritage. The life story worker connected Kiri to a Maori cultural caseworker who visited Kiri in her placement and helped her learn about her Maori culture. Kiri was keen to share what she was learning with her sister and to begin to learn some of the Maori language, further strengthening their bond with one another.

When the life story worker first started work with Kiri, she was asked to complete an eco-map outlining the people in her life with whom she was connected and the level of connectedness she felt with each person. Kiri initially found this activity very challenging, rushing through the activity and finding it difficult to talk about each person. The initial eco map is shown in Figure 16.2.

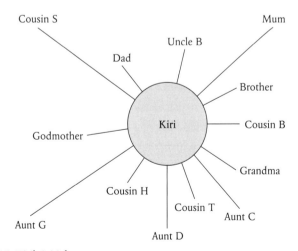

*Figure 16.2 Kiri's initial eco map*

At the conclusion of life story work the initial eco map was reviewed and the exercise was completed again. During the second experience, Kiri was much more positive; she spoke about each person, and added her sister and even a new friend. People in her life were now positioned much closer to her on the map, demonstrating the increased closeness she now felt to them. The final eco map is shown in Figure 16.3.

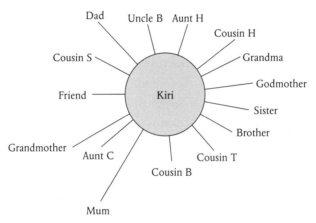

*Figure 16.3 Kiri's final eco map*

Towards the end of life story work it was reflected to Kiri that some of the information shared during sessions, particularly about her mother, must have been very difficult and may not have matched her initial hopes and expectations. Kiri agreed, saying that life story work had been hard at times but she appreciated having the opportunity to learn more about her family.

## Process and practice lessons

A number of systemic practice issues have been considered during the development of the Metro ISS life story team. First, it is acknowledged that the system around the child should understand and support their experience. As each child is referred to the life story team the key support people are identified – this generally includes the caseworker and manager casework from Metro ISS, any current therapists and key staff from the placement agency. This group is included in regular communication from the life story caseworker. Before sessions begin, a session plan is prepared, and although this remains flexible and may be modified as sessions progress, it informs the team about the planned life story work. Following each session a basic outline of what was covered is distributed to the team. This form has been developed based on the session plan and appraisal outlined by Rose (2012, pp.101–102) and enables the team around the child to provide additional support if needed.

To ensure there is a clear and accurate record of the life story process, the life story team records each stage of the work on the FACS Key Information Directory System (KIDS), with particular disclaimers around the confidentiality of the information. This includes interviews that have taken place with family, former carers and schools, any photos or mementos collected along the way, as well as photos of their wallpaper and an electronic copy of their life story book. As such, if a child misplaces their life story book, it remains available and accessible to them in the future.

Finally, the team aims to build capacity across Metro ISS. When caseworkers are providing life story work to children on their own caseload, they will often consult with the team around planning, engaging and sharing stories with children. The third position on the team allows caseworkers to join the team for a 12-month period. During this time the caseworker develops their skill in therapeutic life story work, and when they return to casework they take with them enhanced skills in life story work practice which can enhance their casework practice more generally.

Skye and Kiri were two of our first life story work cases. Being new to the role and somewhat unsure about our ability to make a difference, these children showed us patience and helped us learn. From our work with these children we identified some key lessons, which have continued to influence our practice.

Skye taught us about a child's capacity to manage those distinctly different accounts about contentious issues such as how they came into care. Initially, Skye's life story worker was worried that she had been unable to create an agreed narrative between the Department's version and Skye's mother. The life story worker had underestimated the process of providing Skye with an opportunity to explore all sides of the narratives around her removal, including what she had heard. Skye explained that she did not have the expectation that there would be an agreed version around her entry into care.

When working with Kiri, one of the challenges her worker encountered was that Kiri's mother did not want to participate in an interview. The life story worker faced the issue of how to include her mother's voice during sessions. Providing some psychosocial education to Kiri around her mother's mental illness supported Kiri to gain some perspective around her mother's challenges. Kiri had many questions for her mother and the worker struggled with not being able to provide the answers. To acknowledge Kiri's questions a scroll was drawn on the wallpaper where Kiri could write down the questions she had for her mother. This then became a process of externalising and validating Kiri's thoughts and feelings. The life story worker also tried to bring Kiri's mother's voice into the narrative through asking Kiri questions such as 'What do you think mum would say about that?' or 'What do you think mum was thinking when…?' This was powerful for Kiri and helped bring her mother into the narrative. This experience helped us understand that we can still include the voice of those people who decide not to participate in a direct interview.

We have also learned that working with a child with an intellectual disability is not a barrier to doing life story work. Rather, the life story worker can be creative around how to present the information to the child in a format that is accessible and still allows for exploration and processing information.

## Concluding remarks

The life story team has been a really valuable addition to the support provided for children's cases managed by Metro ISS. We were committed to the importance of this approach and have been able to provide this support within existing resources. Through this work we have recognised that issues such as intellectual disability, significant trauma or challenging information are not barriers to the benefits that therapeutic life story work has to offer. We have seen that when children learn more about their family and their wider family history and have the opportunity to work through issues of their past it can impact positively on their sense of identity. This can provide an individual with a sense of pride, purpose and belonging (Kidd and Teagle 2006). A number of children have also been able to reconnect with members of their family, another factor that can contribute to a positive sense of identity for children in out-of-home care (Mendes *et al.* 2012).

Habermas and Bluck (2000) believe that the identity that is developed in adolescence remains with the individual into adulthood. The implications for those adults who have not been supported to develop their identity during childhood are significant. Watson, Latter and Bellew (2015) state that they tend to lack a sense of purpose and self-esteem, are less likely to form sustaining and positive relationships, may be less likely to engage in education or employment and may also suffer from impaired decision making and reasoning. Supporting children to test and explore their identity while they are still in out-of-home care may well contribute to more positive outcomes for this group as adults.

At Metro ISS we are committed to supporting the children we work with to explore their life story and identity. It is hoped that by embedding this work in our practice we will create more positive outcomes for the children we work with both in the short and long term.

# References

Australian Bureau of Statistics (2012) 4433.0.55.003 – *Intellectual Disability, Australia*.

Cook, A., Blaustein, M., Spinazzola, J. and van der Kolk, B. (eds) (2003) 'Complex trauma in children and adolescents.' White Paper from the National Child Traumatic Stress Network Complex Trauma Task Force. Los Angeles, CA: National Child Traumatic Stress Network.

Cook, A., Spinazzola, J., Ford, J., Lanktree, C. *et al.* (2005) 'Complex trauma in children and adolescents.' *Psychiatric Annals* 35(5), 390–398.

D'andrea, W., Ford, J., Stolbach, B., Spinazzola, J. and van der Kolk, B. (2012) 'Understanding interpersonal trauma in children: why we need a developmentally appropriate trauma diagnosis.' *American Journal of Orthopsychiatry* 82(2), 187–200.

Delima, J. and Vimpani, G. (2011) 'The neurobiological effects of childhood maltreatment: an often overlooked narrative relation to the long-term effects of early childhood trauma?' *Family Matters, Australian Institute of Family Studies* 89, 42–52.

FACS (2014–15) *Family and Community Services, Statistical Report 2014–2015*. Family and Community Services, 10.

Gaskill, R.L. and Perry, B. (2012) 'Child Sexual Abuse, Traumatic Experiences, and their Impact on the Developing Brain.' In P. Goodyear-Brown (ed.) *Handbook of Child Sexual Abuse: Identification, Assessment, and Treatment.* New Jersey: John Wiley & Sons Inc.

Habermas, T. and Bluck, S. (2000) 'Getting a life: the emergence of the life story in adolescence.' *Psychological Bulletin* 126(5), 748–769.

Hollingworth, A. (2015) 'A modest proposal for treating children with respect in care proceedings.' *Communities, Children and Families Australia* 9(1), 5–16.

Humphreys, C. and Kertesz, M. (2015) 'Making records meaningful: creating an identity resource for young people in care.' *Australian Social Work* 68(4), 497–514.

Humphreys, C., McCarthy, G., Dowling, M., Kertesz, M. and Tropea, R. (2014) 'Improving the archiving of records in the out-of-home care sector.' *Australian Social Work* 67(4), 509–524.

Intensive Support Services (2011) *Statewide Services*, Casework Manual, Family and Community Services, unpublished manual.

Kidd, W. and Teagle, A. (2012) *Culture and Identity* (2nd edition). London: Palgrave Macmillan.

Mendes, P., Johnson, G. and Moslehuddin, B. (2012) 'Young people transitioning from out-of-home care and relationships with family of origin: an examination of three recent Australian studies.' *Child Care in Practice* 18(4), 357–370.

Murray, S. and Humphreys, C. (2014) '"My life's been a total disaster but I feel privileged": care-leavers' access to personal records and their implications for social work practice.' *Child and Family Social Work* 19, 215–224.

Osborn, A. and Bromfield, L. (2007) 'Outcomes for children and young people in care.' Research Brief 3, Australian Institute of Family Studies.

Perry, B. (2004) 'Maltreatment and the Developing Child: How Early Childhood Experience Shapes Child and Culture.' The Margaret McCain Lecture Series.

Perry, B.D., Pollard, R.A., Blakley, T.L., Baker, W.L. and Vigilante, D. (1995) 'Childhood trauma, the neurobiology of adaptation, and "use-dependent" development of the brain: how "states" become "traits".' *Infant Mental Health Journal* 16(4), 271–291.

Rose, R. (2012) *Life Story Therapy with Traumatized Children: A Model for Practice.* London: Jessica Kingsley Publishers.

Swain, S. and Musgrove, N. (2012) 'We are the stories we tell about ourselves: child welfare records and the construction of identity among Australians who, as children, experienced out-of-home "care".' *Archives and Manuscripts* 40(1), 4–14.

van der Kolk, B. (2003) 'The neurobiology of childhood trauma and abuse.' *Child and Adolescent Psychiatric Clinics* 12, 293–317.

Watson, D., Latter, S. and Bellew, R. (2015) 'Adopted children and young people's views on their life storybooks: the role of narrative in the formation of identities.' *Children and Youth Services Review* 58, 90–98.

# PART 4

# WRAPPING UP THE STORY

# Chapter 17

# SPREADING THE PRACTICE OF THERAPEUTIC LIFE STORY WORK

## WE ARE ALL STORIES IN THE END

*Kendra Morris-Jacobson, MA, Director of Oregon Programs*

## Introduction by Richard Rose

*In this chapter, Kendra Morris-Jacobson has written a very glowing (if not for you, definitely for me) account of 'spreading the word' of the therapeutic life story process. I was asked a few years ago if I would allow Toni Ferguson, one of the most dedicated social workers I have ever had the privilege to walk alongside, to use a PowerPoint presentation that I had delivered a year before in Australia. I was intrigued by the request, and then found that Toni and her colleagues in ORPARC (Oregon Post Adoption Resource Center) were providing vital support services to a wide range of communities in the State. I was travelling to the USA as I had been asked to talk at a conference on the East Coast and so offered to come and present on therapeutic life story work to those who might be interested. ORPARC offered to cover my cost of travel and within a few months I was in Portland…the rest, as they say…*

## The Oregon Tale: therapeutic life story work with Richard Rose

Oregon Post Adoption Resource Center (ORPARC), a program of Northwest Resource Associates, Portland, Oregon, USA.

We have very little scientific information about the belonging-ness need, although this is a common theme in novels, autobiographies, poems, and plays and also in the newer sociological literature. From these we know in a general way the destructive effects of children moving too often; of being without roots, or of despising one's roots, one's origins, one's group; of being torn from one's home and family, friends and neighbors; of being a transient or a newcomer rather than a native. We still underplay the deep importance of the neighborhood, of one's territory, of one's clan, of one's own 'kind,' one's class, one's gang, one's familiar working colleagues. And we have largely forgotten our deep animal tendencies to herd, to flock, to join, to belong. (Maslow 1954, p.20)[1]

When Richard Rose asked if we would contribute a chapter on behalf of Oregon for his compilation of therapeutic life story work's application around the world, I was stumped.[2] It is not that there isn't ample material about Oregon's child welfare system and our state's relationship with the transformative value of a child's life story. Oregon has promoted the use of life story books for years, embraces trauma-informed care and grasps the powerful ramifications of unresolved grief and loss. It is more so that for us, here at the Oregon Post Adoption Resource Center (ORPARC), Richard is that story.

Our infatuation with Richard is recent. It by no means diminishes the historical contributions of the social work pioneers, therapists, psychologists and families themselves who have been thoughtfully framing and reinforcing the conceptual foundation for life story work in Oregon for decades. We celebrate Massachusetts-based social worker, life book author and adoptee and adoptive parent Beth O'Malley, who has made the process of creating life books a tangible, meaningful record of a child's adoption journey accessible to so many. We salute child welfare trainer, social worker and consultant Darla Henry's insightful 3-5-7 model, an approach to loss, identity and reconciliation

---

1   Maslow, A. (1954) *Motivation and Personality* (third edition). New York: Harper and Row.
2   Portland's rapid mid-19th-century growth led to many un-cleared tree stumps, thus the nickname 'Stumptown'.

so respected in Oregon that it has been formally integrated by the state into child-specific permanency planning services. Of course, no adoption discussion is complete without paying homage to legendary paediatrician and psychotherapist Vera Fahlberg and her keen child-focused perspective. We must also not forget Pacific Northwest treasure Deborah Gray – therapist, author, consultant and founder of Nurturing Attachments, to whom we are gratefully and eternally attached.

All of these experts, and many others (Bruce Perry, Daniel Siegel, Dave Ziegler, Heather Forbes and Karyn Purvis, to name just a few), have helped prepare Oregon for these ongoing healing efforts with children.

We literally shape ourselves to the environment that surrounds us.
(Richard Rose)

Held together by the volcanic high desert expanse of eastern Oregon, the rugged Pacific coastline, the chasm of the windswept Columbia River gorge bordering Washington to the north, and sun-drenched California below, Oregon rests on the far northwestern side of the United States, perched on the Pacific Rim. Its majestic mountain ranges, starring the postcard-perfect and snowy-peaked Mt. Hood, are blanketed by towering evergreen forests of spruce, hemlock and fir. Host to America's deepest lake, Crater Lake,[3] and with cascades of waterfalls and ample 'liquid sunshine' (aka rain), our state's geography is grand, diverse and harsh, but well loved. Established formally as a 'state' in 1859, Oregon is the ninth largest but only the 27th most populous US state.[4]

Like almost every settled area, Oregon has witnessed or even perpetrated its fair share of geographical trauma. The landscape and wildlife have been ravaged or endangered over the years through environmental degradation. Natural disasters, including wildfires, floods, small earthquakes, ice and wind storms, and St. Helen's 1980 eruption in nearby Washington, have also reshaped the land, which in turn naturally moulds and scars its inhabitants.

---

3 'Crater Lake', National Park Service, https://www.nps.gov/crla/faqs.htm.
4 'Oregon' Wikipedia, last updated 9 November 2016.

The vast majority of Oregon's four million plus residents live under the perpetual umbrella of the rainy, mild climate that covers the lush and verdant Willamette Valley. The valley's three major cities, Eugene, Salem and Metro Portland, essentially escort the Willamette River along the populated I-5 highway corridor from its mountainous origins up and out to where it departs into the Columbia River on its way to the ocean.

Who in the world am I? Ah, that's the great puzzle. (Lewis Carroll)

As Oregonians, we flaunt a proud patchwork history of Lewis and Clark exploration, Oregon Trail resilience and American Wild West bravado. Modern metropolitan spins on our unique Pacific Northwest identity include our obsession with quirky coffee shops, craft breweries, food carts and commuter biking. On screen, we play host to television's *Grimm* occult fairy tale series, along with the infamous sketch-comedy *Portlandia*[5] where Oregonians smirk and twitter at themselves.

We also hide beneath an equally shameful and fragmented legacy of tribal displacement and destruction, white privilege and pervasive racism. It is not without surprise that our largest metro area was recently crowned 'Whitest City in America' by *The Atlantic*.[6] Our current statewide population is primarily white/Caucasian at 76.6 per cent, with 12.7 per cent Latino/Hispanic, 4.4 per cent Asian, 2.1 per cent African American, 1.8 per cent American Indian/Alaskan Native, and the remainder a mix of other races.[7] Approximately 5 per cent of Oregon's adult population is LGBT (lesbian, gay, bisexual and transgender).[8]

…it is our duty to ensure there is an outstanding system of public care. (Richard Rose)

Back in the mid-1800s, the early practices of indentured servitude and the arrival of the 'Orphan Trains' first brought impoverished foster children west, outsourcing them from crowded eastern urban cities to

---

5    According to *Rolling Stone*, January 2015, 'Put a Bird on It' is *Portlandia*'s top all-time sketch.
6    Samuels, A. (2016) 'The Racist History of Portland, the Whitest City in America.' *The Atlantic*, 22 July.
7    U.S. Census, 2015.
8    LGBT Movement Advancement Project, 2016.

rural placements. Over time, similar to other US states, Oregon would eventually transition away from foster child labour and orphanages to our current system of formalised family foster care. However, like so many other so-called 'developed' places around the world, we, too, still struggle with how best to care for our most vulnerable.

Oregon claims one of the highest rates of autism in the US and the tenth highest suicide rate.[9] We are the 13th hungriest state and one in each of our six families experiences food insecurity.[10] The devastating ratio of children of Native American heritage in care – one in five in Oregon's most populous county[11] – harkens back to generational impacts of tribal decimation, acculturation and assimilation. At the time of writing, nearly 8000 children are in foster care, and of those children approximately 70 per cent are white/Caucasian, 16 per cent Hispanic or Latino, and 7 per cent African American, with other races comprising the rest.[12] Oregon's foster children are also almost evenly split between females and males.[13]

For children in state care who are unable to reunite safely with birth parents, and for whom adoption or guardianship becomes the plan, the majority find permanency with relatives, kin or foster parents. Oregon finalises close to 1000 combined adoptions and guardianships each year. In fact, Oregon has far more children living in adoptive and guardianship families than in foster care, emphasising the importance of long-term post placement supports. Fortunately, the majority of these placements are successful. Nearly 97 per cent of children adopted in Oregon stay adopted![14] In this regard, as a state we have had tremendous success. However, for those who remain at risk, or for those whose tragic trajectory is to age out of the system without a permanent family resource, there is still serious work to be done.

We all have stories that make us who we are. (Richard Rose)

---

9   American Foundation for Suicide Prevention, 2016.
10  Oregon Center for Public Policy, 2016.
11  Native American Youth and Family Center, 2016.
12  Oregon Department of Human Services, Child Welfare Data Book, 2015.
13  Transgender statistics not available at the time of this writing.
14  Ibid.

As I drive over the Willamette River on an uncharacteristically sunny, early spring Portland morning, diamonds dance across the water under the striking panorama of Bridgetown's nine consecutive spans.[15] I am reminded of how Richard Rose himself burst in like brilliant Oregon sunshine on a stereotypical grey day. A seemingly ordinary arrival to our aptly named 'City of Roses', he dazzled and swept us away.

We Oregonians didn't know quite what to expect from this unassuming, soft-spoken British gentleman; he basically appeared on ORPARC's doorstep. His presentations lack the usual slick videos, eye-candy infographics or toe-tapping background music audiences have come to expect. There are no glossy brochures, flyers or even business cards. He uses quaint, unfamiliar British terms like 'colours' (magic markers), 'nappies' (diapers), 'carers' (foster parents) and 'lorries' (trucks). Yet, he captivates us with his own story – Liverpool football fan, PS4 gamer, loyal customer of See's Candies, moving from humble beginnings as a chocolate-smitten child of a large, struggling, poor family in a three-bedroom house, to his work as a green 17-year-old social worker on the child welfare front lines, and now a world-renowned life story expert. We grew quickly and inextricably fond of Richard.

> It is true, we shall be monsters, cut off from all of the world; but on that account we shall be more attached to one another.
> (Mary Shelley, *Frankenstein*)

No conversation representing Richard's application of therapeutic life story work would be complete without a monster reference. He reminds us that the spectres and monstrosities trapped in the painful histories of the children we serve – and sometimes in ourselves – are universal. They call out to us for help, for release and integration into an understandable, cohesive narrative. In essence, the life story.

As Richard explains, the hallmark of life story work lies in the mutual sharing, the safe haven where the therapeutic relationship is patiently built and solidified. This playful exchange of trust and truth becomes the bridge across which the deeper therapeutic life story work advances,

---

15    Bridgetown is another of Portland's endearing nicknames.

and then ideally transitions over to remain with the permanent caregiver of the child – or, in Oregon's case, philosophically from Richard to us.

Just as he endears himself to the children, Richard persistently endears himself to Oregon. He has delivered over a dozen trainings around the state from top to bottom, each time to resounding refrains of: 'This was the best training I have been to in my entire professional career.' 'Can't wait for Oregon to get on board with this!' 'This training should be required.' 'Wish more foster parents and therapists could experience it.' 'I would attend all his trainings if he lived in the US.' 'Would love to take the training again. Bet I'd learn something new every time.'

When he wraps up a training series in Oregon, ORPARC Family Support Specialist Toni Ferguson and I muse, 'Just what is it about Richard?'

Everyone is in awe of his rolls of wallpaper featuring the children's heartbreaking and heart-warming illustrations. We admire the many tangible activities (Jenga, squiggles, air balloon, memory jar, Mirror of Erised, behaviour tree, hangman, family tree, and so on) he has collected and adapted to help children access elusive puzzle pieces of their history. His handy repertoire of tools for workers (such as chronology boxes, ecomaps, questions) that organise, store and categorise information in preparation for helping the child discern fact from fantasy are equally as impressive. From a stance firmly rooted in neuroscience, he demonstrates how consistency counteracts even profound developmental paralysis and mitigates damage from trauma. Richard confirms that when offered repetition paired with regulation, the brain can access miraculous, reparative abilities.

Is all of this rich, compelling content what makes Richard's approach so mesmerising? Absolutely. But it is more than that. Richard lives his therapeutic life story work model.

He is consistent in his workshops, reinforcing faith and confidence in the therapeutic life story process as a catalyst for change. With doses of self-deprecating humour, he speaks honestly about his own vulnerabilities, drawing parallels between his personal life and his present work. As an audience, together we gasp at his immortal fear of flying, marvel at his triumphant six-hour London Marathon, and murmur sympathetically with his psoriasis. Secure in this sharing, he demonstrates to us repeatedly that he is safe and non-judgemental, that he understands boundaries and that he maintains the utmost respect for children and their healing capacity. He is patient with Oregon's slow contemplation of his philosophies, knowing we will ultimately be 'happy'[16] and understand, just like the children. And, of course, we do; he shows us how.

...when we begin to see our suffering as a story, we are saved.
(Anais Nin)

In child welfare systems, enlightenment comes at a literal financial cost. Oregon is extraordinarily pleased to have launched a more formal implementation of therapeutic life story work. Richard's core training has been added to the biannual seven-course education series offered through the Adoptive and Foster Family Therapy Post-Graduate Certificate Program, a partnership between Portland State University's Child Welfare Partnership, the Oregon Department of Human Services Adoptions Unit and the Oregon Post Adoption Resource Center (ORPARC). This unique state-of-the-art programme enables therapists and state workers to earn a specialty certificate in advanced-level work, specifically with foster and adoptive families. Since the training series is free for in-state professionals (and available online at a fee for those out of state), it provides an excellent opportunity for practitioners to hone adoption competency and become better equipped to meet state families' needs.

When funding permits or when he is passing spontaneously through North America, ORPARC also continues to bring Richard to Oregon for supplementary training for state caseworkers and community partners. Our state's many involved voices, from professionals to parents, welcome his expertise with a passion that makes us proud. It is their investment in this work that will impact generations of Oregonians. In each of Richard's therapeutic life story work trainings, there is always more to

---

16    Richard frequently checks in with audiences to see if they are 'happy' and grasp the material.

learn. Additionally, ORPARC's own information packet, thoughtfully focused on life story books, reflects Richard's influence.

Therapeutic life story work teaches that a truly important tale grows more meaningful in the telling. Oregon's child welfare story is, of course, never-ending. Likewise, Richard's efforts in our state will continue to grow – for a rose…is a rose…is a rose.[17] We thank you Richard.

If history were taught in the form of stories, it would never be forgotten. (Rudyard Kipling)

---

17   Stein, Gertrude. 'Sacred Emily', 1913.

# EPILOGUE

The aim of this book has been to present therapeutic life story work as an intervention that is universal in its approach. The skill of the practitioner in using narrative approaches with children alongside their carers is paramount and, when this is done confidently, the intervention is applicable to many areas of social care and education. I have been impressed with the contributors' approaches and their commitment to best practice, and am extremely grateful for their involvement in this work. There have been many reported positive outcomes for the children and families who have been involved in the work, and some become frustrated that they cannot work with more children and families in need.

Once upon a time, there was a wise man who used to go to the ocean to do his writing. He had a habit of walking on the beach before he began his work.

One day, as he was walking along the shore, he looked down the beach and saw a human figure moving like a dancer. He smiled to himself at the thought of someone who would dance to the day, and so, he walked faster to catch up.

As he got closer, he noticed that the figure was that of a girl and that what she was doing was not dancing at all. The girl was reaching down to the shore, picking up small objects, and throwing them into the ocean.

He came closer still and called out, 'Good morning! May I ask what it is that you are doing?'

The girl paused, looked up, and replied, 'Throwing starfish into the ocean.'

'I must ask, then, why are you throwing starfish into the ocean?' asked the somewhat startled wise man.

To this, the girl replied, 'The sun is up and the tide is going out. If I don't throw them in, they'll die.'

On hearing this, the wise man commented, 'But, young lady, do you not realise that there are miles and miles of beach and there are starfish all along every mile? You can't possibly make a difference!'

At this, the girl bent down, picked up yet another starfish, and threw it into the ocean. As it met the water, she said, 'It made a difference for that one.'

Adapted and based on the poem "Starfish"
by Loren Eiseley (1969)

In much the same way, all of us in the social care world are picking up starfish, brushing them down and putting them back in the world where they may be safe and 'start again'. We all know that there are very many children and young adults in need whom we are unable to respond to, and sometimes it does feel that it is hard to make a difference. In therapeutic life story work, we make a difference to one and sometimes to those connected to the one we work with as we see placements grow stronger and closer together as they begin to understand each other.

My last ten years have been spent travelling the world and promoting therapeutic life story work as an intervention of choice. I have picked up many 'starfish' and, together with those who have adopted this approach, we have helped recover many more to safety.

I hope that this book has been informative and reassuring. If I can be of any help, please contact me, www.childtraumaintervention.com. and together we can help even more 'starfish'.

*Richard Rose*
*www.childtraumaintervention.com*

# INFORMATION ABOUT CONTRIBUTORS

**Joan Moore** is a freelance dramatherapist, play therapist and adoption support provider with foster and adoptive families. She is currently undertaking doctoral study on the use of narrative and drama to support permanent placements and is an accredited supervisor. Her background is in social work with children and families, adoption, fostering and youth justice.

Her publications include: Corrigan, M. and Moore, J. (2011) *Listening to Children's Wishes and Feelings*, British Association for Adoption and Fostering; Moore, J. (2012) *Once Upon A Time…Stories and Drama to Use in Direct Work with Adopted and Foster Children*, British Association for Adoption and Fostering; 3Moore, J. (2014) *Emotional Problem Solving using Stories, Drama and Play*, Hinton House. Her peer reviewed articles include a chapter in Jennings, S. (ed.) (2009) *Dramatherapy and Social Theatre*, Routledge.

Contact details: Email: joanmoore@ntlworld.com

Website: http://www.adoptedchildtherapyservice.co.uk

**Dr Jodie Park** is an accredited mental health social worker who has been working in the child protection/out-of-home care field for 17 years. In this time, Jodie has worked in a number of practice, quality and management roles for statutory and non-government child protection and out-of-home care services. Currently Jodie is in private practice and specialises in providing direct intervention to children and families that is underpinned by a trauma-informed and evidence-based framework. Jodie provides training to staff and foster carers about attachment, therapeutic life story work, reparative care, birth family contact dynamics and sexualised behaviours, as well as providing clinical supervision to social work students, caseworkers and managers.

In addition to Jodie's practice history, she is a casual academic and teaches at the University of Wollongong and Western Sydney University.

**Paula Price** studied for her Master's Degree in Life Story Therapy and Play Therapy, specializing in Life Story Therapy, and becoming the first person to qualify as a Life Story Therapist. In her life story training Paula was taught and supervised by Richard Rose.

Paula has worked as a Learning Mentor since 2000 at St. Patrick's Primary School in Toxteth, Liverpool, mentoring and supporting children and their families and delivering therapeutic provision.

Since achieving her MA Paula has delivered therapy in her own school, and created a therapeutic service, Creative Child Therapy@ St. Patrick's, delivering life story therapy and play therapy for schools, social care and other agencies across the North West.

**Richard Rose** is a consultant and trainer on life story work. He is founder of Child Trauma Intervention Ltd, a Fellow of Berry Street Australia, and an Adjunct Associate Professor of Social Work and Social Policy at La Trobe University, Australia.

# SUBJECT INDEX

# AUTHOR INDEX

## Life Story Therapy with Traumatized Children
## A Model for Practice
*Richard Rose*

Paperback: £19.99 / $32.95
ISBN: 978 1 84905 272 6
eISBN: 978 0 85700 574 8

192 pages

Life Story Therapy is an approach designed to enable children to explore, question and understand the past events of their lives. It aims to secure their future through strengthening attachment with their carers and providing the opportunity to develop a healthy sense of self and a feeling of wellbeing.

This comprehensive overview lays out the theory underlying life story therapy, including an accessible explanation of contemporary research in neurobiology and trauma. Featuring tried and tested ideas, with tools and templates illustrated through instructive case studies, the author identifies how life story therapy can be implemented in practice. Finally, the relationships between life story therapy and traditional 'talking' therapies are explored.

*Life Story Therapy with Traumatized Children* is essential reading for those working with children and adolescents, including social workers, teachers, child psychotherapists, residential care staff, long-term carers, psychologists and other professionals.

**Richard Rose** is the Director of Child Trauma Intervention Services Ltd and an Adjunct Associate Professor of Social Work and Social Policy at La Trobe University, Melbourne, Australia. He is also a Fellow of the Berry Street Childhood Institute, part of Berry Street, Australia and Lead Consultant for Clinical Practice at SACCS, UK. He undertakes consultancy and training on Life Story Therapy and working with 'hard to reach' children and adolescents, and develops academic training programmes in the UK and internationally. He is co-author of *The Child's Own Story: Life Story Work with Traumatized Children.*

# The Child's Own Story
## Life Story Work with Traumatized Children
*Richard Rose and Terry Philpot*

Paperback: £15.99 / $29.95
ISBN: 978 1 84310 287 8
eISBN: 978 1 84642 056 6

160 pages

Helping traumatized children develop the story of their life and the lives of people closest to them is key to their understanding and acceptance of who they are and their past experiences. *The Child's Own Story* is an introduction to life story work and how this effective tool can be used to help children and young people recover from abuse and make sense of a disrupted upbringing in multiple homes or families.

The authors explain the concepts of attachment, separation, loss and identity, using these contexts to describe how to use techniques such as family trees, wallpaper work, and eco- and geno-scaling. They offer guidance on interviewing relatives and carers, and how to gain access to key documentation, including social workers' case files, legal papers, and health, registrar and police records.

This sensitive, practice-focused guide to life story work includes case examples and exercises, and is an invaluable resource for social workers, child psychotherapists, residential care staff, long-term foster carers and other professionals working with traumatized children.

**Richard Rose** is Deputy Director of Practice Development in SACCS and is responsible for life story work. During his seven years as a senior child protection worker he achieved the Practice Teacher award and a PGCE in social work education. He also has experience in residential care work, and has a PQSW child care award and a BPhil in child care. Terry Philpot is author and editor of several books, including (with Anthony Douglas) *Adoption: Changing Families, Changing Times*. He writes regularly for *The Times Higher Education Supplement*, *The Tablet* and other publications, and has won several awards for his journalism. He was formerly the editor of Community Care.